The First World War and Popular Cinema

THE FIRST WORLD WAR AND POPULAR CINEMA

1914 to the Present

Edited by Michael Paris

EDINBURGH UNIVERSITY PRESS

© Copyright the contributors, 1999

Edinburgh University Press Ltd
22 George Square, Edinburgh

Typeset in 10½ on 12½ pt Melior
by Hewer Text Ltd, Edinburgh, and
printed and bound in Great Britain by
the University Press, Cambridge

A CIP Record for this book is
available from the British Library

ISBN 0 7486 1099 5 (paperback)

Contents

Acknowledgements

Firstly to the contributors who responded so positively to the proposal for this collection: to Pierre Sorlin for his help and hospitality when this project was in the planning stage; to Bob Matson for his continued interest and advice; to Esther O'Neill for her word-processing skills; and to the translators Liz Hart, Margit Slosser and Susan Anna Gunther.

The editor and publisher are also grateful to the following for permission to reproduce illustrations: Artificial Eye, Australian National Film and Sound Archive, the Imperial War Museum (London), Museum of Modern Art (New York) and Oesterreichisches Film Museum.

List of Illustrations

Notes on Contributors

Ina Bertrand is Associate Professor in the Department of Media Studies at La Trobe University, Bundoora, Australia. She edited *Cinema in Australia: A Documentary History* (1989) and has published many articles, both on the history of Australian film and television and on the way history has been represented in these media. She is currently editor of *Screening the Past*, an electronic journal of visual media and history.

Franz Marksteiner is Editor of Meteor (Vienna), publishers of books and journals on film and media. He has written a number of essays on film, literature and history. He is at present engaged on a research project on Austrian cinema funded by Fonds zur Foerderung Wissenschaftlicher Forschung.

Ewa Mazierska was a lecturer at the Institute of Methodology in Warsaw and is now Senior Lecturer in Film and Media Studies at the University of Central Lancashire. She has contributed to academic journals in Poland and Britain and is the author of *Jim Jarmusch* (1991) and *Peter Greenaway* (1992). Her most recent work on the films of James Ivory will be published in 1999.

Leslie Midkiff DeBauche is Professor of Communications at the University of Wisconsin-Stevens Point. She is author of *Reel Patriotism, the Movies and World War I* (1998) and of many articles on film and history.

Michael Paris is Senior Lecturer in History at the University of Central Lancashire and specialises in the field of war and popular culture. His most recent publications are *Winged Warfare: The Literature of Aerial Warfare in Britain, 1859–1917* (1992) and *From the Wright Brothers to 'Top Gun': Aviation, Nationalism and Popular Cinema* (1995). *Warrior Nation: British Youth and the Image of War, 1850–1992* will be published in 1999.

Nicholas Reeves has worked on the history of film propaganda for many years. His *Official British Film Propaganda during the First World War* was published in 1986, while his most recent work, *The Power of Film Propaganda: Myth or Reality?*, will be published in 1999. He is currently exploring the legacy of Second World War propaganda in post-war Britain.

Rainer Rother has taught at the universities of Hannover and Saarbruecken and is now Curator of Exhibitions at the Deutsches Historisches Museum in Berlin. His publications include: *Die Gegenwart der Geschichte* (1990) and *Der Historiker im Kino* (1991) as well as many articles and exhibition catalogues.

Pierre Sorlin is Professor of Sociology of the Audiovisual Media at the Université de la Sorbonne Nouvelle, Paris. He is the author of many books and articles on film and history, including *The Film in History* (1980). *European Cinemas, European Societies* (1991) and *Italian National Cinema* (1996). *L'immagine e l'evento* will be published by Paravia in 1999.

Tim Travers is Professor of History at the University of Calgary. He has published extensively on the First World War including *The Killing Ground: The British Army, the Western Front, and the Emergence of Modern Warfare, 1900–1918* (1987) and *How the War Was Won: Command and Technology in the British Army on the Western Front, 1917– 1918* (1992), and has contributed to the *Oxford Illustrated History History of World War One* (1998). He is currently preparing a book on the Gallipoli Campaign of 1915.

Giovanni Nobili Vitelleschi teaches Film Studies at the Foundazione di Studi Storia dell' Arte Roberto Longhi in Florence. He has published a number of articles on Italian film and history and has made a special study of Italian war films.

Denise J. Youngblood is currently Professor of History at the University of Vermont and Director of the Russian and East European Studies Programme. Among her many publications are *Soviet Cinema in the Silent Era, 1918–1935* (1985–1991) and *Movies for the Masses: Popular Cinema and Soviet Society in the 1920s* (1992). She is currently working on *Movies and Modernity in Russia, 1896–1918*.

Introduction

Michael Paris

The cinema and 'total' war are both products of the machine age, spawned by the rapid developments in technology at the end of the nineteenth century. Both came of age during the First World War, one of the most dramatic, disruptive and controversial events of the twentieth century. 1914–18 was not the first war to be recorded on film, that distinction probably belongs to the Anglo-Boer war of 1899–1902, but it was the first war in which cinema was used as an agent of mass persuasion by the governments of the combatant nations and the first to be extensively recorded by the cine camera. The War had considerable impact on the cinema, creating an enormous market for films, a need for mass entertainment which would, if only for an hour or two, provide audiences with distraction from the dangers and hardships of everyday life. The cinema had never been so popular, and the involvement of government agencies in film-making provided much needed respectability for the medium. As Furhammar and Isaksson have pointed out, '[F]or the first time, the cinema managed to shake off its cultural inferiority complex. It was lifted out of the fairground and attained a significance beyond that of cheap entertainment . . .'[1] The War also acted as a forcing house for the development of national cinemas but equally brought to those industries an increased awareness of national identity and the understanding that patriotism could go hand-in-hand with profitability. Yet, in the long term, the closed frontiers of a Europe at war enabled the American film industry to establish a dominance in the production and distribution of films that has never been seriously challenged. But if the War was the seminal event in the development of cinema, film has also played a major part in how we remember that War.

While we still live with the consequences of the War, the living memory has all but faded and today we increasingly rely on the cultural artifacts of the war generation and of those who came later to unravel its meaning. In his fascinating and influential study of British war culture, *A War Imagined*, Samuel Hynes suggests that it is mainly through literature that the conflict has been 'imagined', that it is through the written word that the popular memory of the Great War has been recalled and influenced.[2] Although Hynes was writing specifically about the British experience, his comments have been echoed by scholars of all the combatant nations, suggesting that literature has pride of place in shaping our memory of the War. However, what is implicit in this present volume is the suggestion that, from at least the mid-1920s, if not before, the filmic image was equally, if not more, influential for reconstructing that memory. And film continues to provide the dominant popular national interpretation of that War for most people, simply because of the ability of film to reach a far greater public than the printed word – not just with the initial exhibition of a film, but through subsequent re-release, through television screenings and the video cassette. Today, as Pierre Sorlin suggests in his introductory essay, for those generations who have no direct experience of war, the cinema screen provides their dominant impression of what 'war' is.

Yet despite the central importance of the Great War in shaping the twentieth century and an ever-growing number of scholars making use of film to explain the past, historians have devoted comparatively little attention to films about that War. The development of film as national propaganda during the conflict in Britain and elsewhere has been documented to some extent,[3] but the, arguably, more influential post-1918 feature films have, until recently, received scant attention. There is evidence to suggest that this is now beginning to change and some excellent national studies have started to emerge.[4] However, there is, as yet, no comparative trans-national introduction to the subject – an omission that this volume seeks to rectify.

The specially commissioned essays presented here explore some of the ways in which film was used during the war years as an agent of national persuasion and how film-makers have subsequently attempted to reflect and perhaps mould the dominant national perception of the War. Pierre Sorlin's introductory essay, 'Cinema and the Memory of the Great War', sets the scene, as it were, by examining the connections between cinema and war, mapping the contours of this interaction and the shifting filmic interpretations of 1914–18. The essays that follow then examine in detail the experience of the major combatant nations: Britain and the Dominions – Canada and Australia, France, Italy and the United States; Russia, Germany and Austria, and Poland. The essays on Italy, America and Canada, and the essay by Nicholas Reeves on Britain offer detailed comparative studies of how film-makers became an essential part of the propaganda effort during the years of conflict, while others focus more on the fictional reconstructions of the War in the post-war world. In some instances the essays here represent the first systematic attempt to explore how the popular perceptions of the War were reflected in national cinemas – Canada and Poland, for example. Others offer new or revised interpretations of more familiar topics. Overall they attempt to chart some of the neglected waters of the interaction between the Great War, cinema and the popular memory of 1914–18. If they stimulate debate and encourage further research they will have succeeded in their purpose.

NOTES

1   Leif Furhammar and Folke Isaksson, *Politics and Film* (London: Studio Vista, 1971), p. 12.
2   Samuel Hynes, *A War Imagined: The First World War and English Culture* (London: Pimlico, 1990).
3   See M. L. Sanders and Philip M. Taylor, *British Propaganda during the First World War* (London: Macmillan, 1982); Nicholas Reeves, *Official British Film Propaganda during the First World War* (London: Croom Helm, 1986); *The Historical Journal of Film, Radio and Television*, 13:2 (1993) First World War Issue; Larry Ward, *The Motion Picture Goes to War: The United States Government Effort during World War 1* (Ann Arbor: University of Michigan Press, 1985); Leslie Midriff DeBauche, *Reel Patriotism: The Movies and World War 1* (Wisconsin: University of Wisconsin Press, 1997).
4   Karel Dibbets and Bert Hogenkamp (eds), *Film and the First World War: Papers from the Fifteenth Conference of the International Association for Media and History* (Amsterdam: Amsterdam University Press, 1995); Andrew Kelly, *Cinema and the Great War* (London: Routledge, 1997); Peter C. Rollins and John E. O'Connor, *Hollywood's World War 1: Moving Picture Images* (Bowling Green: Kentucky University Press, 1997). Equally, historians have started to explore what might be considered key films, most notably *All Quiet on the Western*

Front. See, for example, Modris Eksteins, 'War, memory and politics: The fate of the film "All Quiet on the Western Front" ', *Central European History*, 13 (1980), and Andrew Kelly, *Filming 'All Quiet on the Western Front'* (London: I. B. Tauris, 1998).

1

Cinema and the Memory of the Great War

Pierre Sorlin

Letters, verbal accounts, narratives, speeches and books were long the only media through which people were advised of what was occurring in the outer world. Newspapers widened the horizon and standardised the telling of events without modifying the primacy of words over any other sort of information. And then, as movies took on more importance during the first decades of the twentieth century, important changes occurred. Not only were proper names associated with expressive faces and means of transport with moving objects, not only were minds flooded with new images, but the pictures offered another vision of reality; they looked so precise and alive that they were considered a genuine reproduction, a perfect imitation of life. The modern experience of the world was shaped by the new technology which was especially good at conveying impressions of speed, action and violence.

WAR AND THE BIRTH OF THE MOVIES

The diffusion of moving images was particularly effective in modifying people's awareness and understanding of military events. Public screenings had only begun two years before when spectators were offered a few pictures of the Spanish American War, in the spring of 1898. Shortly after, the same audiences could watch a series of documentaries dealing with the Boer War. Feature films followed very soon and it is not by chance that the first masterpiece in the history of cinema, *The Birth of a Nation* (1915), focused upon a conflict. From now on the close relationship between war and cinema was embedded in the memory of individuals and, throughout the twentieth century, collective celebrations made an extensive use of pictures. Our awareness of what 'war' is and of what any specific war was in previous centuries is closely linked to records which were made then. Before photography, how was it possible to conceive of war in countries where most men and women had never witnessed an actual conflict? Some regions were regularly devastated but large areas of the world experienced no fighting for more than a century. Between the defeat of Prince Charles in 1745 and 1914, Britain was almost constantly at war but soldiers constituted less than 1 per cent of the population and spent much more time in barracks than on the battlefields. Information about fighting came from soldiers returning from the front, from books and magazines, from drawings and paintings. Hand-made illustrations reveal a great deal but they are often poor on facts. Goya's depiction of the Napoleonic war in Spain had a tremendous impact on imaginations throughout Europe during the nineteenth century, few people would dispute their ability to convey the atrocity of a merciless conflict, but Goya tells us little about the actuality of war. Despite the invention of photography, the most popular kind of picture, up to the end of the nineteenth century, was still the cheap wood-engraving. Thousands of them, widely diffused in Europe, represented the wars fought during that period. Following very old patterns, these stereotyped fictions were more revealing of an earlier period than of their own. The dominant model was that of hand-to-hand combat, gallant soldiers with bayonets confronting other soldiers: it was unreal, childish, terrifying and archaic.

Things began to change drastically with the invention of the cinema. By 1914, city dwellers were regularly attending picture-houses all over the world: travelling shows went through most countries offering one-hour programmes consisting of news, documentaries and short stories. Films gave their audience the opportunity to see an imitation of life, to observe, for instance, artillery fire or an infantry attack. Films were not merely a mirror of what was happening; they showed people what they must know; they contributed in moulding their vision and instructing them in how to behave in war.

Most actuality film-makers conceived of themselves as 'concerned' workers and were keen to make excellent pictures. However, right from the start, they were hampered by the problems that photographers had previously faced. War correspondents[1] and photographers had been sent to various battlefields since 1856; they had roughed it, but they had seldom been allowed to visit the war zone and many of them had given up after a while. Photographic or cinematographic equipment was heavy, cumbersome and costly: it was a burden for the cameramen to bring equipment to where the action was and they avoided situations where it could be lost or broken. Good, efficient operators were not easily found or replaced; furthermore in the case of the death of a film-maker, the studios might be liable for enormous damages. As a consequence cameramen tended to film scenes which did not place them in danger. This resulted in the emergence of a few recurring patterns. There is no shortage of films about the conflicts which took place between 1898 and 1914 but we must look at them sceptically. Far from displacing the role of art and trying to catch 'the real' directly, photography was enhanced by touching up devices to improve the appearance of people. Pictures of the period are thus primarily evidence not of how soldiers behaved but of what film-makers were able to shoot.

Before 1900, postcards, drawings and photographs representing some aspect of military life made the company the key operational unit. Of course small groups are better adapted to the limited space available on a postcard than regiments or divisions. But we must also take into account military theory which, during the last third of the nineteenth century, reshaped itself by reference to the pattern of colonial warfare. When his country was about to attack Ethiopia, an Italian tactician, Alberto Guglielmotti, defined a new style of war, 'lead outside the rules, in which soldiers, harassing the foe from all sides, with careful firing, hold up its advance'.[2] The cinema expanded upon this doctrine, showing again and again the self-contained, self-sufficient unit as appropriate to modern war; it celebrated small groups heroically defending a position or hardy professionals leap-frogging forward and attacking in open formation. War in the head, imaginary war, was represented as the sum of heroic actions carried out by a handful of individuals.

The early decades of the twentieth century, the years of the armaments race, brought complications which tacticians had to take account of. Films are significant inasmuch as they reflect part of these transformations, while simultaneously concealing them. In all European countries a new theme emerged with the presentation of navy or army manoeuvres or the prospect of war. Some were dramatised, such as the *Invasion of England* from March 1909, a movie produced by the Rosie Film Company showing the rapid advance by car from Hastings to London. This imaginary war was entirely concentrated on the front line, and especially

1.1   Filming from the trenches. A photograph from the
Illustrated London News, 1916 (Michael Paris Collection)

on infantry or cavalry charges; nothing was shown about the delivery of ammunition; soldiers seemed to carry with them all that was needed. The pictures themselves, even without commentary, pointed to a very short conflict won within a few days. There was nothing about fire-power, nothing about the function of railroads in bringing up troops quickly to reinforce a position or counter-attack. Little footage from the Russo-Japanese war of 1904–5 was screened in picture-houses and no lessons were learnt from that experience, at least from cinema coverage. That is to say that, unwittingly, cameramen and photographers supported the cult of the offensive which was the dominant view among general staffs and that officers, after going to the pictures, were convinced that troops had to be sent charging forward in a great number. This was not intentional, merely that there was a congruence between the ideas of officers and the practice of film-makers. In August 1914 all the armies launched massive offensives which resulted in terrible losses. A better strategy would have been to let men attack in small formations. But, as films show, such was not the conception of what an attack ought to be. In July 1914 nobody could foresee what was about to happen. Who could even have described it? Military representations showed regiments advancing with fixed bayonets. How is it that this misrepresentation surfaced so quickly after 1900? There is no clear-cut answer but certainly films helped spread the dominant image of massed battle.

A very important aspect of the cinema, in its early decades, is that it grew up as a cosmopolitan business. People interested in the modish medium rushed to the main production centres, while technicians from these places were anxious to go and work in other locations. The development of cinema came about through permanent exchanges. The Lumière brothers were the first to send cameramen throughout the world, instructing them to film everything which could be of interest for the public. In this respect, parades, reviews, army exercises and military operations looked particularly exciting and were extensively photographed.

In the first decade of the century cinematic programmes combined, at random, fictions and newsfilms. The French firm Pathé, which had subsidiaries in most European countries, as well as in America, hit upon the idea that spectators, instead of seeing movies made at different times and casually assembled, might be willing to be informed about current issues. In April 1908, Pathé launched the *Pathé Newsreels* which were distributed everywhere that they had an agency. The news, which lasted about twelve minutes, consisted of short films delivered from different parts of the world and dealt mostly with kings or other important people, and of items concerned with local events. A few American or French companies followed suit, but Pathé was by far the most important producer of newsreels and, in some countries, they even had a monopoly. In Germany, for instance, spectators saw, every week, Pathé's *Look at the Week* (Wochenübersicht). Pathé's only competitor, the German producer Oskar Messter, who had acquired the rights to take pictures of the Kaiser, was content with celebrating the glory of the Hohenzollern Dynasty, and did not attempt to produce newsreels.

HOW THE GREAT WAR WAS FILMED

Oddly enough, during the first weeks of August 1914, it was thanks to Pathé that German audiences could watch the mobilisation of their country and observe regiments parading in the streets or soldiers gathering in train stations. Of course, Pathé were soon expelled from the country but it took Messter two months to organise a newsreel, the *Messter Week* which would be the main source of visual information in Germany until 1917. The German example highlights a problem that all belligerents had to face: nobody ever thought that, some day, it would be necessary to control the diffusion of moving images. In the early weeks of hostilities operators were allowed to cover events relatively freely; for instance, when Belgium was invaded by the Germans, Pathé filmed the exodus of civilians: the exhibition of these dramatic images was hardly likely to raise the spirits of the British or the French. Following this period of panic, a tight system of official censorship developed. Initially staff headquarters were content with supervising the shootings but, after a while, the authorities took film production in hand.

Once under government control the private film companies could no longer export and were reduced to concentrating on the domestic market. The subsidiaries of big firms like Pathé became practically independent and the films ceased to circulate from country to country. Not surprisingly the hostilities witnessed an outburst of nationalism in Europe. The glorification of national values was accompanied by elimination of what did not concern the homeland, newsreels celebrated exclusively 'the deeds of our soldiers', 'the strategic genius of our generals', 'the firepower of our guns'. All governments, including the most backward, such as the Austro-Hungarian Empire or Russia, recruited the best operators to set up military film crews and provided them with up-to-date equipment. Quantitively, the amount of visual evidence on war is gigantic and, from a technical point of view, most footage is excellent. However, we should not be surprised that this material is tediously repetitive, mostly parades, long files of prisoners, tracking-shots of the seemingly inexhaustible build-up of supplies accumulated before offensives. A few shots deal with military actions but, when scrutinising them, we guess that they were taken during a period of training or were re-enacted. Film archive catalogues show us that the War was extensively filmed but there is so little variety in this material that the television series dealing with the period have always to resort to the same cluster of images.

When watching these newsreels, we are surprised by their slowness and monotonous regularity. For instance, we see an interminable shot of a landscape, a caption interrupts the shot and tells us that a long-range gun is about to fire, we return to the landscape and, after a while, we notice far away a plume of smoke which is, likely, the gun smoke. If there is a sequence dedicated to an attack, we are only shown the soldiers getting out of the trench and beginning to run. And, since none of them falls down, we, today, understand that this was a drill. Spectators at the time were less critical; they had not yet got used to watching, every night, on their television set, mountains of dead bodies. In the French newspaper L'Oeuvre, an anonymous writer explained that on the 26 February 1918 he had gone to a movie theatre in order to observe 'the trenches and the mutilated forest, the ground ploughed by the shells, the explosions that make a monstrous smoke, the changing of the guards, the slow muddy men treading along a communication lane up to the trench'. His is rather a good description of an ordinary newsreel which hides neither the destruction nor the suffering of the soldiers but never reveals a corpse, a mutilated body or a wounded man.

While guessing that this was a softened version of what was really happening, spectators generally were very keen on watching the war newsreels, and the German playwright Herman Kraus could note, in October 1916, that 'seeing a battle on film is part of the daily bread of the German film-goer'. We have little evidence about the reactions of audiences but in the few cases where inquiries were made after the projections we see that people attended in batches, veterans and civilians, and that they came out deeply moved. This was, presumably, because those who had not been mobilised, but who had had one of their dearest killed, wounded or shell-shocked wanted to 'see' what had happened, wanted to understand and at the same time to 'participate'. A good many articles in contemporary papers demonstrate how anxious people were to get 'involved'. How was it possible to imagine what soldiers went through, what sort of life was theirs? After the projection spectators believed that, now they knew. To a large extent the screenings were ways of collective mourning.

Artificial though they were, the filmed operations were not totally fanciful; the cameras recorded aspects of what was actually taking place in the war zone. Between 1914 and 1918, the nature of military operations changed radically. In the picture-houses, the civilians discovered these transformations, they saw the heavy guns, the gas masks which, some papers claimed, made them laugh, the mountains of ammunition, the walls built with empty gun cartridges, the goods trains, the reconnaissance aircraft and the Zeppelins, the first air fights and that great novelty, the tank. *The Times* was right when it noted on the 28 January 1915, that 'the realities of this war are being more truly brought home to the British public through the agency of the picture palace than by any other means'. It was the cinema which introduced people to modern warfare and, despite their inaccuracy, newsreels were effective in telling their viewers that they had entered a new world.

The cinema was also used to move the neutral nations and, possibly, implicate them in the conflict.[3] The French could use endless footage of ruins, burnt-out houses, destroyed cathedrals and skeletons of trees. The other countries were obliged to focus more on their war effort than on their losses. Special reels, addressed both at the domestic and the international market, were devoted to a particular event. Interestingly, in a few cases, the adversaries gave their respective versions of an operation, as happened for the Battle of the Somme (July-October 1916), screened first by the British, with their *Battle of the Somme*, then by the Germans who produced, shortly after, *With our Heroes at the Somme*. Both sides aimed at showing that they were perfectly honest, told nothing but the truth and, therefore, proved that they were stronger than their enemy. Commenting upon *The Battle of the Somme* Captain Bromhead, who was entrusted with making propaganda in Russia, said: 'I am particularly pleased with the artillery work, especially the intense bombardment . . . this part of the film will do much to hearten [the Russian officers] and confirm what I have often told them of our new guns'. Bromhead was right: there is much shelling in the propaganda movies. However, what strikes us, today, is the lack of cohesion. The shots, very well filmed, seem to have been edited at random or, more likely, because they had to do with the same topics (heavy guns, ammunition, infantry men), there is no organised narration, merely a succession of mixed snapshots. This is not a criticism, only a way of stressing the fact that the contemporaries, who appreciated these movies, did not receive them as we do. We are aware of the intervention of an operator who, by framing a fragment of the world at a given time, already interprets it. Spectators, at the beginning of the century, had not seen many pictures and believed that, on the evidence of the image alone, they could tell exactly what had happened. And it is this point that matters. The newsreels are a second-rate source of evidence for any history of the Great War, but they are of paramount importance for what they reveal about the construction of a memory of the conflict.

The First World War was the first war to be extensively filmed for huge national audiences. But the period 1914–18 was also the first time when entire populations involved in a conflict could witness, indirectly, what was occurring in the war zone. The newsreels established what we might call the accepted version of the War. Since 1918 countless generations have seen the same pictures which, having no precise origin, have become quotations without reference, ill-defined memories of what people have seen before so that spectators accept them as authentic, as traces of what life was like on the front line. It is even due to them that fiction films dealing with the War are labelled realistic – or unrealistic when a film on the Great War fails to use documents of this sort.

WHY DID WE FIGHT?

In Europe, the years following the end of the Great War saw the rise of the motif of a cataclysmic, apocalyptic horror that had marked the end of any idea of historical progress or possible improvement of the human condition.[4] This theme of absolute trauma was accompanied by an inclination to grant authenticity only to those who had endured the ordeal. Both Jay Winter[5] and Samuel Hynes[6] note that most visual or literary accounts of the First World War were produced more than ten years after the Armistice. There were of course exceptions, *Under Fire* published by Henri Barbusse in 1916 or Abel Gance's *I Accuse* released in 1919, but, until the end of the 1920s, knowledge of the horrors of the war was a grim secret whose communication was delayed.

A fundamental difference between the two world wars, at least in Europe, is that, with the exceptions of Portugal, Sweden and Switzerland – Spain had its own nightmare – no European country was spared between 1939 and 1945 while, in 1914–18, millions of men fought in a few limited areas without affecting the majority of the population. As the war dragged on, soldiers at the front became increasingly bitter about those at home who did not seem to care about what they were suffering. Robert

Graves confessed that while on leave he 'found serious conversations with my parents all but impossible'. In *Under Fire*, which is filled with hostile references to the 'Rear', one of the characters complains: 'We are divided into two foreign countries, the Front where there are too many unhappy and the Rear where there are too many happy'.[7] Even after 1918, ex-servicemen were reluctant to speak. For them, truth, reality lay back in the trenches, they did not believe they would be understood: 'they will never know, they cannot imagine'.[8]

It is something that we can easily conceive since it is still our problem: is there a way of speaking of the unspeakable? Veterans could not talk; Samuel Hynes stresses the similarity of most reports made, afterwards, by soldiers at the Front: 'The accounts are composed mainly of things all rather small-scale, all randomly disposed and all rendered without judgement or expressed emotion'.[9] Emotion, in fact, could not be re-created, let alone shown on the screen. 'Why didn't you tell them?' Leslie Smith asked Robert Graves who answered: 'You couldn't. You can't communicate noise. Noise never stopped for a moment'.[10] 'The roaring chaos of the barrage', Eric J. Leed comments, 'affected a kind of hypnotic condition that shattered any rational pattern of cause and effect. This state was often described in terms of a loss of coherence'.[11] There was also the stench of rotten flesh, urine, dead rats, sweat and verminous clothes which announced the Front a mile away; there was the mud, damp and dirt. A few film-makers attempted to fill the screen with filth and dampness but there remained an unbridgeable gap between film and reality. Most of the war was endured as endless waiting. There were attacks, at times, but there were many more empty days spent waiting for food to arrive, for shells to fall and kill, for time on the front line to end.

Things were different in the United States, where the losses, individually dramatic, were statistically negligible, where nothing had been destroyed and where, as was made clear in *The Big Parade* (1925), army contractors made a great deal of money. Hollywood, which had worked hard during the conflict, was well ahead of all the other film producers. Movies had become, in America, the first true mass entertainment, appealing to everyone, but especially to the educated people of the middle class,[12] those who, like James Apperson, the protagonist of *The Big Parade*, had enlisted and, after coming back home, were wondering what they had fought for. While the Europeans were radically unable to raise that sort of question, the Americans did not hesitate to ask them and movies were one of the most effective forms through which to debate the problem. In 1920 Hollywood people, from directors to cameramen, mostly young and often cosmopolitan, were keen to discuss the pros and cons of American intervention in Europe. During the 1920s Hollywood had a near monopoly of films dedicated to the War. This would have been of little importance if, because of the closing of most European studios, Hollywood had not gained control over the international film market. The first visual accounts of the conflict were of American origin. Hollywood produced and disseminated the first elements of what would become the 'imagery' of the War and its influence was so decisive that we cannot help explaining how it was formed.

Most soldiers were shattered psychologically by the conflict. However, as Samuel Hynes notes in his challenging book,[13] there were young men who were eager to experience war because it looked exciting and would make a break in the humdrum of daily tasks. According to the accounts that they gave afterwards some volunteers thoroughly enjoyed their war years, especially the thrill of risk, the camaraderie of the mass, the pleasure of having a unit under one's command. One of the veterans quoted by Hynes did not hesitate to write: 'I *adore* war. It is like a big picnic without the objectlessness of a picnic. I have never been so well or so happy'. What may sound slightly exaggerated is better understood when one remembers that people had to face fairly different situations. The first contact with the front line was often devastating; *The Big Parade* exemplifies perfectly the panic and terror of recruits hastily trained and suddenly caught under enemy fire in the forest of Bois Belleau. Such an unexpected encounter with reality accounts for much of the sense of revulsion adopted by some veterans when they came back home. But those who were not mutilated learnt that it was possible to survive and, on their return to the United States, they boasted that they had tested their personal courage. In particular, during the American phase of the conflict new opportunities for individual exploits had arisen in the aerial battles. The chances of being shot down in flight were high but it was a romantic fight where individual skill counted, a sphere of 'aces' and victory celebrations.

American films made in the wake of the hostilities illustrate the contradictions of public opinion which was unable to come to terms with the significance and consequences of America's participation in the War. The American intervention had its positive aspects. To begin with, innocent civilians had suffered, villages had been destroyed, women had been assaulted by the Huns. Allied propaganda had been effective in this respect; all films since *Hearts of the World* (1917) explored collapsed buildings and ruined church towers; most of them had a strong anti-German background and stereotyped Germans as uncivilised barbarians who deserved punishment.[14] Fighting in Europe was not only defending a just cause, it was also a chance to visit a far-away country and for making comrades. The relationship with local people (women, since men were seen mostly as extras filling the background) was often emphasised, but the most important thing was the bond of friendship created by the common danger. *What Price Glory* (1926) is entirely built upon the camaraderie of two tough guys. In *The Big Parade* as in *Wings* (1927) initially reluctant recruits soon become comrades and enjoy being together. Howard Hawks, who had been a pilot during the War, and then made films, had pleasant memories of the contacts he had formed behind the front line and tried to express them in *The Dawn Patrol* (1930), while *Wings* was excellent at communicating the sheer excitement and satisfaction of flying over the trenches and seeing the startled infantrymen try to find shelter.

Films did not conceal the moments of pleasure, humour and even happiness but all of them stressed the hellish aspect of the conflict. Did film-makers depict exactly what they had gone through? Or did they comply with the widespread mood which saw the Great War as an archetypal example of war horror? There can be no clear-cut answer to the question and we must be content with emphasising the constancy of the anti-war theme in the Hollywood movies. Killing appeared to be random, accidental, arbitrary and brutal. A soldier in *The Big Parade* has managed to silence a German mortar but he is hit, casually, while he is crawling back to his hole. One of the heroes of *Wings* is shot down by his best chum who has mistaken him for a German. In *What Price Glory?* a very young boy, mortally wounded by a grenade, does not stop crying, while dying, 'enough with blood', and a caption directly addresses the audience: 'And now, what price glory?'

Down with *that* War. However, no film-maker dared explain why the United States had gone to war and the movies did no more than mourn the sacrifice of the young men. It is interesting, from that point of view, to compare *The Four Horsemen of the Apocalypse* (1921) and *The Big Parade*.[15] The former was one of the biggest hits of the 1920s, comparable in viewers' response only to the best films of Griffith. The shooting was exceptionally sophisticated, with a clever use of deep focus. But there was, above all, young Valentino, a slim, fragile lad, romantic and inconsiderate, a perfect victim for the war Moloch. Spectators were enthralled because Valentino's destiny was unjust and accidental, like the fate of those who had been killed in Europe. The depiction of battle, in *The Big Parade*, was also horrific but its protagonist was not a dupe of fate; he enlisted under the pressure of his home environment.

1.2   The Hollywood battlefield, *All Quiet on the Western Front*
(Michael Paris Collection)

   Hollywood participated in the debate about the American involvement
in war by combining realism and melodramatic romanticism. Hollywood
productions were soon conceived as vehicles for narratives, ways of
carrying fictitious characters from one place to another; every American
movie had, necessarily, its protagonist who was going toward a (sad or
happy) end which the public expected. This tradition of emphasising
private destinies at the expense of collective concerns helped American
film-makers to transform the problem of war responsibility into a moral
conflict, the resolution of which was, by definition, psychological. American movies never tackled the tricky question of cause but their depiction
of warfare was extremely impressive. It is through these pictures rather
than historical studies that successive generations have learnt the
history of the conflict.

AGONISING IN MUD

It was only in the late 1920s that Europe was at last able to begin facing
the past. Germany came first. She was keen on screening the conflict for

two reasons: she wanted to prove that she had no responsibility for the outbreak of hostilities, and to show that, having resisted up to the last minute, she had not been defeated – which implied, obliquely, that she had been stabbed in the back by revolutionaries. Here movies used footage shot in 1914–18 alongside documentary-like footage taken after the War; in some instances, the protagonists played their own part and re-enacted what they had done during the operations. The difference between the two types of material was, at times, absolutely unnoticeable and even nowadays it is frequently difficult to decide which are the 'genuine' pieces and which are the 'fake' ones. Despite their precision and apparent objectivity, these movies did not do very well. I mention them only to make it clear that spectators were not interested in cold, unemotional documentaries.

The sensation of the period was *All Quiet on the Western Front* (1930). The depiction of the horror of war in this movie was not very different from what could be found in previous pictures, some scenes were even borrowed from *The Big Parade*, but there were important innovations. Violent, unrestrained, the soundtrack transformed the movie theatre into a battlefield; spectators were overwhelmed by the gun shots, the rattling of machine-guns and the whistling of bullets, and dazzled by the glare of the Very lights. Then, the action took place on the other side, in German trenches and the boys there were as scared as their foes. More significantly, there was no hero; the characters were ordinary boys who merely aimed at surviving; there was neither glamour nor romance and no predictable end except death.

Although it was neither polemical nor judgemental, the film was passionately discussed in Europe; it was even banned for some time in Germany and truncated in different countries according to the prejudices of the local censors.[16] The fact that it was a vehicle for fierce political controversies proves that the Europeans were ready to open a debate about the conflict. Spectators who, in those days, had a weakness for pictures which concealed their artificial nature and projected a coherent, complete and moving story suddenly accepted films which provoked a reassessment of their individual experience. Within a few months, most of the ex-belligerents released war pictures in which characters were compassionately observed. We do not need to list them here, suffice to mention the most noticeable ones: *Journey's End* (Britain 1930), *Westfront* (Germany, 1930), *The Wooden Crosses* (France, 1931). These were big hits. Expanding upon patterns and images already used in American films, unifying and simplifying them, they contributed to establishing an iconography, in other words a series of stereotypes endlessly re-used to the present to depict the First World War.

1.3   The recent video release of
All Quiet on the Western Front still carries *Variety's*
original endorsement for the League of Nations (Paramount)

What can we say about the relationship between cinema and the actual world? That a picture is simultaneously reliable and deceiving. It is reliable because it is a reflection, a duplication of a fragment of our universe. It is deceiving because it isolates part of the continuous space we live in and freezes the flow of time. The images of war which emerged in the 1930s were neither true nor false, they were partial and limited. We may call them 'stereotypes' not because they lie but because they restrict the memory of war to a few recurring pictures. Clichés offer a repertoire of stock images which orientate the viewer without any tedious effort, introduce him into the movie and, however dramatic they are, allow the audience to focus its attention on the most important aspects of the action. Being markers of the already known, they provide spectators with a familiar background against which to make sense of what is going to happen on the screen.

There are, in the films of the 1930s, three main clichés and one recurrent pattern. The first cliché is the trench. Of course trenches were a characteristic feature of the First World War, a defensive position which had seldom been used previously and was not systematically employed in subsequent conflicts. So the trench there was. But, in many cases, the trench had an appearance of squalid improvisation; there was no parapet or sand bags or earth to protect the men from the enemy's fire; and, sometimes, there was no trench at all. Pictures taken as late as the summer of 1917 or the spring of 1918, and found at London's Imperial War Museum, show pits hastily prepared where men cannot entirely hide. When Wilfred Owen joins his regiment at the beginning of 1917 there are no dugouts and his platoon has 'to lie in the snow under the deadly wind'.[17] A few months later Major Edmund Allhusen has no dugout either and is obliged to share a hole 'like a torture cage, too small either to sit up or lie down'.[18] 'What were our trenches like?' Robert Graves asks.

> Like air-raid shelters hastily dug in a muddy field, fenced by a tangle of rusty barbed wire, surrounded by enormous craters; subjected to constant attacks by professional killers, and without any protection against flooding in times of heavy rain. No trees; no birds; no crops; no flowers, except an occasional rash of poppies; no wild animals except rats.[19]

The repeated images of trenches that we see in films are correct. They are also incorrect. How can one film the men in their trench without standing back from them? Up to the 1960s the conventions were that characters must be clearly situated inside the framework of the picture so that spectators were led to believe that the trenches were quite wide and that soldiers could always hear each other. Trenches became symbols of another life, a hidden, subterranean life, opposed to the visible world of our homes, buildings and monuments which stand above ground. Soldiers were underground beings.

The second cliché is a night patrol caught in barbed wire. Not an unlikely accident but one that men had learnt to avoid. Patrolling was a dangerous, organised operation but not necessarily fatal. In order to represent night reconnaissance, movies combined three cinematic devices, artificial lighting, close-up of menacing barbed wire, plus the sound of human breath in an otherwise agonising silence to create an impression of fear and despair. A good trick perhaps, but a trick nevertheless.

The third cliché is a disfigured landscape with broken trunks, ruins, shell-holes and craters filled with water. This nightmare can be found in all the photographic archives, but men could hardly see it because they had to lie down in holes or find shelter behind parapets. What soldiers could see was a restricted piece of ground shored up by branches and filled, in places, by dead rats, rations, discarded weapons and, sometimes, fragments of corpses. Above all there was the omnipresent mud that summer could not dry and which became a lake in September. It is possible to film the mud but one must, to make the take understandable, show a man walking knee-deep in slush or dirty water. In their trenches, soldiers could not move; they had to remain idle for hours, while dampness was seeping up from the ground.

Beside recurrent stereotypes the films of the 1930s showed preference for a narrative pattern which, at the time, seemed very original. These movies have no protagonist; spectators are introduced to a group of characters and follow sometimes one of them, sometimes another. These men are identical and commutable; they do not differ from each other since they are all doomed to die. When the picture comes to its end nobody had been spared. The characters introduced at the outset have been eliminated, one after another. But, once the last of them has fallen, the film continues on, showing upsetting images, taken at random by an anonymous camera. It is like a world's end; no story can be told; there is not even any possibility of history. Compare the conclusion of Great War and Second World War movies. In the latter, someone, a friend, an officer, a comrade remembers; his companions, his men have been killed but it has not been in vain; their memory will survive. In First World War films nobody cares to tell what happened and there is no memory. The message is the more devastating for being delivered with no comment from the film-makers. The emptiness of the shots give them an impact, an intensity that tends to overwhelm the spectators and make them feel they have been caught up in some vast, impersonal, meaningless disaster.

Paul Fussell believes that the trauma of the Great War has moulded the self-consciousness of people belonging to the belligerent countries.[20] War imagery supports his assumption. The stereotypes we have identified are forceful and weak, effective and fragile. It is as if the signs which allow us to identify the Great War had all been petrified. The strength of the clichés can be seen in their periodic recurrence. Many decades after 1918 the same pictures, the same patterns, were re-used by film-makers born many years after the hostilities ended and whose knowledge of the Great War was mostly borrowed from previous movies. Consider for instance *Paths of Glory* (USA, 1957), a film which had considerable impact when it was released: it uses all the clichés that we have identified. If we do not take into account the scenes which take place at French headquarters, we have: the trench, then a night patrol, then the trench again; we witness an attack filmed as charges were filmed in the 1930s; we attend a court martial which looks like any tribunal in a Hollywood movie and it is only with the execution that we get rid of stereotypes. This was neither weakness nor lack of imagination. On the contrary, the film-makers had recourse to conventional images in order to lure their public onto familiar ground and then shock them violently. They did it because they knew that, however arguable they are, the clichés of the Great War are part of the accepted knowledge about the conflict. In pictures, the War has been turned to myth. It is like a Greek tragedy: we can tell the story again and again; we can create new characters and new circumstances; but we can change neither the plot nor the symbols which define the period. Complex, gripping films camouflage their background but, once one begins to look for it, simply repeat old images which cannot move us deeply since we have long been accustomed to them. Veterans' anguish has been translated into a few visual formulas.

AND NOW?

Paths of Glory was the first in a series of movies which, in the 1960s, reopened the debate about the Great War. The other pictures were *The Great War* (Italy, 1959), *King and Country* (Britain, 1964), *Oh! What a Lovely War* (Britain, 1969), *The Men Against* (Italy, 1970), *Johnny Got His*

Gun (USA, 1971) and, a bit later, *Gallipoli* (Australia, 1981). The fact that these movies arrived in a batch is significant; it suggests that, after fifteen years during which attention had been focused on the Second World War, and before the long series of pictures dedicated to the Vietnam War, different film companies thought that it was possible to look back at the conflict which had opened the century.

During the 1950s various 'New Waves' of films began to blossom in all European countries, in South America and, slightly later, in the USA. These pictures were based on another conception of film-making; they made nothing happen and were no place for events or adventures. What their viewers must care about was not the things pictured but the way of picturing. Although they were directed by leading film-makers, who were perfectly aware of what was going on in the business, the movies we have just listed did not indulge in the new fashion. They were basically personal and historical in as much as they attempted to reconstruct an authentic background and had central, well-defined characters, whose fate they illustrated. We have noted that, in the 1930s, the individual heroes had been substituted for small groups of more or less interchangeable fellows. To a large extent, focusing on a protagonist, as was the case in the 1960s, was a way of being 'revisionist', in other words of reactivating outmoded narrative patterns in order to question their validity.

To be precise, we must note that *Oh! What a Lovely War* had no protagonist. It was a slapstick comedy which mixed historical figures with fictitious characters. But this was no novelty. This picture, as well as *The Great War*, were burlesque stories which, for the first time, made fun of the conflict. Adopting a mock-heroic tone, *Oh! What a Lovely War* ridiculed the ruling class, especially the monarchs and generals, likening them to gangsters and criminals, and also the ordinary parents ready to let their son enlist and who enthusiastically attend the fight in which he would be killed. Less sarcastic, *The Great War* constantly fluctuated between comedy and melancholy, alternating hilarious episodes with horrifying scenes borrowed from the stock of Great War clichés. Against a conventional background of war images, it presented two men whose only concern was to survive at any price, be it by cheating or letting their comrades die in their place. It was funny and terrible but the spectators' pleasure was shadowed by the unavoidable death of both men.

Instead of merely mourning the destiny of the rank and file, the films we have listed above strongly contrasted on the one hand the stereotypes and the way infantrymen lived the routine of war and on the other the gigantic gap between the headquarters and the trench. In the previous films some officers could be cowards or inhuman martinets, but this was due to their individual personality. In the films of the 1960s there were no exceptions because the difference was of a social order. The movies featured two classes, radically opposed, which were obliged to fight in the same camp, and they explained how the ruling class, which hated and despised the plebeians, sent them to their death. It was a radical reconstruction of the past, consistent with the Marxist interpretation of history which was prevailing at the time. We do not have to discuss this version since we are not concerned here with explaining the Great War, but only with studying how it was represented on cinema screens. Did the provocative movies of the 1960s change the dominant image of the Great War? We may doubt it. They did not aim to challenge the clichés and even used them to prove that they were dealing with that conflict, not with fanciful hostilities born from their imagination. In doing so, they reinforced the existing conventions.

There are at least two reason which account for the viability of the stereotypes. One was the quick reaction of Hollywood and its ability to sell its vision to the rest of the world. There was also something specific to the First World War which was, between December 1914 and July 1918, an endless non-event. Compared with the Second World War during which things did not stop changing, thus providing scriptwriters with an inexhaustible collection of incidents. It does not come as a surprise that more than one thousand films have been dedicated to the Second World War, about five times as many as for the Great War.

The First World War began in August 1914. The point is not only this fact, but the way people expected it, were told of it, appreciated it. Words such as 'war', 'fight', 'army' enable us to account for military situations. However, for contemporaries, these abstractions were related to clues that everybody at the time could identify. In dealing with a few cinematic representations of the Great War we have tried to detect some of these images. We are now in a position to assume that the cinematic representations, screened every week in picture houses, were central to contemporaries' understanding of the events. We may also think that fiction films, mostly coming from Hollywood, moulded people's comprehension of what they had gone through and created the stock of images long associated with the memory of the Great War.

NOTES

1   The expression 'war correspondent' was coined during the American Civil War. 'War film' appeared in 1897, less than two years after the first film was released, in the magazine *Animated Photography*. Oddly enough, 'War photography' came later, in 1907.

2   *Vocabulario marino e militare* (Turin, Molinaro, 1889), p. 162.

3   Michael L. Sanders and Philip M. Taylor, *British Propaganda during the First World War* (London: MacMillan, 1982); Hans Barkhausen, *Filmpropaganda in Deutschland im Ersten und Zweiten Weltkrieg* (Hildesheim: Olms, 1982); Nicholas Reeves, *Official British Film Propaganda during the First World War* (London: Croom Helm, 1986; 'Britain and the cinema in the First World War', special issue of the *Historical Journal of Film, Radio and Television*, edited by Philip M. Taylor and Andrew Kelly, XIII, 2, Fall 1993.

4   A question amply tackled in: *Facing Armageddon: the First World War Experienced*, edited by Hugh Cecil and Peter H. Liddle (London: Pen and Sword/Leo Cooper, 1996).

5   *The Experience of World War I* (London/New York: Oxford University Press, 1989).

6   *A War Imagined: The First World War and English Culture* (London: Bodley Head, 1990).

7   Many other references are to be found in Paul Fussell's *The Bloody Game: An Anthology of Modern War* (London: Abacus, 1991). See also John Terraine, *The Impact of War, 1914–1918* (London: Leo Cooper, 1993), and John Glover and John Silkin (eds), *The Penguin Book of First World War Prose* (London: Viking, 1991).

8   The difference between survival in the trenches and survival after the War, the feelings of many survivors who were not sure that they had really come back, are analysed by Joanna Bourke, *Dismembering the Male: Men's Bodies, Britain and the Great War* (London: Reaktion Books, 1995).

9   Hynes, *War Imagined*, p. 423. This is confirmed by the testimonies collected by Lyn Macdonald in *Somme* (London: Michael Joseph, 1983).

10 Quoted in *Listener*, 15 July 1971, p. 74.

11 *No Man's Land: Combat and Identity in World War One* (London/New York: Cambridge University Press, 1979), p. 129.

12 Kathryn H. Fuller, *At the Picture Show: Small-Town Audiences and the Creation of Movie Fan Culture* (Washington/London: Smithsonian Institution Press, 1996).

13 *The Soldier's Tale* (New York: Allen Lane, 1997). In the same way Michael Paris shows ('A different view of the trenches: Juvenile fiction and popular perceptions of the First World War, 1914–1939', *War*

Studies Journal, 3, 1, Winter 1997, pp. 32–46) that juvenile war stories written by veterans offered a heroic, rather exciting view of the battle-field.

14   A film was titled *The Hun within* (1918); in another film, *The Heart of Humanity* (1918), a German officer shoots at the doll of a little girl.

15   See Michael Isenberg, 'The Great War viewed from the Twenties: *The Big Parade*', in John E. O'Connor and Martin A. Jackson (eds), *American History/American Film: Interpreting the Hollywood Image* (New York: Ungar Film Library, 1979), pp. 17–37.

16   For instance the sequence in which four Germans flirt with French girls was cut in France.

17   *Collected Letters*, II (London/New York: Oxford University Press, 1967), p. 430.

18   Quoted in Philip Warner, *Passchendaele* (London: Sidgwick & Jackson, 1987), p. 114.

19   *The Crane Bag* (London: Cassell, 1955), p 55.

20   *The Great War and Modern Memory* (London/New York: Oxford University Press, 1975). An interesting view of cinema as a critical tool is to be found in Andrew Kelly, *Cinema and the Great War* (London: Routledge, 1997).

2

Official British Film Propaganda

Nicholas Reeves

The inclusion of an essay on wartime film propaganda in a book looking at the way in which the First World War has been constructed in popular cinema may seem a little out of place, if only because propaganda films have so often failed to be popular enough to win access to the mass audiences at which they were targeted. For while cinema was already well established as an enormously popular medium of mass entertainment before the First World War, and continued to hold that position until it was displaced by television in the 1950s, propagandists always found it extraordinarily difficult to exploit that popularity for their own, very different, ends. Audiences proved remarkably resistant to propaganda films, both in the obvious sense that they avoided them wherever they could and, when such films did reach them, they proved much more able to resist the ideology of those films than the propagandists had anticipated.[1] Yet, an effective discussion of the role of cinema in Britain during the First World War should not be unduly influenced by a late twentieth-century scepticism about the power of film propaganda. At the time the official films were made, the propagandists were entering virgin territory and, given the speed with which cinema had so recently built up its mass audience, there was every reason to be optimistic: film-makers had demonstrated that audiences were interested in a wide variety of different kinds of films. Why should propaganda films prove any different?

Certainly, many were convinced that cinema could make an important patriotic contribution to the war effort. Before the War was a month old, the trade paper, *Kine Weekly*, was arguing that film was uniquely placed to 'arouse patriotism' and could play an important part in military training.[2] A week later, an editorial in another trade paper made a more sophisticated case: the people had a right to be kept properly informed about the conduct of the War, and cinema, with its special ability to record the 'actual likeness of events', was especially well placed to play this role.[3] In the months that followed, the trade continued to press its case, and news that the French government had decided to combat German film propaganda with its own official films provoked a fresh chorus of demands for action.[4] But, on this occasion, the special pleading of the cinema trade won support from a much less likely source – an article in The Times argued that, because so many of those who went to the cinema were young men of military age, appropriate films could make a dramatic impact on military recruitment.[5]

Throughout these early months of the War, comparable arguments were being put by those responsible for propaganda within the wartime administration. For, notwithstanding the fact that the British declaration of war had provoked a huge outpouring of enthusiastic patriotic support, Asquith's Cabinet had decided very early on that there would be a need for official propaganda, albeit targeted exclusively at public opinion outside Britain and conducted in the strictest secrecy.[6] The man given the task of implementing this strategy was the journalist, writer and Liberal politician, Charles Masterman, and the secret organisation that he established soon became known within government by the name of the central London offices in which it was located – Wellington House. Masterman quickly identified the unique role that film could play in the world-wide propaganda war that was fast emerging, partly because he recognised the need to counter German film propaganda, but also because he understood that cinema had a unique ability to reach those 'immense illiterate populations'[7] who constituted such an important part of the target audience in many parts of the world. In sum, before the end of 1914, those responsible for official propaganda had reached precisely the same conclusion as the cinema trade: official films had an important and distinctive contribution to make to the war effort. And yet, in spite of this consensus, the first official film was not screened until a full year later, a delay that prompted Britain's diplomats overseas to add important additional weight to Masterman's case. In the summer of 1915, for example, the ambassador in the United States drew attention to the very great effect of the German films, 'considering the popularity of the cinematograph shows and the mentality of their patrons', and urged the importance of appropriate British films to counter these German films.[8] Barclay in Bucharest was even clearer: 'real British war films, as distinct from faked war dramas' were what was needed and their production should be 'facilitated by his Majesty's Government'.[9]

Although he probably did not know it, Barclay's insistence on the importance of 'real British war films' was shared by both Masterman and the cinema trade, for all were agreed that the staged war films that had been made in earlier wars (notably the Boer War) would no longer be accepted by the audience. As the *Kine Weekly* columnist H. B. Montgomery put it, 'any suspicion of faked pictures in connection with the present war would do the picture theatres serious injury and any proof of "faking" would almost certainly have a damaging effect on kinematography generally'.[10] Yet it was just this commitment to the factual film that was largely responsible for the enormous delay in producing the first official films, for the production of such films would, of necessity, require the active co-operation of the War Office and the Admiralty – only with their agreement would cameramen be allowed to film Britain's servicemen in France, at sea, or indeed anywhere else. And such an agreement proved extraordinarily difficult to secure. Two separate sets of negotiations were conducted with the service departments, and both dragged on for months: one, initiated by Wellington House, resulted in the production of a single film, *Britain Prepared*, which had its premiere in London on 29 December 1915; the other, initiated by the trade, led to the appointment of official cameramen who would work at the front, regularly sending back footage for subsequent exhibition in Britain and around the world. The first two official cameramen finally left for France in early November, and their first films were shown to the trade early in January 1916.[11] Thus, if the character of the War had provoked the wartime British government into an unprecedented commitment to official propaganda, the implementation of this most novel form of that propaganda demonstrated just how formidable were the obstacles that such novel practices would have to overcome. Why then were the service departments so obdurate in their opposition to film propaganda?

In essence, their opposition was grounded in two quite different concerns. Most obviously, decision-makers at the Admiralty and the War Office shared with their peers across Whitehall a profound distaste for the cinema, which they regarded as a second-rate, even disreputable, form of working-class entertainment, which could not possibly make a contribution to the desperately serious business of winning the War. Cinema had established itself by pricing its product low enough to attract an almost exclusively working-class audience – as one middle-class film manufacturer admitted in 1914, 'The cinemas are not for people like ourselves, we do not go to them; the poor people go to them'.[12] Indeed, in making the new medium their own, working-class audiences had imposed a noisy, boisterous culture on the auditorium in which the audience engaged actively and loudly with the events unfolding before them on the screen – not an environment designed to attract a middle-class clientele. Certainly, almost all those who were required to make decisions about film propaganda did not have firsthand experience of the cinema and, not least for that reason, could not accept that such a vulgar activity could play any part in the war effort, believing that it was 'infradig for this country to allow its forces to be portrayed for the delectation of foreigners'.[13]

But if social conservatism was one source of their hostility to film propaganda, a rather more modern preoccupation with news management provided the other. British studies of the rigorous censorship that the Japanese had enforced during the Russo-Japanese War of 1904–5 concluded that such censorship had given the Japanese a distinct advantage over their enemy and, in the absence of an agreement with the press about a voluntary code of wartime censorship, the government determined that, at the outbreak of the war, it would impose the strictest censorship on any and all information related to the conduct of the war. Moreover, the new Secretary of State for War, Lord Kitchener, had a long-standing distrust of journalists, not least because of his own experiences of Winston Churchill's work as a journalist during the Boer War, and he was personally determined to ensure the most careful management of news within the army.[14] As a result, even accredited war correspondents were not allowed anywhere near the front until May 1915, and it took the army some time to learn the importance of cultivating good relations with journalists and newspaper proprietors. In such a climate, it was perhaps remarkable that the service departments were ever persuaded to allow movie cameramen access to the front, although it soon became clear that those charged with implementing this decision remained deeply suspicious about everything the official film-makers tried to do. Thus, for example, the cameramen filming on board HMS *Queen Elizabeth* for *Britain Prepared* found that every time they set up a shot with land in the background, one of the ship's officers would put his hand over the lens or catch hold of the man's arm so that he could not crank the camera, and it took several days before sufficient trust was established to allow any effective work to be done.[15] This particular encounter did not last long enough for any long-term progress to be made, although the cameramen who worked on the Western Front did eventually work out a *modus vivendi* with the intelligence officers who supervised their work, albeit one in which GHQ remained firmly in control. Thus not only did GHQ determine precisely what could be filmed, all the resulting footage was subject to rigorous military censorship at home, as well as at the front.[16]

The long delay in initiating official film propaganda was largely the product of a conviction that factual film was incomparably better suited to the purposes of propaganda than any other form of film, and that conviction proved remarkably durable. Indeed, for most of the remaining three years of the War, the official propagandists proved extremely reluctant even to question the assumptions on which it was based, and it was not until the closing months of the War that any serious discussion of the alternatives took place.[17] In the event, the War ended before these discussions were concluded, and thus wartime official film propaganda was dominated by the factual film. The form in which such footage was released changed significantly over time: *Britain Prepared* was a huge, rambling film, with a running time of no less than three hours, forty minutes. In marked contrast, it was followed (over the first six months of 1916) by twenty-six films from the Western Front, most of which ran for less than ten minutes. Then, in August 1916, everything changed once more with the release of the feature-length *Battle of the Somme*, not only the most successful propaganda film of the War, but arguably the most successful British film of all time.[18] Like film producers everywhere, the propagandists could not resist the temptation to exploit a winning formula and two further 'battle' films followed. *The Battle of the Ancre and the Advance of the Tanks* was released in January 1917 and *The German Retreat and the Battle of Arras* in June 1917; *The King Visits His Armies in the Great Advance*, released before both these films in October 1916, was a forty-minute film of the King's visit to the Somme battlefields.

Battle of the Somme broke all box office records but, by the time the *Battle of Arras* was released ten months later, it was clear that audiences had lost interest in feature-length battlefront films, and for the remainder of the War the propagandists reverted to their earlier strategy of releasing such footage in the form of short factual films. From May 1917, much of it also found its way into a new official newsreel, the *Official War Office Topical Budget*,[19] while this regular bi-weekly newsreel was supplemented by fifteen-minute films which focused attention on the work of colonial or allied troops and a series of shorter films about individual British regiments. Over the last eighteen months of the War, a further five films focused on the war in the Middle East, while nine explored different aspects of the work of the navy. *The King Visits His Armies* was followed by another five films about the royal family, while eleven more explored disparate aspects of life on the home front, including a film about German prisoners of war, a film that set out to demonstrate how little London had been damaged by German bombing, and a number of films that explored women's new wartime roles in munitions and the services. The closing months of the War saw one final innovation, namely the introduction of 'film tags', one- or two-minute films that were tagged on to the end of the newsreel.[20] Whatever approach the propagandists took, however, they were never able to recover the mass audience that had watched the first two battle films and, in some desperation, they decided in 1918 to try to reach the target audience a different way. Lorries equipped with a generator and a film projector would stage free film shows in localities which lacked a cinema and, after an experimental tour in February 1918, two major 'cinemotor' tours were arranged in April and May and again in September and October. While the size of the audience at these shows varied enormously, the surviving evidence suggests a mean audience of three thousand – large enough perhaps, until one remembers that at the time *Battle of the Somme* was so successful, some twenty million tickets were being sold in British cinemas each and every week.[21]

In the three years in which official films were produced, some 240 films were released, together with 152 issues of the official newsreel.[22] In the absence of any earlier tradition of official film propaganda, that represented a significant achievement in its own right, but what is even more remarkable is the way in which the official films avoided the hysterical and deeply chauvinistic 'propaganda of hate' that was so dominant in the wartime propaganda constructed by the press and the innumerable private patriotic organisations that came into existence as soon as war broke out.[23] Such propaganda revelled in presenting the Germans as barbaric Huns who routinely mutilated children, raped women and indiscriminately slaughtered all who crossed their path, and it would have been a comparatively easy matter to use the fiction film for propaganda of this kind – indeed, cinema's ability to construct 'realistic' narratives made it especially well suited for such a task. But not only did the propagandists refuse to indulge in invented atrocity stories, their factual films were characterised by a remarkable ideological restraint, presented in a measured, unemotional, almost objective manner. Nowhere is this more clear than in the inter-titles which, in the silent film, perform much the same function as the spoken commentary in the sound film and, as such, go a very long way towards constructing the film's ideology. Yet, almost without exception, the titles in these films are conspicuous by their brevity and their factual approach. The tone was set in the very first film, *Britain Prepared*, where footage of the King visiting a Vickers factory was introduced, not with patriotic words celebrating the event, but with the simple words: 'The visit of His Majesty King George V to the Ordnance Works of Messrs. Vickers Ltd'. Indeed, the titles introducing the three immediately following sequences were even more sparse: 'Visiting various shops. Testing shrapnel. Testing quick firing guns'.[24]

Moreover, when the first films from the Western Front were released precisely the same strategy was pursued. Nowhere is this more clear than in *Ypres – The Shell-shattered City of Flanders* (March 1916), for its footage of the terrible devastation of the city surely provided an ideal opportunity to instruct the audience in the barbarities of the evil Hun. In fact, this five-minute film contained just seven inter-titles, namely: General panorama of the City; The remains of the Grande Place (City Square); All that remains of the Cloth Hall; The exterior of the Cathedral; The Western Door; The interior of the Cathedral – the broken organ; and, Left amidst the ruins.[25] 'General panorama of the City' – those very words must have been used in innumerable travel films before the War, and yet they are used here to introduce scenes of unprecedented destruction. While this might have been the result of a sophisticated recognition that the images were able to 'speak for themselves', it can probably be explained in rather more mundane terms. The agreement under which official film-making took place insisted that the titles would be 'supplied' by the War Office[26] and, in their determination to ensure that the films did not reveal anything to the enemy, those responsible may well have judged that extremely short, factual titles would be least likely to cause problems. Whatever the explanation, this very particular approach to *titling* (which was sustained throughout the War)[27] clearly distinguished the official films from the hysterical hyperbole of most other wartime propaganda, and indeed from very many of the propaganda films that have been made since. For such subsequent films invariably went to very great lengths to ensure that audiences were left in no doubt what meaning they should construct in the images that were being presented to them – to a quite remarkable extent, the official British films of the First World War leave that construction of meaning to the audience.

At the beginning of 1916, when the first official films were released, wartime public opinion was still broadly supportive of the war effort; the passionate enthusiasm of the early months had passed, but the new mood could still be characterised as one in which everyone was 'quietly content to persevere – even unto the end'.[28] In such an environment, in which cinema audiences had not yet seen any wartime footage, the propagandists must have expected that their first films would be well received. Certainly, it would be difficult to explain the moderate success enjoyed by *Britain Prepared* in any other terms, for the film made considerable demands on its audience. Precisely as its title suggested, the film offered audiences images only of Britain's preparedness, presenting the navy, the army in training and the manufacture of munitions and, while much of the military and naval footage was new, the images of munition-making were provided by Messrs Vickers Ltd from footage that had been shot before the War.[29] Much of the film is slow and repetitive and it is not difficult to imagine that even the most patriotic audience would not have had difficulty in sustaining interest throughout its three hours, forty minutes. That said, a good deal of the Vickers' footage of the manufacture of munitions was impressive while some of the naval footage is both repetitive and under-exposed, but it is this latter section that contains some of the film's most striking images, notably in footage of battleships firing their guns broadside. The film enjoyed enthusiastic reviews in the quality press,[30] sustained six weeks of

2.1   'Firing broadside salvoes', from *Britain Prepared* (IWM 580)
(Imperial War Museum, London)

afternoon performances at London's prestigious Empire Music Hall in Leicester Square and enjoyed a limited national release, being booked by over a hundred cinemas nationwide.[31] It was a competent, if modest, start.

If *Britain Prepared* was marketed honestly enough as a film about Britain's preparedness for war, the advertising for the first films from the Western Front, released during the first half of 1916, aroused very different expectations. Claims that they would present the first images of 'The British Army in France'[32] suggested that British audiences would at last see the kind of battlefront footage that had led so many to make the case for official film propaganda in the first place. But, in practice, the intensely cautious approach of the GHQ intelligence officers who supervised the filming, coupled with the constraints inherent in the equipment with which the cameramen worked, resulted in footage that focused entirely on events away from the front line.[33] Cinema audiences were given their first taste of a variety of aspects of life at the front (British artillery in action, the physical destruction caused by German artillery, the logistical and medical aspects of war and so on) but the continuing lack of battlefront footage eventually provoked a sharp sense of disappointment. Thus, while the press was initially enthusiastic about these films, by April the *Manchester Guardian* was arguing that they offered so little access to life at the front that they 'might as well have been taken in this country'.[34]

All these reservations were swept aside in August 1916, however, with the release of the feature-length film, *Battle of the Somme*. For, while much of its emphasis was also on life away from the front line, it included a short sequence that apparently showed British troops going 'over the top' into action and this was followed at greater length by unprecedented footage of the human consequences of war. The first third of the film was full of already-familiar images (happy, smiling soldiers who waved at the cameramen as they marched past the camera), but much of the remainder gave contemporary audiences their first authentic images of the horrors of modern war. The pain and trauma of the fighting can be read all too clearly on the faces of these soldiers returning from the front line, who invariably fail to respond to the camera, too exhausted or too distraught to care.[35] Moreover, it is not always easy to distinguish German prisoners-of-war from British soldiers,[36] and the audience is left with an overwhelming sense of the *common* experience which all have endured. The most harrowing moments in the film come in a two-minute sequence that presents explicit and detailed images of the dead.[37] A slow pan across a heap of bodies at the bottom of a crater is followed by a succession of shots of individual dead soldiers, and the sequence ends with footage of the unceremonious manner in which the German dead are buried on the battlefield – the British soldiers, smoking as they work, stack the bodies side by side to await burial in common graves. But none of this makes a chauvinistic point; once again it is the horror of war, regardless of the nationality of its victims, that makes such a powerful impact on the audience, an impact that has not diminished with the passage of time.

If audiences at the end of the twentieth century are still moved by *Battle of the Somme*, the film made an incomparably larger impact on contemporaries. Not only did it break every kind of box office record, but also its unprecedented images of war on the Western Front resonated powerfully with audiences and thus, in marked contrast to the way in which films were usually viewed, they watched *Battle of the Somme* with silent, almost religious, attention. I have discussed the domestic reception of the film in detail elsewhere[38] – suffice it here to make two important points. Firstly, the twenty-one second sequence that undoubtedly made the single largest impact on the audience apparently showed men going

2.2 'Tending the dead', from *Battle of the Somme* (IWM 191)
(Imperial War Museum, London)

'over the top' into action, and yet we now understand that, in all probability, this sequence was faked.[39] Important as this is, however, any proper understanding of the film's contemporary reception has to start from the recognition that this was not how it was seen at the time. At the time, this was, as the *Manchester Guardian* put it, 'the real thing at last'.[40] Surrounded on all sides by visual and literary rhetoric that presented the War as a heroic, romantic adventure in which the forces of good would inevitably triumph over the forces of evil, *Battle of the Somme* gave contemporaries their first opportunity to understand just how different this war really was, and time and again they commented on the 'realism' of the film – as the trade paper *The Cinema* put it, 'There is no make believe. This is the real thing. This is war, rich with death'.[41]

Secondly, notwithstanding the powerful, unprecedented character of *Battle of the Somme*, the film served above all else to reinforce and strengthen existing attitudes towards the War. By and large, public opinion in Britain in the summer of 1916 was still entirely convinced of the justice of Britain's cause – this was a war that Britain had to win. Thus, where a late-twentieth-century audience sees *Battle of the Somme* as powerful propaganda for the horror and futility of war, fitting the film into its own firmly established views about the special character (and special pointlessness) of this particular war, audiences of 1916 fitted the film just as successfully into their (very different) notion of the War. Far from undermining or weakening popular commitment, the film served only to strengthen popular resolve to carry the War through to a victorious conclusion – Lloyd George may well have been right in asserting that it would make munitions workers work even harder.[42] Yet the film also played an important personal role for many of those who had struggled to come to terms with the death of a close relative, enabling them to place that event in a world which, through the film, acquired some kind of reality. Even Frances Stevenson (Lloyd George's secretary and mistress), who, more than most, had access to detailed information about the course of the War, wrote that she had often tried to imagine what her brother Paul would have gone through in the last hours before his death – it was only after seeing *Battle of the Somme* that she felt, for the first time, that she knew what had happened.[43] In short, in addition to meeting its political objectives, the film met many people's individual needs as well. For an official propaganda film, it was a remarkable and unique achievement.

Moreover, the next two official films also proved very popular. *The King Visits His Armies in the Great Advance* (October 1916) took audiences back to the Western Front, but this time alongside King

2.3   'The King in captured trenches and dugouts', from *The King Visits His Armies in the Great Advance* (IWM 192) (Imperial War Museum, London)

George V as he visited the Somme battlefields. This forty-minute film presents a remarkably intimate portrait of the King, the informal mood being established in an early sequence where he poses for the cameraman with the French President Raymond Poincaré, unashamedly pointing to the camera and laughing.[44] In spite of the fact that the King is always in uniform, this sense of informality is always sustained as, for example, in a sequence at a casualty clearing station, where the camera dwells on the King admiring a puppy. The invariably smiling King carries out his official functions with a surprising lack of formality, an informality that is sustained even when he visits the battlefield itself. Thus, the camera observes him climbing into a trench and then being pulled out by two officers, after he has tried unsuccessfully to clamber out on his own. In subsequent propaganda films (even in this War) such a sequence would have ended up on the cutting room floor, but here it retains its place because it serves powerfully to underline the sense of 'royalty with a human face' that is so central to the film. All of this reaches its climax in a sequence in which the camera dwells on the King lighting and smoking a cigarette as the features of the scarred landscape are pointed out to him, a shot that epitomises the film's construction of the soldier-king, linking him explicitly and directly to the ordinary soldier who had been at the very heart of *Battle of the Somme*. For, in the iconography of the official films, the image of the British soldier and his cigarette was constantly repeated – men smoke as they march to the front, they smoke on return, they smoke while they wait to have their wounds treated.[45] Moreover, the fact that none of the other senior officers who accompany him is smoking serves only to underline the film's very distinctive characterisation of the King. In startling contrast to the formal, regal images that featured so regularly in the newsreels, *The King Visits His Armies in the Great Advance* offered contemporary audiences unparalleled access to their King and, as such, it proved hugely popular.

Rounding off a trilogy of successful films, the *Battle of the Ancre and the Advance of the Tanks* was released in January 1917 and, while it broadly followed the successful formula of *Battle of the Somme*, one important addition was probably enough to persuade audiences to go back to the cinema once more. Thus, it gave them their first sight of Britain's new 'implement of war',[46] and, while tank footage only amounted to some 9 per cent of the film, the novelty of the new

2.4   'Nearing advanced gun positions', from *Battle of the Ancre and the Advance of the Tanks* (IWM 116) (Imperial War Museum, London)

technology was probably sufficient to bring the audience in – indeed, according to one report, *Battle of the Ancre* earned more in its first three months at the box office than *Battle of the Somme*.[47] While the film reworked much familiar ground, it also included a number of sequences that achieved a visual quality quite unprecedented in the earlier official films. In one sequence, for example, the camera observed a file of horsemen making their way through a barren, war-devastated landscape, populated only by tree stumps, mud and standing water.[48] The shot opens with the horsemen in the foreground, and the camera then pans slowly to the left to follow as they turn right and then left again to cross the screen along a small ridge above water-filled craters. The strength of the composition and the slow, steady pace of the camera serve precisely to convey the realities of this very particular environment, forcing the audience to confront the harsh, battle-scarred landscape, while empha-sising at the same time the quiet dignity of the men who must go about their appointed tasks in this God-forsaken land. Indeed, it is this sense of ordinary men retaining their dignity and their humanity in these most dreadful and extraordinary of circumstances that represents perhaps the most remarkable characteristic of both *Battle of the Somme* and *Battle of the Ancre* – small wonder, then, that these films evoked such a powerful response in the domestic audience.

Popular as these first two battle films, were, however, the propagan-dists found it impossible to repeat that success in any of their subsequent films. The third battle film, *The German Retreat and the Battle of Arras* (June 1917), was such a complete box office disaster that no further feature-length battlefront films were ever made and, as we have already seen, the propagandists spent the rest of the War in an increasingly desperate search for an audience that had in fact abandoned them for good. Those who had flocked to see *Battle of the Somme* in such huge numbers in the late summer and autumn of 1916 abandoned the official films just as quickly and dramatically in the spring of 1917, and part of the explanation for that volte-face must be found in the changing character of battlefront reporting. For while *Battle of the Somme* was distinguished by the (comparative) honesty with which it reported the horrors of modern war, with each successive film the propagandists apparently became increasingly unsure about the wisdom of such an approach. Thus where over 14 per cent of *Battle of the Somme* focused on the dead and wounded, there were no images of the dead in *Battle of the Ancre*, although images of the wounded still made up 13 per cent of the film. With *The Battle of Arras* the change was even more dramatic – a short sequence did include footage of dead German soldiers, but this, together with all the footage of wounded soldiers, amounted to less than 2 per cent of the whole film.[49] Moreover, in the eighteen months of war that followed the release of *The Battle of Arras*, the propagandists scrupulously maintained this new, sanitised approach to the reporting of the battlefront. Time and again these films presented anodyne images of happy, smiling soldiers. Nearly half of the twenty-five short films made about individual regiments, for example, featured the preparation and distribution of food – the men invariably smiled as they ate![50] In all, these later official films were a direct throwback to the representation of the army that had characterised the very first films from the Western Front. Such footage had proved unpopular in the first half of 1916; it proved even more unpopular in the last eighteen months of the War.

But while the changing character of the films themselves provides one explanation for the new unpopularity of the official films, an even more important explanation has to be found in the changing state of public opinion in the second half of the War. For while popular commitment to the war effort was still secure when *Battle of the Somme* was screened in the summer of 1916, by the end of the succeeding winter a very different situation was developing. In part, the new attitude was a product of a recognition of the character of the War itself, not least as the much-heralded Somme offensive failed to deliver the dramatic victory so many had anticipated. But the changing domestic situation was just as important, for it was in 1916 that the War began to intrude more and more directly in people's lives. That year saw the introduction of military conscription and, while wartime increases in economic output reduced levels of unemployment to the point where some of the most disadvantaged members of society enjoyed real improvements in their standards of living, there were many others who saw their standards of living fall, trapped in the twin grip of growing shortages and restrictions on the one hand, rising prices on the other.[51] The growing bitterness of those who experienced this fall in living standards was profoundly exacerbated by the fact that, in spite of the War, the more privileged classes seemed able to continue to live very much the same, comfortable lives they had enjoyed before the War began. Indeed, as the War dragged on, more and more people came to believe that an unscrupulous minority was exploiting this situation for their own personal gain and, as Trevor Wilson has argued, 'the word "profiteering" entered working-class language as one of the war's most potent forms of abuse'.[52]

None of this undermined the dominant sense of the essential justice of Britain's cause – the tiny minority who opposed the War root and branch remained a tiny minority; the vast majority remained convinced that

Germany had to be defeated. But alongside that conviction, a new pessimism about the lack of progress at the front was reinforced by a growing sense of injustice about the way in which the war effort was being managed at home. Mounting inflation, growing shortages and, above all else, the unequal way in which the burdens of war were being shared, appeared to reveal a fundamental unfairness in the domestic conduct of the War. Whatever the precise causes, the consequences were all too clear. Industrial unrest, which had been such a distinctive feature of pre-war British life, began to reappear.[53] A first wave of strikes took place in May 1917, to be followed by further strikes in August and November, reaching a climax in January and early February 1918.[54] The government watched these developments with growing anxiety and, from mid-April 1917, detailed, regular reports on the labour situation were prepared for the War Cabinet which revealed that it was resentment at the worsening food situation that was the primary cause of this mounting popular anger.[55] And that, from the government's point of view, was very good news, for it meant that the solution was in its own hands. For the problem was not one of an absolute shortfall in food supplies, but rather was a product of the way in which food was being distributed – a fair and efficient system of rationing would meet the workers' needs. The foundations for such a scheme were in place by February 1918; a uniform, nationwide system completed by mid-summer.

The rapid collapse of the strikes in the spring of 1918, however, was not merely a product of these domestic developments. It coincided with the Bolsheviks finally agreeing peace terms with the Germans at Brest Litowsk in March 1918, for the nature of the terms that the Germans exacted provided a sharp reminder of the extent of German ambitions. Moreover, on 21 March, the Germans launched their long-anticipated offensive. The scale of the German advances reawakened fearful memories of the opening weeks of the War and, while such developments might have weakened popular commitment to the War, in the event they had the opposite effect; it was one thing to go on strike when the War appeared to be bogged down in interminable stalemate, it was quite another when the German armies were on the march. Thus, not only did the strikes collapse, the nation united once again in resolute opposition to the enemy. A tide of xenophobia swept the country, more passionate, more hysterical than anything that had gone before, and that xenophobia dominated the public mood through to the very end. In November 1918, the people's determination to defeat Germany was perhaps even more passionate, even more implacable, than it had been in 1914. In all this, the official films played little or no part. They lost their audience in the spring of 1917 as the first strikes gave expression to the new popular mood and, no matter how ingenious the propagandists were in the way in which they presented their films to the domestic audience thereafter, they never won them back again. The unparalleled success of the earlier trilogy of official films can only be explained by the fact that they gave the domestic audience its first images of the terrible physical devastation of war – the ruined buildings, the battle-scarred landscape and, much more important, a sense of the human cost of war. Within a few short weeks of the release of the *Battle of the Ancre*, however, the public mood changed dramatically and, in those new circumstances, the newly cautious official films lost their audience and thereby lost the ability to influence domestic wartime public opinion thereafter.

Official wartime propaganda had originated in an attempt to manipulate public opinion overseas and Wellington House and its successor organisations, the Department of Information (DoI) and the Ministry of Information (MoI),[56] attempted to ensure that the films were seen as widely as possible outside Britain. In the first instance, embassies and consulates were asked to look after the distribution of the films ensuring, wherever possible, that they would be given a commercial release and, in this way, *Britain Prepared* was seen extensively in Europe, Asia, the Americas and Australasia.[57] As time went on, however, it became increasingly clear that very few diplomats had either the time or the specialist knowledge to discharge these responsibilities effectively, and the DoI tried to develop a more professional approach. From the middle of 1917, it offered advice on how best to exploit the films, while requiring the submission of detailed reports on the state of the local film industry.[58] At the same time, it announced a more radical departure: in future, responsibility for film propaganda would be taken out of diplomatic hands altogether. New, professional cinema agents would be appointed, chosen for their knowledge of the local film industry, and they would be sent out from London to supervise the work in the field. By the middle of 1918, many of these new men were in post and, in almost every case, they proved deeply critical of the amateur efforts of the diplomats who had preceded them – when a Mr Slade took over responsibility for film propaganda in Central and South America in February 1918, for example, he immediately urged the DoI to disregard the pessimistic advice that it had been given by local diplomats; much could be achieved, if only sufficient films were made available.[59] Slade may well have been right, but it is clear from other evidence that relations between these newly-appointed 'experts' and the local diplomatic establishment were strained and difficult – the British diplomat with overall responsibility for propaganda in America described his new cinema colleagues as 'a cunning lot of rogues' and 'snide movie people'.[60]

Just how successful these various approaches were in ensuring that Britain's official films reached their target audiences is far from clear – what evidence there is is fragmentary and woefully incomplete. Indeed, as late as September 1918, the MoI was complaining to the Foreign Office about the inadequacy of diplomatic feedback about the films.[61] But it may well be that the decision to appoint cinema agents derived from a recognition that the longer the War lasted the more difficult it became to place official British films in overseas markets. Indeed, what evidence there is appears to suggest a pattern not wholly dissimilar to that which the films enjoyed on the domestic market. Thus, they appear to have done good business up to and including the release of the *Battle of the Ancre*, but thereafter the position was much more mixed, with some successes but many, equally spectacular, failures. Indeed, the decision in the last year of the War to distribute commercial films with the official films probably indicated an increasing reluctance to book the official films.[62] Certainly many elementary mistakes were made: diplomats in Mexico complained that the films they received were acceptable, but only after errors in the Spanish titles had been corrected and appropriate lantern slides prepared to strengthen the propaganda message; five copies of *Battle of the Somme* were returned from Tangier because the poor quality of the prints made them unusable.[63] In all fairness, however, mistakes like these were not common and, in contrast, there were some remarkable achievements. Against all the odds, the official films were screened in Russia in 1916, both to the royal family and to service audiences on the various Russian fronts, and these shows were judged so successful that extravagant plans were laid to take ten mobile film units to Russia in the autumn of 1917. In the event, such plans were thwarted by the Bolshevik revolution and the equipment (which had reached Stockholm) had to be transported back to England, to be used eventually in the cinemotor tours later in the year.[64] A report on film propaganda in China revealed that between September 1917 and the end of the War the films had been screened on no less than 593 occasions and had been seen by nearly four-hundred-thousand people.[65]

Yet that report also reveals wildly different responses to the films in different parts of China, and that was in fact the central problem for all British film propaganda overseas. It was difficult enough to construct films that met the (changing) public mood at home; how much more difficult was it to construct films that would be equally well received in St Petersburg and Rio de Janeiro, Peking and New York. Throughout the late summer and autumn of 1917 British diplomats from all around the world reported that audiences had grown tired of war films and yet, within weeks, Mallet (in Panama) was arguing that what was needed was as much actual fighting as possible, while Willis (in Khartoum) demanded films 'showing lots of dead Germans and Turks'.[66] Moreover, even that most successful of British official films, *Battle of the Somme*, enjoyed a mixed reception overseas. When it was shown at the Apollo Cinema in the Hague, Red-Cross slides were interpolated urging support for the anti-war league, and a senior DoI official was forced to admit that the film could be seen as 'an excellent piece of peace propaganda on account of the vivid way in which it shows the horrors of war'.[67] Even without the addition of anti-war propaganda slides, so many American audiences read the film in a similar way that it was quickly withdrawn and 'subjected . . . to a strong censorship' before going back into the cinemas.[68] Wartime propagandists may have embraced the new medium of the cinema because they believed that film spoke a universal language which all would understand; the profoundly different way in which the same films were received by different audiences demonstrates all too clearly that the construction of meaning in film is an interactive process in which the audience always plays a critical role.

For all that, the official British films of the First World War constitute a remarkable and unique achievement. For a few short months they constructed an image of war on the Western Front with which tens of millions of British people could identify and the films carried some sense of that unprecedented conflict to very different audiences all around the world. Moreover, even after the films had lost their mass audience at home, they were seen by a wide variety of different audiences around the world, invariably offering them a more powerful representation of the character of the European war than that provided by any other medium. And last, but by no means least, the footage shot by the handful of official British cameramen during the First World War offers us now, at the end of the twentieth century, a uniquely direct access to a part of the experience of those men and women who endured so much on the battlefields of Europe. The medium of television has already given millions access to those, tantalisingly short, extracts from their work that appear with such regularity in programmes about the War. It may be that the new technologies of the twenty-first century will enable a more complete access to their work, so much of which survives in the remarkable collection held by the Imperial War Museum Film Archive in London.[69] And maybe, then, these film-makers will achieve the recognition that has for so long been accorded to their peers who worked in the very different media of painting, poetry, drama and the novel.

NOTES

1 By and large, propaganda films were only well received when their ideology confirmed and endorsed the audience's already established ideology. For further discussion of the difficulties propagandists encountered in reaching the mass audience see Nicholas Reeves, *The Power of Film Propaganda: Myth or Reality?* (Cassell: London, 1999).

2 Its full title was *The Kinematograph and Lantern Weekly*, but it was invariably referred to as *Kine Weekly*: 27 August 1914, p. 63.

3 *Bioscope*, 3 September 1914, p. 859.

4 See, for example, an editorial in *Bioscope*, 15 April 1915, p. 179.

5 'The film as an aid to recruiting. Bringing home the realities', *The Times*, 14 April 1915, p. 5.

6 For detailed discussion of wartime official propaganda see M. L. Sanders and Philip M. Taylor, *British Propaganda during the First World War* London: Macmillan, 1982); a brief discussion can be found in Nicholas Reeves, *Official British Film Propaganda during the First World War* (London: Croom Helm, 1986), pp. 8–43. Hereafter referred to as Reeves (1986).

7 The phrase is Masterman's own, quoted in his wife's biography of her husband: Lucy Masterman, *C. F. G. Masterman: A Biography* (London: Nicholson and Watson, 1939), p. 283.

8 Public Record Office, FO 371, Vol. 2538/89982/89982, Sir C. Spring Rice to the Foreign Secretary, 24 June 1915.

9 Public Record Office, FO 371, Vol. 2573/127947/127947, Sir G. Barclay to Foreign Office, 24 August 1915.

10 *Kine Weekly*, 13 August 1914, p. 27.

11 For further discussion of these negotiations see Reeves (1986), pp. 50–56.

12 Quoted in Nicholas Hiley, 'The British cinema auditorium' in Karel Dibbets and Bert Hogenkamp (eds), *Film and the First World War* (Amsterdam: Amsterdam University Press, 1995), p. 161.

13 The words are Lucy Masterman's describing the character of the opposition which her husband encountered: Masterman, *C. F. G. Masterman*, pp. 282–3.

14 Philip Towle, 'The debate on wartime censorship in Britain 1902–14', in Brian Bond and Ian Roy (eds), *War and Society: A Yearbook of Military History* (London: Croom Helm, 1975) pp. 103–16.

15   'Civilian on fleet seeking Germans', *New York Times*, 4 June 1916, p. 3.

16   For further discussion of the circumstances in which official filming took place see Reeves (1986), pp. 89–113.

17   For an analysis of that debate see Reeves (1986), pp. 79–81.

18   Precise audience figures for the film do not exist, but Nicholas Hiley has calculated that the film was seen by audiences of twenty million in its first six weeks, and may have eventually been seen by a majority of the domestic population – Nicholas Hiley, 'The *Battle of the Somme* and the British news media', a paper presented at a conference held at the Centre de Recherche de l'Historial de la Grande Guerre, in Péronne on 21 July 1992, pp. 10–11.

19   The word 'official' was soon dropped and in February 1918 its title was changed to *Pictorial News (Official)*. For further discussion of the wartime official newsreel, see Luke McKernan, *Topical Budget: The Great British New Film* (London, British Film Institute, 1992), pp. 19–63.

20   At least twenty film tags were made, and many urged people to grow their own food, though some also promoted the various savings schemes that were such a prominent feature of wartime life.

21   For further discussion of the cinemotor tours see Reeves (1986), p. 28 and p. 226.

22   For a comprehensive discussion of the entire range of official film production, see Reeves (1986), pp. 140–221.

23   The phrase is Cate Haste's and her monograph remains the most comprehensive discussion of unofficial wartime propaganda and the wide variety of organisations that produced it: Cate Haste, *Keep the Home Fires Burning* (London: Allen Lane, 1977).

24   Imperial War Museum Film Archive, *Britain Prepared* (IWM 580), Reel 3, 00–354.

25   Imperial War Museum Film Archive, *Ypres – The Shell-shattered City of Flanders* (IWM 206).

26   House of Lords Records Office, Beaverbrook Papers, Series E, Box 1, File 4, *Agreement between Sir R. Brade and Gaumont and Jury's*, October 1915.

27   The only exception was the group of nine naval films released in the last twelve months of the War, where a rather more wordy and propagandist style was followed. For further discussion of the character of titling in these films see Reeves (1986), pp. 175–7.

28   These words were written by the Conservative MP, Holcombe Ingleby, in a letter of his written on Christmas Day 1915, quoted in Trevor Wilson, *The Myriad Faces of War: Britain and the Great War 1914–1918* (Cambridge: Polity, 1988), p. 169.

29   For further discussion of the circumstances of the film's production, see Reeves (1986), pp. 89–94.

30   *The Times*, for example, commented on 31 December 1915 that the film was simply 'the finest thing ever produced in this country'.

31   Public Record Office, INF 4, Vol. 2, J. Brooke-Wilkinson, 'Chapter XI, The war years', undated typescript, pp. 305–6. This is apparently part of the manuscript for a book 'Films and Censorship in England', by Brooke-Wilkinson (Secretary of the Kinematograph Manufacturers' Association), that was never published.

32   The phrase was used in the title of a full-page advertisement: *Bioscope*, Vol. XXX, No. 483, 13 January 1916, p. 190.

33   For further discussion of the circumstances under which the official cameramen filmed, see Reeves (1986), pp. 94–113.

34   'The picture-houses', *Manchester Guardian*, 19 April 1916, p. 3. The trade press had been critical from the outset, with *The Cinema* arguing, for example, that the way in which the films were marketed represented nothing less than 'a fraud on the long-suffering British public': *The Cinema*, Vol. X, No. 170, 17 January 1916, p. 2.

35   The film's ability to convey much of its meaning through the expressions on the soldiers' faces is lost almost entirely in the video print – it is only when the film is seen on the screen that the image achieves the level of definition in which this becomes clear.

36   In fact, German prisoners of war can be recognised by the absence of their helmets.

37   This sequence comes at the end of Part IV of the film – Imperial War Museum Film Archive, IWM 191, Reel 4, 734–868'.

38   Nicholas Reeves, 'Cinema, spectatorship and propaganda: "Battle of the Somme" (1916) and its contemporary audience', *Historical Journal of Film, Radio and Television*, Vol. 17, No. 1, 1997, pp. 5–28.

39   The debate about the authenticity of this and a small number of other problematic sequence in the film is rigorously explored in Roger Smither, ' "A wonderful idea of the fighting": The question of fakes in "The Battle of the Somme" ', *Historical Journal of Film, Radio and Television*, Vol. 13, No. 2, 1993, pp. 149–69.

40   'Film pictures from the Somme', *Manchester Guardian*, 11 August 1916, p. 4.

41   'War's reddest side', *The Cinema*, Vol. XI, No. 200, 10 August 1916, p. 26.

42   Reported in: 'War history on the cinema. The British offensive', *The Times*, 11 August 1916, p. 3.

43   In her diary, published as: A. J. P. Taylor (ed.), *Lloyd George: A Diary by Frances Stevenson* (London: Hutchinson, 1971), p. 112.

44   Imperial War Museum Film Archive, *The King Visits His Armies in the Great Advance* (IWM 192).

45   There is even a sequence in *Battle of the Somme* in which a doctor, who is dressing an arm wound, gives the wounded soldier a cigarette during the course of his treatment!

46   The phrase is Major H. E. Trevor's in a letter to his parents, written from the Somme battlefield on 16 September 1916 – quoted in Malcolm Brown, *The Imperial War Museum Book of the First World War* (London: Sidgwick and Jackson, 1993), p. 84.

47   It was reported in May 1917 that it had earned £35,000 compared to the £30, 000 earned by *Battle of the Somme: War Office Cinematograph Committee Revenue Account up to 4 May 1917*, House of Lords Record Office, Beaverbrook Papers, Series E, No. 14, File, 'Cinema general May 1917'.

48   Imperial War Museum Film Archive, *Battle of the Ancre and the Advance of the Tanks* (IWM 116).

49   There is no definitive indication in the surviving evidence why this change took place, although it seems probable that the propagandists became increasingly wary about the inclusion of explicit images of the dead and wounded. Certainly, General Rawlinson claimed that he had cut 'most of the horrors in dead and wounded' from *Battle of the Somme* (Rawlinson's diary entry quoted in Trevor Wilson, Myriad Faces, p. 739) and this claim was substantiated many years later by one of the official cameramen in an interview with Kevin Brownlow – Brownlow's interview is discussed in Reeves (1986), pp. 96ff. By 1918 the inclusion of such material was opposed by the War Office on the grounds of its deleterious effect on the public. For further discussion of these issues see Reeves (1986), p. 105.

50   For a discussion of these films see Reeves (1986), pp. 169–74.

51   See J. M. Winter, *The Great War and the British People* (London: Macmillan, 1985), especially pp. 279–82.

52   Trevor Wilson, *Myriad Faces*, p. 529.

53   In reality it had never disappeared, but in the first two years of the War it had been largely limited to the Clyde (in south-west Scotland) and South Wales.

54   In all, five-and-a-half million working days were lost in 1917, with a further six million lost in 1918, both more than double the number for 1916, although still far short of the ten million lost in the first seven months of 1914.

55   See Wilson, *Myriad Faces*, pp. 519–30.

56   The Department of Information took over from Wellington House in February 1917; it was replaced by the Ministry of Information in March 1918.

57   Public Record Office, FO 395, Vol. 37, 104484/8403, *Report by Cinema Committee on 'Britain Prepared'*, 25 May 1916.

58   Public Record Office, FO 395, Vol. 149, 135331/135331, *Memorandum for the Information of H. M. Ambassadors, Consular Officers and Others*, undated; despatched 28 July 1917 – ibid., 141398/135331.

59   Slade's comments are reported in a letter from T. L. Gilmour (at the DoI)

to Stephen Gaselee at the Foreign Office – Public Record Office, FO 395, Vol. 248, 26754/698, 9 February 1918.

60   Public Record Office, FO 395, Vol. 66, 49064/329, Captain Gaunt to C. H. Montgomery (DoI), 21 February 1917.

61   Public Record Office, FO 395, Vol. 233, 240657/994, Northam (MoI) to Gaselee (FO), 18 September 1918.

62   The evidence of the reception of the films overseas is discussed in Nicholas Reeves, 'Film propaganda and its audience: The example of Britain's official films during the First World War', *Journal of Contemporary History*, Vol. 18 (1983), especially pp. 474–7 and pp. 488–9.

63   Public Record Office, FO 395 Vol. 78, 205101/125435, Cummins (Mexico) to Foreign Office, 25 September 1918; Vol. 163, 240803/47357, White (Tangier) to Foreign Office, 16 September 1918.

64   For a detailed discussion of film propaganda in Russia see M. L. Sanders, 'British film propaganda in Russia 1916–1918', *Historical Journal of Film, Radio and Television*, Vol. 3, No. 2, 1983, pp. 117–29.

65   Public Record Office, FO 395, Vol. 269, 003893/0026, *Report of the Work of the British War Information Committee for China during 1918*, 31 March 1919.

66   Public Record Office, FO 395, Vol. 248, 35530/698, Mallet to Foreign Office, 25 January 1918; Vol. 163, 87475/19324, Willis (Khartoum) to Gaselee, (FO) 13 April 1918.

67   Public Record Office, FO 395, Vol. 38, Gowers (DoI) to Montgomery (FO), 25 November 1916.

68   Public Record Office, FO 395, Vol. 80, 17307/132634, Butler (USA) to Buchan (DoI), 9 August 1917.

69   Some sense of the extraordinary extent and scope of the collection can be gained by looking at the published catalogue: Roger Smither (ed.), *Imperial War Museum Film Catalogue – Vol. 1: The First World War Archive* (London: Flicks Books, 1994). DD Video, in conjunction with the Imperial War Museum, has also published video cassette recordings of both *Battle of the Somme* and *Battle of the Ancre*, and there is also a compilation video, *War Women of Britain – Women at War 1914–1918*, which features a number of official films that focus attention on the new wartime roles of women.

3

Enduring Heroes: British Feature Films and the First World War, 1919–1997

Michael Paris

In the popular television series *Blackadder Goes Forth*, Captain Edmund Blackadder, a regular soldier from the old pre-1914 army is serving on the Western Front. In the final episode, set in 1917, he is called to HQ and informed by General Hogmanay Melchett that the Germans somehow appear to know all the British battle plans. Blackadder looks surprised, 'I didn't know we had any battle plans', he explains. 'Of course we have,' replies the General, 'how else do you think the battles are directed?' 'Our battles are directed, sir?' asks a quizzical Blackadder. 'Yes of course they are, Blackadder; directed according to the Grand Plan'. Blackadder considers this for a moment before replying. 'Would that be the plan to continue with total slaughter until everyone's dead except Field Marshal Haig, Lady Haig and their pet tortoise Alan?' 'Great Scott!' exclaims the General, 'Even you know it!' At the end of the episode, unable to wangle his way out of the trenches, Blackadder and his companions go 'over the top' to certain death in another meaningless offensive, yet more sacrificial victims to the High Command's 'Grand Plan'.[1]

This episode perfectly encapsulates what has now become the popular interpretation of the First World War in Britain – futile struggle directed by dull-witted generals whose only strategy was to waste young lives in a series of pointless attacks in the hope that the enemy would be the first to tire of the slaughter. As Gary Sheffield has pointed out, *Blackadder* required only minimal scene-setting to make the series intelligible to a mass-audience born long after the conflict itself ended – trenches, incompetent generals, and long-suffering but good-humoured 'Tommies' resigned to the inevitable fate awaiting them in 'No Man's Land'.[2] But such a negative interpretation of 1914–18 really only took hold of the popular imagination during the 1960s when a flood of revisionist popular histories, novels, documentaries and films was created to mark the fiftieth anniversaries of the conflict.[3] Before then, British cinema had generally been reluctant to portray the War as unmitigated disaster and had adopted a far less critical approach which sought to find some meaning in the conflict. The purpose here, then, is to examine the manner in which the British film industry reconstructed the Great War after 1918, and to consider why film-makers believed such ambiguity was necessary in dealing with the subject.

Long before 1914 war had become a major theme in British popular culture and the nation's little wars of empire were invariably portrayed as romantic and heroic adventures when reconstructed in popular novels, illustrations and films. In 1914 the public expected the European war to conform to the same glamorous scenario. But when the conflict turned out to be far longer and far more brutal than anyone could possibly have imagined, the film industry, like the rest of the media, happily conspired to maintain an image of the War as 'the Great Adventure'. Yet despite the best efforts of the propagandists, after 1916 it became increasingly difficult to conceal the fact that this was no romantic adventure – an excitement to savour from the safety of the auditorium – but a total war that directly impacted upon the whole population. Those at home, appalled by the hardship, suffering and the seemingly endless casualty lists, needed no reminders of the War and looked to cinema for an escape from everyday reality. Thus by the Armistice, feature films about the conflict had almost disappeared from the screen.

It is often suggested that when films about the Great War did re-emerge in the 1920s they reflected the same bitter view of the War as the memoirs and novels of the disillusioned young survivors, such as Siegfried Sassoon and Richard Aldington, and the poetry of Wilfred Owen and the other young martyrs of the Western Front. By the end of the 1920s, we have been told, this disenchantment permeated society and, later wedded to the pacifist/appeasement movement, became the dominant popular view of the War. The problem with this explanation, however, is that those who have advanced it have based their argument upon limited sources – the novels and memoirs of a handful of bitter veterans who felt betrayed because the War had neither restored the

'Golden Summer' of Edwardian England nor created the brave new world of the politicians' promise – and have taken these as the representative view of the nation as a whole.[4] Yet the work of the disenchanted was only a small part of the outpouring of war-related material during the inter-war period, most of which took a far more positive view of what the War had been about. Certainly no one sought to deny the horror of the trenches or the shocking loss of life, but it was more commonly believed that such sacrifice had not been in vain. After all, the War had ended in victory; Europe had been freed from German tyranny; and the British Empire preserved, even extended. The dead, then, had given their lives for something worthwhile – and here we must remember that this was a far more comforting idea for hundreds of thousands of bereaved families than accepting that their loved ones had died for no good reason. One simply had to believe that the War had been justified in order to give their death meaning.

What is suggested here, then, is that during the inter-war period there were in fact two perceptions of the War co-existing in an uneasy balance: a minority view held by the disenchanted, a response by some battlefield survivors – mostly officers from the social elites, who mourned their fallen contemporaries, the golden youths who, it was believed, would have been the future leaders of the nation; and a more common view, which endured at least until the Second World War, and which believed, or tried to believe, that the War had been justified and which emphasised its heroic and sacrificial nature – another bloody but glorious page in the history of the British Empire. This interpretation of the War was expressed, not in the writings of an intellectual elite, but in mass culture – in war memorials, in adventure fictions, boys' stories, magazine illustrations and in popular histories.[5] Here cinema provides a useful case study, for film was a popular art playing to a vast audience. Cinema was frequently condemned by the social elites for pandering to the masses but it is exactly this dependence upon a mass audience that makes film such a valuable reflection of popular opinion. While many film-makers themselves came from the upper classes, Anthony Asquith or Ivor Montagu, for example, they were aware of their dependence upon the audience, thus British feature films dealing with the Great War struck an uneasy balance, reflecting the dominant public mood of wanting to remember the War as worthwhile and the dead as heroes, yet often tinged with the disenchantment that film-makers shared with others of their class.

It has been commonplace to suggest that following the Armistice war films were unpopular with audiences, that they virtually disappeared from the screen. While it is certainly true that Britain produced far fewer films about the War than some nations, particularly America, this was due more to the financial constraints on the industry than a general distaste for the subject. The War had had such dramatic impact upon the nation and its consequences were so far reaching that film-makers were frequently drawn back to the subject throughout the inter-war period. War films were popular with an audience who wanted to know what it had been like and who needed reassurance that it had all been worthwhile.

The first post-War release was Maurice Elvey's *Comradeship* (1919), a patriotic tale of a young tailor initially inclined to pacifism. However, when persuaded to do his duty by the daughter of a wealthy landowner, he serves bravely on the Western Front until blinded by an enemy shellburst. Back home he is nursed by his young friend and gradually their 'comradeship' turns to love. *Bioscope* suggested that the story embodied the 'spirit', the sense of duty to King and Empire, that had inspired so many young Englishmen to fight for their country: '[T]he sense of camaraderie which made the British people one united national army of comrades, is shown in the film as effectually destroying those social barriers which would have been insurmountable in peace time'.[6] The War, then, not only resulted in the defeat of Germany but had also created a new society at home. A popular and financial success, *Comradeship* deals in stereotypes: brave soldiers driven by a sense of duty, brutal Germans and patriotic girls. The film started life before the Armistice and was clearly intended as morale-boosting propaganda. Nevertheless, it established a number of cinematic conventions for dealing with the War that would prove influential throughout the period.

The prolific Elvey went on to make a further three films in the 'war as romantic adventure' style. *Mademoiselle from Armentieres* was released in 1926, and starred Estelle Brody and John Stuart. A straightforward romance in which a beautiful and patriotic French girl helps a plucky British soldier escape from his German captors, the film was uncomplicated, unrealistic and immensely successful. Elvey also produced *Roses of Picardy* – an attempt to dramatise part of R. H. Mottram's *Spanish Farm* trilogy dealing with the love affair between a British officer and a Flemish farmer's daughter – and *Mademoiselle Parlay-Voo*, another romantic adventure, but equally popular with audiences. At this time, Elvey was one of the most prolific and successful directors in Britain but, as Rachael Low points out, this was due more to his understanding of public taste than any real creative flair – a telling point for our purposes, suggesting that Elvey was reflecting exactly how his audience wanted to remember the War.[7]

Romance and adventure were also the key elements in Arthur Maude's 1928 feature *Poppies of Flanders*, based on a story by Sapper. According to the film's publicity it contained 'all the qualities that make for a popular success – love, laughter, patriotism and self-sacrifice'.[8] The *Guns of Loos* (1928), a more lavish production, told the story of the soldier son of an armaments manufacturer. In France, the young officer is accused of cowardice when in fact he is suffering from shell-shock. Yet he redeems his honour by saving his guns during a German attack, but is blinded in the action. Returning home he again saves the day by persuading his father's workers to call off a proposed strike, by appealing to their patriotism. The well-constructed and realistic battle scenes were much praised by critics, but more interesting was the suggestion that what appeared to be cowardice was in fact caused by battle fatigue – thus even those who might appear cowardly were essentially heroic.[9] During the 1920s, such positive reconstructions of the War were powerfully reinforced by a series of elaborate and popular documentary-dramas from British Instructional Films (BIF) and produced by that ardent imperialist, Harry Bruce Woolfe.

Beginning with the *Battle of Jutland* in 1921, Woolfe, himself a veteran, produced a number of celebrations of the great battles of the War, including *Ypres* (1925) and *Mons* (1926).[10] *Jutland* used actuality footage with animations and models, but the later films were mostly re-enactments which included fictional episodes to add to the drama. The films were made with men and equipment supplied by the Army and Royal Navy. In return for this assistance, BIF virtually surrendered control to the Army Council, and what resulted was very much an 'official' interpretation. Indeed, so closely was BIF connected with the Establishment that in 1927 the prime minister was quizzed in the House of Commons on how far the Government was subsidising these productions and what was the return on its investment? However, as Samuel Hynes has pointed out, the questioner missed the mark, for the point was not that the government was interested in profit but with monument-making and using willing film-makers for that purpose. As he goes on to suggest, the BIF reconstructions were propaganda, 'intended to tell the story of the war in heroic, value-affirming terms that monuments traditionally express'.[11] However, we should note that these films told essentially the same story as the popular fictions of the period.

What BIF put on the screen were sanitised, heroic images, testaments to courage, patriotism and the nobility of sacrifice. *Mons*, for example, was sub-titled *The Story of the Immortal Retreat* and suggested a heroic vision of the British Expeditionary Force's first battle. The brochure for

3.1   Comrades in Adversity, *Mons* (Michael Paris Collection)

the film tells us that the retreat of the 'Old Army' is one of the most glorious memories of the War, 'more splendid than any victory'. The film does more or less acurately re-tell the story of how the BEF, heavily outnumbered, was forced back after the initial clash with the German Army at Mons, but focuses mainly on the episodes in which individuals performed outstanding acts of bravery. We see: Lieutenant Dease continuing to fire from his artillery position despite his many wounds; the stand of the King's Own Yorkshire Light Infantry who, surrounded and outnumbered, did the only honourable thing – attacked the enemy; the wild bayonet charge of the Argyll and Sutherland Highlanders which shattered the attacking Germans; and the final stand that stopped the enemy advance. The captions read like sub-headings from some pre-1914 adventure story from the *Boys' Own Paper* – 'How mention valorous deeds when all alike are valiant' and 'The 2nd. Suffolks outshine their own proud history'. What is so striking in the film is the emphasis on how these young Britons gave their lives so unhesitatingly, so willingly, for King and Country.

BIF portrayed the War as a national achievement – an adventure in which brave young Britons won immortality. They did not seek to disguise the human cost, but suggested that those who fell died in a noble cause. *Picturegoer*, in an article on the director of many of these

epics, Walter Summers, claimed that *Mons* and *Ypres* were two of the
'finest war pictures' ever produced anywhere and that few men were as
well qualified as Summers to reconstruct these great battles. Here it was
alluding to Summers's war record for he was a highly-decorated veteran
who had fought on the Western Front.[12] Summers himself, as Rachael
Low tells us, was a man obsessed with the idea of bravery, and this
concern is very evident in his view of the War.[13] But while these films
were extremely popular with audiences,[14] their critical reception varied.
The trade and popular press were generally enthusiastic while more
intellectual journals denigrated their emphasis on patriotism and heroic
incident. In *Bioscope*, for example, the reviewer had nothing but praise
for *Mons*, a 'tragic and glorious' saga of the British Army – a 'Homeric
struggle' with photography of 'the highest standard'.[15] However, in the
avant-garde *Close Up* 'Bryher' (Winifred Ellerman) suggested that the
same film was badly photographed, 'blurred and out of focus', and that it
suffered from 'the kind of sentimentality that makes one shudder . . . a
mixture of a Victorian tract for children and a cheap serial in the sort of
magazine one finds discarded on the beach'.[16] Her attitude to the series
was summed up in a later review of *The Battles of the Coronel and
Falkland Islands*. Here she suggested that the films suffered from a
romantic and sentimental approach to the conflict that ignored the
disease, discomfort and horror of the War. In order to fully understand
the meaning of war, she argued, it was essential to 'get away from this
nursery formula that to be in uniform is to be a hero; that brutality and
waste are not to be condemned provided they are disguised in flags,
medals and cheering'.[17] *The Battles of the Coronel and Falkland Islands*,
a lavish spectacle made with the full co-operation of the Admiralty, was
the last of Woolfe's reconstructions, but his heroic conception of the War
was inherited by New Era films which went on to produce a further three
re-enactments, *The Somme* (1927), *Q Ships* (1928) and *Blockade* (1932), a
re-edited version of *Q Ships* with added soundtrack.

But while more thoughtful film-makers eschewed the romanticism of
BIF their films were not without ambiguity. The veteran film-maker
George Pearson had spent the war years producing propagandist pictures such as *For the Empire* (1916) and a film version of Bruce
Bairnsfather's play *The Better 'Ole*, which he hoped 'would strengthen
the nation's will to carry on to the bitter end'.[18] However, by 1924, he was
in more reflective mood when he began work on a film about the effects of
the War on the poor, a 'scrapbook of pictures of life . . . My characters
must be of humble folk, for they had given most and suffered most in the
Great War'.[19] *Reveille* revolves around a widowed shopkeeper, who has

lost her three sons in the War, Mick, a young seamstress and her brother Fred who lodge above the shop, and 'Nutty' and Whelks, the soldier friends of the widow's sons. We meet them first in September 1918 when the boys are home on leave. Later, amid the celebrations of Armistice Night, the Widow receives the news that the brothers and Fred have all been killed in action. Then, as Pearson has explained,

> [t]he third and concluding phase of my narrative was an exposition of initial disillusionment, but eventual courage that came with War's aftermath. On Remembrance Day five years later, Whelks and the embittered Nutty visit the widow. As they climb the stairs to her room, they are overtaken by the 'Great Silence'. They pause, remembering their dead comrades. Then the first notes of the Reveille. 'Whelks staring at a strangely different Nutty . . . a man with eyes lit by a kinder light. The rousing call of the distant bugles for a new and inspiring courage . . .'[20]

What exactly did Pearson intend here? Has Nutty realised that his comrades did not die in vain, that the War did have meaning, or simply that he cannot allow his bitterness to dominate the remainder of his life? The film provides no more clues, nor does Pearson's autobiography. Certainly it is a deeply emotional film, particularly in the representation of the two-minutes silence – which is played in real time – and which still exercises considerable impact upon the viewer. Yet the film was premiered in June 1924 at a special performance on behalf of the British Legion and attended by the Prince of Wales, suggesting that it was seen as supporting the official view of the conflict. Critics almost unanimously praised the film, with the *Sunday Express* calling it a 'National Film'. It was equally popular with audiences, perhaps because it could be interpreted as supporting both the disenchanted and those who believed such sacrifice had been necessary. Pearson later made the curious '*East Lynne' on the Western Front* (1930) in which a group of bored Tommies, at rest behind the lines stage a burlesque version of the play in a derelict French theatre to amuse themselves.

The meaning of the War is also unclear in Adrian Brunel's 1927 production *Blighty*, but deliberately so. Brunel had worked for the Film Section of the Ministry of Information during the War. His attitude to the conflict, he later wrote, was based upon a 'sincere conviction that ours was a better cause than theirs'.[21] After the War he started Minerva Films with Leslie Howard and worked as both director and writer. In 1926 he was persuaded to make *Blighty* for Michael Balcon based on a script by Ivor Montagu. Brunel was initially unhappy with the idea because he believed that 'nearly every war film was based upon the chivalry, bravery and sacrifice of men in the fighting forces, and inevitably was pro-war propaganda'. He also believed that the public were tired of such films.[22] Balcon, however, thought the story 'touched on patterns of behaviour at the time . . . the realisation that the outbreak of the First World War was the end of an era and more, perhaps most, important, it suggested the breaking down of class barriers'.[23] The film tells the story of an aristocratic English family during the war years. Their son and chauffeur both volunteer. The son meets and marries a French girl but is subsequently killed. The chauffer, however, distinguishes himself and is commissioned. At the end of the War he returns to his old job. His employers, however, devastated by the death of their son, are only consoled when his widow and her infant son are brought home. A year later the widow marries the chauffeur who is welcomed into the family. While the film uses newsreel battle footage to provide some idea of the War, the main focus is the Home Front and the effect of war on what the publicity called an 'average family'. It offered the view that such sacrifice had not been in vain for the War had broken down class barriers and produced a more consensual society.

While it was popular with audiences, Roy Armes has suggested that *Blighty* omits the 'dirt and squalor' and 'uses the love affairs of the younger generation not to probe the problems posed by class and nationality but to celebrate the myths of the British aristocracy: gallantry in action and tolerance in behaviour, patriotism and self-sacrifice . . . Other critics, however, have suggested that it it was one of the few films of the period to make a comment about the War.[24] The truth is that Brunel and Montagu, perhaps sensing that disenchantment with the War was on the increase, attempted to play to both views. As Brunel candidly explained,

> It fulfilled the requirements of a popular patriotic picture, in that it showed a decent English family behaving decently, and while being resolute in what they believed to be the cause of right and justice, they refused to join in the singing of either 'Land of Hope and Glory' or The Hymn of Hate . . . It also fulfilled the requirements of a 'war' picture, although we never showed the war, but rather the reactions to it on the Home Front. And it was, quietly, an anti-war picture rather than a pro-war picture.[25]

Clearly, then, like all the war films produced during the 1920s, *Blighty* was ambiguous, offering different readings to different audiences. In this case, Brunel deliberately tried to play to both camps but with *Dawn*, released the following year, the director's stated purpose was widely misinterpreted.

Made by Herbert Wilcox, *Dawn* retold the story of Nurse Edith Cavell and became one of the most controversial films of the decade. The German Government, apparently hearing that the film was in production, became concerned that the reconstruction of such an emotional episode might well upset Anglo-German relations and asked the British Foreign Office to intervene. Their cause was taken up the Foreign Secretary, Austen Chamberlain, who approached the British Board of Film Censors (BBFC) and the film was banned.[26] Wilcox, however, was prepared for a fight and arranged for a private viewing for the London County Council which ruled that the film could be seen in London. The film opened in April 1928 to considerable public interest. Over the next few months, most local authorities sided with the LCC, a deliberate snub to the government and the BBFC. Wilcox always strenuously insisted that *Dawn* was intended as an anti-war film and indeed his German soldiers are neither sinister nor barbaric. Many sympathise with Cavell's predicament. The death sentence is only arrived at after careful deliberation and even then one young member of the firing squad refuses to shoot. Yet despite the careful handling of the story, the fact remains that Cavell, a civilian, and one who had nursed German as well as Allied soldiers, was executed for simply aiding her countrymen to escape. We must accept that Wilcox, as he claimed, did indeed make the film as an anti-war statement, yet it seems surprising that he should use such a notorious and emotionally charged episode to do so. Even more curious is that in 1939, on the eve of the Second World War, he should remake the film – again claiming it was a plea for peace! The German occupation of Belgium was also the subject for less ambiguous films, *The Burgomaster of Stilemonde* (1929), based on a story by Maurice Maeterlink about German atrocities inflicted upon helpless civilians, and *I Was a Spy* (1933), the true(?) story of Belgian heroine Marthe Cnockeart, a nurse who was also an Allied spy (see below). Clearly, then, while the 1920s certainly witnessed a growing trend towards pacifism in British society and an increasing sense of the futility and waste of the Great War in particular, films which portrayed the War in traditional and patriotic terms far outnumbered those that raised even some ambiguously phrased doubts about whether such sacrifice could ever be justified.

In his highly readable survey, *The War Film*, Ivan Butler entitles the chapter that deals with the 1930s 'Disillusion'. Here he discusses those films which are generally regarded as condemnations of the Great War,

All Quiet on the Western Front, Westfront 1918 and *The Grand Illusion*, for example, giving the impression that the decade, in terms of cinema at least, marked some kind of watershed in the way in which the War was portrayed on the screen. Butler's book was published in 1974 but this interpretation is still common. More recently Andrew Kelly went even further telling us that, 'in common with many countries, in the late 1920s and early 1930s there was a turning against war in Britain'.[27] However, as we shall see, while disillusionment with the War did gain ground in Britain, there is scant cinematic evidence to suggest that there was any widespread 'turning away' from war in general. Even the cinematic reconstructions of 1914–18 made in the early Thirties still retained their ambiguity and were followed later in the decade by several films which portrayed the War as straightforward adventure.

Britain's contribution to anti-war cinema centres on one particular film, *Journey's End*, released in 1930. The film, closely based upon the stage version of R. C. Sherriff's play, has attracted considerable attention as the 'definitive' film of the First World War.[28] Set entirely in a dug-out on the Western Front in 1917, the film explores the effects of the War on five British officers: Stanhope, the Company Commander, Osborne, the former schoolmaster, the stoical working class Trotter, Hibbert who has lost his nerve, and Raleigh the young replacement and an old school-friend of Stanhope's. While the film has frequently been seen as an indictment of war, the author was at pains to point out that he wrote not one world of condemnation.[29] The truth is that the film can be read in a variety of ways. Here the War is brutal and tragic; all the officers are eventually killed, Raleigh within a few days of his arrival at the Front. Stanhope drinks heavily to forget that he must order men to their deaths and because he is afraid of being afraid. Osborne is killed leading a completely unnecessary trench raid and Stanhope is cynical about his superiors. Here, too, in Trotter's advice to Raleigh to resist lobbing Mills bombs into the German trenches lest they retaliate, is evidence of the 'live and let live' system, the survival strategy employed by many British and German soldiers.[30] Equally, Raleigh's comment that the Germans are 'quite decent' might well be taken as endorsing the camaraderie of the trench fighters while suggesting that the real enemy are those who have sent them to the slaughter. Yet for all this, *Journey's End* is a film about duty, about enduring; the War is and Englishmen must carry on. As Stanhope tells Hibbert, who pleads to be sent on sick leave so that he will not have to endure another attack, 'Go on, see it through Old Man . . . it's the only decent thing to do'. And Hibbert does, redeeming his honour by dying in battle.

The emphasis on duty is also the key element in Anthony Asquith's *Tell England*, the story of two young officers at Gallipoli.[31] Based upon Ernest Raymond's popular novel of the same title, we first meet Rupert Ray and Edgar Doe at their public school, and while many of the school sequences in the book have been cut from the film there is still the suggestion of the concepts of honour and patriotism which such schools instilled in their boys. Both are enthusiastic to get to war but the realities of Gallipoli dampen their fervour. Doe, like Stanhope in *Journey's End*, begins to lose his nerve and at one point screams that what he would like to tell England is the truth about the War. Nevertheless, he still leads a successful raid on a Turkish mortar position, but is fatally wounded in the attack. On the headstone of his grave in this 'foreign field' is inscribed,

> Tell England, ye who pass this monument,
> We died for her, and here we rest content.

As Jeffrey Richards has pointed out, for Doe and Ray, 'War and indeed death, though messy and a trifle unpleasant, are a small price to pay for the preservation of England . . . the England which they, as public schoolboys, were produced and trained to defend'.[32]

3.2   The enduring Tommy, *Suspense* (Michael Paris Collection)

Made around the same time, Walter Summers's *Suspense*, while demonstrating a similar image of a brutal war and stressing the importance of duty, is nevertheless one of the few British films to focus on the other ranks. An infantry company takes over part of the front line. Four comrades explore their new quarters but Pettigrew, a mere boy, begins to hear strange sounds from the trench floor and realises that German sappers are tunnelling beneath them. This is confirmed when he drunkenly blunders into No Man's Land and captures two German prisoners. Now the men can only wait and listen for the sounds to stop, knowing that when they do the enemy mine will be ready to explode. When the tunnelling stops their anxiety becomes intense; they can only wait and hope. The company are relieved at last, but as they thankfully stumble towards the rear, an explosion tells them that their old trench and the relieving company have been destroyed. *Suspense* reconstructs a cruel war where pure chance decides who will live and who will die. But the Company are enduring, stoical; they know what could happen but there is never any doubt but that they will continue to do their duty. Only Pettigrew is temporarily unnerved, but, as his mad escapade results in the capture of two prisoners, it is overlooked. The War has to be endured, and, just like the officers in *Journey's End* and *Tell England*, they carry on. Of course, what is never explained in this, or in any other British film about the War is why they must endure. But this was hardly necessary for, by the mid-1920s, the dominant view of the War's cause was historical inevitability – The nations slithered over the brink into the boiling cauldron of war', wrote Lloyd George, an interpretation that was endorsed in virtually all the political memoirs of the time. The War, then, was no one's fault, no one wanted it; but once drawn into the conflict, nations struggled to survive or go under.[33] This widely held view relieved film-makers of the necessity for causal explanations or apportioning blame, and allowed them instead to concentrate on the nobly enduring hero of the trenches in the battle for national survival.

Suspense, however, was the last British film to deal directly with the war in the trenches until the 1960s; a tacit acknowledgement, perhaps, that the subject was becoming too painful and too controversial to attract a mass audience. Yet at the same time, film-makers were reluctant to proclaim openly the War's futility. In such a climate they developed oblique ways of dealing with the War which still allowed them to explore heroism but avoid the contentious war in the trenches. A popular alternative was to focus on the dangerous world of the spy.

In popular imagination, the spy was a sinister figure operating in a dark and dishonourable world. Thus film-makers had to remake this despised figure in a more heroic mould. One way of doing this was to have a brave and highly decorated officer undertake a dangerous mission behind enemy lines. In *The W Plan* (1930), for example, Colonel Duncan Grant, a 'lad typical of the breed', is just such a hero. Grant is first and foremost an honourable front-line soldier, a battalion commander, but he unhesitatingly goes behind enemy lines disguised as a German soldier to unravel the mystery of the 'W Plan' – secret mining operation designed to destroy the Allied defences.

Victor Saville's *I Was a Spy*, based on the real-life adventures of Marthe Cnockaert, is introduced with an endorsement by Winston Churchill that serves to elevate spying into something noble and heroic,

> A secret service agent who is not activated by any sordid motive, but inspired by patriotism, and ready to pay the well-known forfeit, deserves respect and honour from those he serves so faithfully.
>
> Marthe Cnockaert fulfilled in every respect the conditions which made the terrible profession of a spy dignified and honourable.

While the film does not flinch from the horrors of war – the Germans unleash a poison gas attack and the British bomb German soldiers at a church parade – it is essentially a romantic adventure. Marthe is told by several of her compatriots that she must learn to hate the Germans, but, despite working for the liberation of Belgium, she is still capable of sympathy for the enemy wounded. According to Rachael Low, years later when the film was shown to a new generation, it was praised as an anti-war film. Victor Saville, present at the screening, was surprised but Michael Balcon, the producer, 'dismissed the idea with a brisk "Nonsense!" '[34]

Alfred Hitchcock's *Secret Agent* (1936) employed the adventure mode even more powerfully. Ashenden (John Gielgud) is the dashing, upper-class officer persuaded to leave off his uniform and seek out and kill a German agent operating in Switzerland. He is reluctant to take on such a distasteful assignment but is persuaded it is his duty. Before the traitor is finally dealt with, Ashenden is responsible for the death of an innocent man, but is not long troubled by his mistake, after all, the film seems to suggest, such things happen in war. This incident, within what is a generally good-humoured adventure, has a certain moral ambiguity. Spies were also featured in Edmond Greville's Anglo-French co-production *Mademoiselle Docteur* the following year, and in Michael Powell's 1939 thriller, *The Spy in Black*. Here Conrad Veidt plays a U-Boat commander on a secret mission to the Orkneys who's downfall is deservedly brought about by a beautiful British agent.[35] Interestingly, no attempt was made to recreate the look of the Great War, and thus the film suggested a certain contemporary relevance.

The only other Great War film made during the later 1930s focused on the heroism of an ordinary British seaman – appropriately called Brown. Walter Forde's *Forever England* (1935), adapted from C. S. Forester's novel *Brown on Resolution*, tells the story of a young Briton, who single-handedly delays the repair of a German battle-cruiser and thus paves the way for her destruction by a pursuing British warship. While *Forever England*, advertised as 'a sea drama to stir the blood of everyone of British stock', was seen by critics as a testament to courage, only the *Monthly Film Bulletin* pointed to its lack of jingoism and the mutual respect for both British and German seamen.[36] Nevertheless, as the film was made with the assistance of the Admiralty, which provided both men and ships, it seems that it was intended as a showcase for the Royal Navy – a timely reminder in an increasingly troubled world that British sea power was still a force to be reckoned with.

As we have seen, it has frequently been suggested that during the inter-war period the British turned away from war and inclined to pacificism – a direct consequence of the horrors of the Great War. Yet film-makers were reluctant to condemn the War openly and risk offending those who, for whatever reason, still wanted to believe that the War had been justified. But there was also the problem of censorship. As Jeffrey Richards points out, 'The subject of pacifism and anti-war feeling came within the BBFC realm of "controversial politics" and so no film on the subject was permitted'.[37] Richards has identified a number of proposals for films about the War that, because of their anti-war message, were banned as too controversial.[38] From the mid-1930s, in fact, and no doubt influenced by re-armament and increasing international tension, films about the Great War began to reflect a far more positive and patriotic attitude to the War, but there seems little cinematic evidence to suggest that the British public were 'turning away from war'. Films dealing with the Great War were often ambiguous but there were no ambiguities in the manner in which British cinema portrayed earlier wars nor the obvious enjoyment of audiences of such entertainments.

Bruce Woolfe, for example, also produced a number of nationalistic epics beginning with *Nelson* and *Boadicea* (both 1926); by the 1930s, even his distribution company was called 'Pro Patria Films'. Nor was he alone in portraying war as patriotic adventure, for throughout the period other studios produced a number of heroic films about Britain's 'little wars' of empire such as *The Flag Lieutenant* (1919 and 1926), *The Four Feathers*

(1921 and 1939), *Tommy Atkins* (1928), *Balaclava* (1930), *Lieutenant Daring RN* (1935) and *OHMS* (1937). These were countered by only a handful of short anti-war documentaries that had limited exhibition and were far outweighed by more popular 'war as adventure' features.[39] Nor should we forget that from the mid-1930s a number of documentary and feature films were made which appear to have been intended to prepare the nation for another war – *The Gap, RAF, Midnight Menace* and *Q Planes*.[40] Clearly, then, while the memory of the Great War created difficulties for film-makers, earlier wars could still be portrayed as high adventure and were well received by the public.[41] It would seem that the nation's pacifism was not perhaps as deeply held as we have been led to believe, or at least did not extend to entertainment.

The Second World War, however, did have a considerable impact on the public perception of 1914–1918; as Brian Bond has suggested, 'the First World War came to suffer by comparison with the Second in terms of moral purpose and beneficial outcome.'[42] The popular understanding of 1939 as the beginning of a moral crusade against the evils of Nazism threw into relief the futility of the Great War, and, although film-makers became almost totally absorbed with contemporary events, references to the futility of that earlier war can be found in the Boulting Brothers' *The Dawn Guard* and Leslie Howard's *The Gentle Sex*, among others.

After 1945, Britain faced an increasingly uncertain future, plagued by economic crisis, the problems of decolonisation and the loss of great-power status. In such a climate, film-makers became almost obsessed with the Second World War – the nation's last great triumph. 1914–1918, often seen as the beginning of national decline, was painful to recall and thus ignored by British cinema. However, as Alex Danchev has noted, the Great War was rediscovered in the 1960s through the fiftieth anniversaries which fell between 1964 and 1968.[43] During this period a spate of controversial monographs and popular works was published and the BBC embarked upon its massive twenty-six-part history *The Great War* (1964), attracting an average eight million viewers for each episode. This attention created considerable public interest in the War, yet film-makers seemed curiously reluctant to take advantage of this renewed interest and only three films dealing with the War were made during the entire decade, *Lawrence of Arabia* (1962), *King and Country* (1964) and *Oh! What a Lovely War* (1969).

Several attempts had been made to film the contentious Lawrence story but all ended in failure.[44] However, in 1960 producer Sam Spiegel acquired the rights to Lawrence's own account of the war in the desert and persuaded David Lean to direct the film version. *Lawrence of Arabia* was released in 1962 to considerable acclaim. Opening with Lawrence's death in a motorcycle accident in 1935, the film uses flashback to unravel his complex character through the events of the Desert Revolt. Lean's Lawrence is both heroic and romantic but equally tormented by the dark side of his personality which thrives on danger and the power to take life bestowed by the War – the massacre of the Turkish column at Tafas, for instance, where Lawrence orders 'No Prisoners' and revels in the slaughter. British films about the Great War, had usually suggested that conflict brought out the best in men – a sense of duty and concern for their comrades, but here we are forced to confront the idea that war can also bring out their worst qualities as well.[45]

Similar ideas are also a feature of *King and Country*, directed by American exile Joseph Losey. This is the story of the court martial of a very ordinary soldier, Private Hamp (Tom Courtney), who has served on the Western Front for three years. Finally, in 1917, during the Battle of Passchendaele, he can stand it no longer and decides to go home. Arrested and tried for cowardice, he is defended by Captain Hargreaves (Dirk Bogarde). Initially, the public-school educated Hargreaves has little sympathy for this 'common little runt' who has failed to do his duty and taken the easy way out. However, as Hamp's horrific experiences begin to emerge, Hargreaves gradually begins to see Hamp as a man who has been psychologically damaged by the War. It is obvious that Hamp is suffering from shell-shock, a fact that Hargreaves tries to introduce into the trial without success. The verdict is inevitable, not because of lack of sympathy for the soldier, but because the unfortunate Hamp must become an object lesson lest other soldiers also walk away from the War. When the unhappy firing squad botch the execution, it is Hargreaves who must adminster the final shot. As much about class relations as about the War, *King and Country* does, nevertheless, convey a powerful sense of the futility of War and questions the whole idea of duty.[46] Interestingly, while the film was critically well-received it was a commercial failure – perhaps even in the 1960s British audiences simply could not accept that such a blatant miscarriage of justice could happen in the British Army?

Richard Attenborough's *Oh! What a Lovely War*[47] breaks away from traditional narrative structure and portrays the War as a series of sketches played out as seaside entertainment – a show on Brighton Pier – 'WORLD WAR ONE, BATTLES, SONGS AND A FEW JOKES', claims the advertising banner – and works remarkably well. The sketches convey a kaleidoscopic impression of the War: the almost hysterical mood of 1914 during which men rushed to the colours to 'get into the war', the incomparable Maggie Smith as the suggestive music hall star enticing men into recruiting with the promise of adventure, glory and sexual favours, and the awful realisation that battle is not glorious and romantic but brutal and bloody. The reconstruction of the 1914 Christmas 'truce' is particularly significant here for it is this incident which makes both sides realise that they are comrades in suffering and leads them to question why exactly they are fighting each other. Here, too, is the suggestion that their real enemies might be those who have sent them into the trenches and the idiotic generals who blindly continue to believe that just one more push will win the War! There is nothing even remotely romantic or heroic here, just a bleak and terrifying experience.

The films of the 1960s broke away from the idea of the nobly enduring hero in an inevitable war and added new, and critical, elements to the story. Now, in this more outspoken decade, film-makers began to blame politicians and generals for the suffering. *Oh! What a Lovely War* was the first British film to even mention the causes of the War – a family squabble between the crowned heads of Europe, it suggests, into which the British government were drawn by self-interest and imperial ambition. The generals, the 'donkeys' of popular 1960s historiography, are condemned – ruthlessly back-biting as they jostle for position in the command structure, and hopelessly incompetent as they sacrifice yet

3.3   FM Sir Douglas Haig (John Mills) in
Oh! What a Lovely War (Michael Paris Collection)

another division in a pointless attack. We do not see the High Command in *King and Country*, but we know they reject Hamp's plea for mercy so that he can become an object lesson for his comrades. The regimental officers here are mostly decent men, but war has inured them to death and suffering and they have shed their moral responsibilities. Even in *Lawrence*, the General Staff mentality is noticeable among many of Lawrence's contemporaries. But far more important here is that the film allows us to see something of the appalling duplicity of the British Government in using the Arab Revolt to further their own imperial ambitions in the Middle East. Lean exonerates Lawrence from such cynicism, for in the film he is ignorant of the Sykes-Picot Agreement – the Anglo-French deal that carved up the Ottoman Empire between the two nations.

Yet even even during this critical and outspoken age the War as adventure was not entirely dead, as *Zeppelin* (1971) demonstrated. Equally curious, was *Aces High*, a reworking of *Journey's End*, and made five years later. Now set in a Royal Flying Corps squadron, the story appeared even more strongly an essay in duty and patriotism. Over

3.4   *Regeneration* (Artificial Eye)

the next decade or so, it was television that produced the most un-compromising documents about the War, most notably Vera Brittain's powerful indictment *Testament of Youth* (1978) and the controversial *Monocled Mutineer* (1986). Not until 1997 did cinema return to the Great War with *Regeneration*.

Based upon Pat Barker's novel of the same title, *Regeneration* explores the psychological effects of modern warfare upon those who are forced to endure it. Set at Craiglockart, the hospital for neurasthenic officers, the film is a re-working of the experience of Siegfried Sassoon. Sassoon, a reckless and highly decorated officer, had been sent to Craiglockart not because he suffered from shell-shock but simply because he had openly protested about the War and must therefore be unbalanced. Here he meets psychologist Dr William Rivers and the young Wilfred Owen, another patient. Rivers represents traditional ideas about duty and honour, for he must cure these damaged officers and return them to the front. Yet his sense of duty is constantly at odds with his humani-tarian instinct to protect these men from further harm. Interestingly, River also displays the symptoms of shell-shock caused by this internal conflict and the constant 'bombardment' of his patients' experiences. He is finally instrumental in helping Sassoon realise that looking after his company in France will achieve more than an isolated protest: a revival of his sense of duty – not to the nation but to his brothers-in-arms. A second theme deals with the meeting between Sassoon and Wilfred Owen and Sassoon's advice that the younger man should use his war experience as the subject for his poetry. At the film's conclusion, both return to France and the film ends with Sassoon's letter to Rivers telling him of Owen's death in battle. Pointedly, he includes a copy of Owen's 'Parable of the Old Man and the Young'. Richly-layered and haunting, *Regeneration* nevertheless returns us, full circle, to the 'inevitable' war and the nobly enduring hero of the trenches.[48]

NOTES

I am grateful for a grant from the Scouloudi Foundation, Institute of Historical Research, London, for assistance with the research costs in preparing this paper.

1   *Blackadder Goes Forth* (six episodes) was originally shown in 1989 and repeated in November 1998. The series is available on a BBC videocas-sette.

2   Gary Sheffield, 'Oh! What a futile war: Representations of the Western Front in modern British media and popular culture', in Ian Stewart and Susan L. Carruthers (eds), *War, Culture and the Media: Representations of the Military in Twentieth Century Britain* (Trowbridge: Flicks Books, 1996), pp. 54–5.

3   See Alex Danchev, ' "Bunking and debunking": The controversies of the 1960s', in Brian Bond (ed.), *The First World War and British Military History* (Oxford: Clarendon Press, 1991).

4   See Samuel Hynes, *A War Imagined: The First World War and British Culture* (London: Pimlico, 1992).

5   See Michael Paris, 'A different view of the trenches: Juvenile fiction and popular perceptions of the First World War', *War Studies Journal*, 3:1, 1997, pp. 32–46.

6   *Bioscope*, 41: 643, 6 February 1919.

7   Rachael Low, *History of the British Film, 1918–1929* (London: George Allen and Unwin, 1971), p. 173.

8   Quoted in, Ivan Butler, *The War Film* (London: Tantivy Press, 1974), p. 36.

9   Interestingly, Michael Balcon's first film, *Woman to Woman* (1923), also dealt with an officer suffering the effects of shell-shock.

10 The series comprised: *The Battle of Jutland* (1921), *Armageddon* (1923), *Zeebrugge* (1924), *Ypres* (1925), *Mons* (1926) and *The Battles of the Coronel and Falkland Islands* (1927).

11 Hynes, *War Imagined*, pp. 445–6.

12 *Picturegoer*, 13: 78, January 1927.

13 Rachael Low, *The History of the British Film, 1929–1939: Film making in 1930s Britain* (London: George Allen and Unwin, 1985), p. 120.

14 Low, *History of the British Film, 1918–1929*, p. 181.

15 *Bioscope*, 68: 1041, 23 September 1926.

16 'Bryher', 'The War from three angles', *Close Up*, 1, July 1927, p. 19.

17 'Bryher', 'The War from three more angles', *Close Up*, 1, October 1927, p. 45.

18 George Pearson, *Flashback: The Autobiography of a British Film-Maker* (London: George Allen and Unwin, 1957), p. 71.

19 Ibid., p. 125.

20 Ibid., pp. 127–8.

21 Adrian Brunel, *Nice Work: The Story of Thirty Years in British Film Production* (London: Forbes Robertson, 1949), p. 47.

22 Ibid., p. 126.

23 Michael Balcon, *A Lifetime in Films* (London: Hutchinson, 1974), p. 25.

24 Roy Armes, *A Critical History of British Cinema* (London: Secker and Warburg, 1978), pp. 71–2; Leslie Halliwell, *Halliwell's Film Guide* (London: Paladin, 1989), p. 115.

25 Brunel, *Nice Work*, pp. 126–7.

26 See James C. Robertson, 'Dawn (1928): Edith Cavell and Anglo-German

relations', *Historical Journal of Film, Radio and Television*, 4: 1, 1984, 15–28.

27   Butler, *War Film*; Andrew Kelly, *Cinema and the Great War* (London: Routledge, 1997).

28   Jeffrey Richards, *The Age of the Dream Palace* (London: Routledge, 1984), p. 289; Kelly, *Cinema and the Great War*, pp. 65–75; William Everson, 'Journey's End', *Films in Review*, 26: 1, 1975, pp. 31–5; Michael T. Isenberg, 'An ambiguous pacifism: A retrospective on World War 1 films, 1930–1938', *Journal of Popular Culture*, IV, 1975, pp. 98–115.

29   Kelly, *Cinema and the Great War*, p. 70.

30   See Tony Ashworth, *Trench Warfare, 1914–1918: The Live and Let Live System* (London: Macmillan, 1980).

31   See Kelly, *Cinema and the Great War*, pp. 75–8; Richards, *Age of the Dream Palace*, pp. 290–1; on the original novel see, Jeffrey Richards, *Happiest Days: The Public Schools in English Fiction* (Manchester: Manchester University Press, 1988), pp. 216–29.

32   Jeffrey Richards, *Visions of Yesterday* (London: Routledge, 1973), p. 154, and Ernest Raymond's later retelling of the Gallipoli story, *The Quiet Shore* (London: Cassell, 1958).

33   See Niall Ferguson, *The Pity of War* (London: Allan Lane The Penguin Press, 1998), pp. xxxvi–xxxviii.

34   Low, *History of the British Film, 1929–1939*, p. 134.

35   See Richards' comments on Conrad Veidt, 'Britain's favourite German', *Age of the Dream Palace*, pp. 291–2.

36   *Monthly Film Bulletin*, 2: 16, 1935.

37   Jeffrey Richards, 'The British Board of Film Censors and content control in the 1930s: Foreign affairs', *Historical Journal of Film, Radio and Television*, 2:1, 1982, p. 45.

38   Ibid., pp. 45–8.

39   The exception was the widely seen *Things to Come* (1936).

40   See K. R. M. Short, *Screening the Propaganda of British Air Power* (Trowbridge: Flicks Books, 1998).

41   See, Michael Paris, *Warrior Nation: Images of War and British Youth, 1850–1992* (London: Reaktion Books, 1999), ch. 5.

42   Bond, *First World War and British Military History*, p. 8.

43   Danchev, ' "Bunking and debunking" ', pp. 263–4.

44   See Jeffrey Richards and Jeffrey Hulbert, 'Censorship in action: The case of Lawrence of Arabia', *Journal of Contemporary History*, 19: 1, 1984, pp. 153–69.

45   See, Kevin Brownlow, *David Lean: A Biography* (London: Cassell, 1996).

46   Kelly, *Cinema and the Great War*, pp. 176–80; see also Dirk Bogarde, *Snakes and Ladders* (London: Peguin, 1978), pp. 242, 245, 266.

47   Danchev, ' "Bunking and debunking" ', pp. 281–6.

48   Andrew Kelly, 'Trench footnotes', *Sight and Sound*, 7: 12, 1997, p. 25.

BRITISH FEATURE FILMS AND THE FIRST WORLD WAR

1919   *Comradeship*
1923   *Woman to Woman*
1924   *Reveille*
        Sideshow of Life
1926   *Mademoiselle from Armentieres*
        Roses of Picardy
1927   *Blighty*
1928   *Dawn*
        Guns of Loos
        Mademoiselle Parlay-Voos?
        Poppies of Flanders
1929   *Burgomaster of Stilemonde*
        The Lost Patrol
        Woman to Woman (a sound remake of the 1923 title)
1930   *Journey's End*
        'East Lynne' on the Western Front
        Suspense
        W Plan
1931   *Tell England*
1933   *I Was a Spy*
1935   *Forever England*
1936   *Secret Agent*
1937   *Mademoiselle Docteur* (Anglo-French co-production)
1939   *Nurse Edith Cavell Spy in Black*
1962   *Lawrence of Arabia*
1964   *King and Country*
1969   *Oh! What a Lovely War*
1971   *Zeppelin*
1976   *Aces High*
1982   *Return of the Soldier*
1997   *Regeneration*

4

The ANZAC and the Sentimental Bloke: Australian Culture and Screen Representations of World War One

Ina Bertrand

C. J. Dennis's long verse narrative 'The Sentimental Bloke' was first published in 1914,[1] it was an immediate best-seller and has not been out of print since. It tells the story of Bill, an urban larrikin, whose life of idleness, gambling, drinking and petty crime is turned around by his love for Doreen, living in genteel poverty with her mother and working in a pickle factory. In 1918 the story was filmed,[2] and from its release in 1919 that, too, was a runaway popular success, well received not only across Australia but also in Britain, and maintaining its reputation today as Australia's main claim to a silent film masterpiece. In between the release of the book and the film came World War One, so the book was too early to incorporate mention of the War and the film does not depict it directly.[3] These two works of popular culture are, however, a useful starting point for this discussion, for both played a part in establishing the mythic foundations of a new nation, officially formed as recently as 1 January 1901 by the federation of six states and two territories into the Commonwealth of Australia.

The love story in 'The Sentimental Bloke' is untypical of the romance form, which is usually powered by female desire. In this romance, it is male desire which structures the narrative: Bill is the 'sentimental bloke', who not only desires a woman but also seeks marriage and children. He is therefore also untypical of the accepted notion of the ocker: Bill expresses emotions – such as love and guilt and shame – which are usually not admitted by the stoic Aussie bloke, but he manages to do so without losing the reader's/audience's respect and sympathy. When Bill and Doreen marry and move from the slums to the country, Bill's language (the ultimate class marker) does not change as he shifts class location. Nevertheless, the movement can be read as transposing class conflict onto the urban/rural division that had for so long been at the centre of Australian narratives.[4] But in this particular narrative this division is also elided, by constructing an urban heroine (Doreen) as a typical 'girl of the bush' – a strong woman, forced by circumstances to take a male (decision-making, bread-winning) role, until the right man comes along to restore the social equilibrium by displacing her into wife and mother roles. And so a social consensus is established within the narrative, by the mythic resolution of gender, class and urban/rural divisions.[5]

This is narrative working as myth, to defuse social tension, functioning 'to transcend, to reconcile and to depoliticise'.[6] the popularity of 'The

4.1   *The Sentimental Bloke*. The Bloke (left of frame) and his
mate Ginger Mick take refreshments with Doreen and the
Stror at' Coot (Australian National Film and Sound Archive)

Sentimental Bloke' across nearly a century is testimony to the powerful
desire within Australian culture for such a consensual myth. For what
both the verses and the film do is represent Australian life as potentially
idyllic, with employment for all who want it, and the possibility of
redemption/inclusion of the outsider through hard work and love. A
pocket edition of the verses was available for distribution to the soldier
in the trenches, reminding him of the 'Australian way of life', for which he
was fighting.

During the War, however, another – much less consensual – myth also
arose. World War One brought a new word into the Australian language
– Anzac, the acronym for the Australian and New Zealand Army Corps,
but also the name given to the landing place on the Gallipoli Peninsula
where that corps for the first time in the nation's short history engaged
an enemy, under Australian commanders, in an international conflict.
Though Australian forces had already been involved in one naval battle,[7]
and there were to be many more land campaigns, the word 'Anzac' came
to encapsulate the experience of the War for Australians, and to define –
in a very different way from the Sentimental Bloke – what it meant to be
an Australian.[8] The first thing it meant was to be an equal partner with
other dominions, within the British Empire. In 1916, The Anzac Book,
'Written and Illustrated in Gallipoli by The Men of Anzac' was published,
'For the benefit of Patriotic Funds connected with the A. & N.Z.A.C.'[9] On
the front cover is an image of a defiant Australian infantryman defending
a tattered Union Jack. On the frontispiece two soldiers hold Australian
and New Zealand flags aloft, while looking up at a Union Jack suspended
above their heads, and King George V is quoted below: 'The Australian
and New Zealand troops have indeed proved themselves worthy sons of
the Empire'.

C. E. W. Bean, war correspondent, editor of The Anzac Book and later
Australia's official historian of World War One, could himself remember
the declaration of war in 1914:

At 11 p.m. on August 4th, English time, Britain declared war on Germany
which was already invading [Belgium and France].
The present writer can remember how, after the following night's work at a
newspaper office, as he walked home in the small hours through Mac-
quarie Street, Sydney, the clouds, dimly piled high in the four corners of the
dark sky above, seemed to him like the pillared structure of the world's
civilisation, of which some shock had broken the keystones . . . The stable
world of the nineteenth century was coming down in chaos: security was
gone . . . Yet people's feeling, in Australia and New Zealand as in England,

was one of relief from that latest and worst anxiety. Had Britain, despite
her pledges, held out of the war, the loyalty of the overseas Dominions to
her would hardly have survived the shock to the Empire's honour.[10]

So, in defence of the Empire's honour, Australia was within hours
committed to support of Britain, and planning to send troops. The mood
of the people was buoyant. Some of the women were fearful, but most
were confident that their boys would 'do the right thing'. And the men
were frankly looking forward to a good stoush – the young men sensing
an opportunity to travel and see the world, the older ones anticipating
looking on with pride.

But since the founding of the Commonwealth, Australia had also been
a nation, proudly independent of its British 'homeland'. And, at the
declaration of war, it was in the grip of election fever: the Cook Liberal
ministry had in June called a double dissolution, intending to solve the
problem of Opposition control of the Upper House. So war news and
political news jostled for attention in the newspapers.

There were reports of the invasion of Belgium, the occupation of
Brussels and heavy casualties on both sides. Headlines telegraphed
the tension: 'Struggle in Belgium. Fiercest Battle in War. Allies Hold
Their Ground. German Attacks Repulsed'.[11] A letter from a Belgian
mother described the German invasion as 'the orgy of the beast of hell in
our country',[12] and alongside the photographs of Australian casualties
(men who had enlisted in Britain) were reports of enemy atrocities such
as firing on the Red Cross or shooting prisoners-of-war.[13]

Labor won the September election, and Andrew Fisher (who had
promised Australia's support of Britain to 'our last man and our last
shilling')[14] was confirmed as Prime Minister and Treasurer. His Attorney-
General was William Morris Hughes, and when, only a year later, on 26
October 1915, Fisher resigned and accepted an appointment as Australian High Commissioner in London, Hughes became Prime Minister and
held that position till February 1923.

Hughes was universally known as 'Billy'. The diminutive suited him:
he was short and slight, pugnacious and voluble, a populist politician
with a large personal following.[15] Billy Hughes greeted the Great War
with enthusiasm: it was an opportunity for the nation and for himself
personally to strut upon the world stage. In the Boer War, Australians
who wished to support Britain had to go 'home' to join up, and in the first
few days and weeks of the Great War many Australians who happened
to be in Britain enlisted there. But this time there was also an Australian
Expeditionary Force, recruited and trained on Australian soil. The first

volunteers went quickly into the new training camps, and in November the first convoy left Albany on the long sea voyage to England via Suez. By the time they reached Aden, Turkey had entered the War, so the Australian troops disembarked and were trained in Egypt, ready for deployment in the Middle East.

Back home in Australia, the cinema was an important player in the game of war: attendance at cinemas soared, and both states and Commonwealth took advantage of this to help fund the war effort by levying new entertainment taxes.[16] But the role of the cinema was more than simply financial: morale-building was an important task. The local picture theatre was not only where the public relaxed with escapist fare, but also where they were re-assured constantly of the justice of the nation's fight and the competence of the armed forces to carry through their obligations to the Motherland. This combination of information and relaxation was illustrated, for instance, by the entertainments pages of the Melbourne daily *Age* on 1 January 1915: West's Pictures were screening an Edison melodrama, *What Could She Do?*, with an actuality film on *The City of Brussels*, advertised as 'the centre of war interest', while Spencer's Pictures were screening a 'stirring war drama', *The Ordeal*, supported by war gazettes, but also by the short entertainment films *Love at the Pound* and *The Mutual Girl*. A similar combination could be found at the Royal, in suburban Windsor, which presented on that day *A Romance of Old Brittany* along with 'the latest war news'. The weekly newsreels showed, so much more graphically than could the words of newspaper reports, the recruitment drives and fund-raising, training camps and street marches, and the farewelling of the departing troops.[17] Battle footage was not always available (or could not be screened because of censorship restrictions), but then the cartoonist could fill in the gaps.[18]

There were also local-filmed dramas, providing a much more complex barometer of attitudes to and emotions about the War. Australia received most of its feature films from overseas, increasingly Hollywood, which took over world markets during the War.[19] But filmic dramatic conventions were developing along similar lines across the world, so locally-produced drama shared conventions with imported film, representing the War through myth and symbol, even when addressing the subject apparently directly. There was certainly no mismatch between the fiction and non-fiction: they supported each other, with no room for alternative views or second thoughts about Australia's participation.

The demonisation of the Germans in Australian dramatic features began early: Alfred Rolfe's *The Day* premiered at the Sydney Stadium on

23 November 1914.[20] This was a dramatisation of the popular poem by Englishman Henry Chappell, with the script prepared by actor Johnson Weir, who recited the poem as accompaniment to the film: it depicted German brutality, confirming the Australian sympathy for 'poor little Belgium'. The irredeemably evil, almost sub-human, enemy re-appeared in *For Australia* (1915) and *If the Huns Came to Melbourne* (1916). This enemy was always, of course, defeated, as in *How We Beat the Emden* (1915), as well as in the newsreel depictions of prisoners-of-war. Australian bravery was represented in the images of young servicemen receiving medals in, for instance, *Murphy of Anzac* (1916) or *The Murder of Captain Fryatt* (1917). The bravery of the nurses was represented in three 1916 films about (the English) Nurse Cavell, who refused to betray her country and was executed (*Nurse Cavell*, *The Martyrdom of Nurse Cavell* and *La Revanche*), and one completely fictional representation of the Australian nurse at war – *Scars of Love* (1918). The danger of saboteurs and spies was represented in *Within Our Gates* (1915), *For Australia* (1915), *Australia's Peril* (1917) and *The Enemy Within* (1918).

But, particularly in the feature films, a new myth was building – of the War as the 'coming of age' of the Australian nation. Central to this myth was the landing at Anzac Cove, just before dawn on 25 April 1915, and the consequent Gallipoli campaign. In comparison with the later European campaigns, it was minor: of the approximately 330,000 Australians who enlisted throughout the War, only about 60,000 fought at Gallipoli. It was also a disaster: confusion and mistakes in the initial landing, about 26,000 casualties over the eight months of the campaign (including 7594 killed), then withdrawal with little achieved.[21] The accusation that Australian troops had been wasted, in 'the wrong place at the wrong time for the wrong reasons',[22] seemed plausible, even to those involved. But the myth overrode all this.

In later years, 25 April was celebrated nationally as 'Anzac Day': Australia's participation in the Great War was commemorated on this day by dawn services at war memorials all over the country, followed by marches of the veterans, in uniform and wearing their medals, and culminating in a ceremony of thanks. Anzac had come to mean not only a specific place where Australian blood had been spilled, nor even the memory of all the sacrifices made in the whole conflict, but something even larger still – something like the spirit of the nation.

This spirit was encapsulated in the idea of the 'digger' – the Australian soldier in his slouch hat, uniting at last the resilience and enterprise of the bushman with the cheeky charm and anti-authoritarianism of the urban larrikin. D. A. Kent attributes the origins of the digger legend to

Bean's selection and editing of the contributions to *The Anzac Book*, as well as to his herculean efforts to distribute the publication, making it a runaway best-seller.[23] Bean continued to develop the image in his official histories, but the earliest public recognition of the fighting prowess of the Australian digger had actually come from English war correspondent Ellis Ashmead-Bartlett, whose despatches were the first to describe the Anzac landing in detail, concluding that 'There has been no finer feat in this war than this sudden landing in the dark and storming the heights'.[24] British Poet Laureate John Masefield also described the campaign in hyperbole.[25] It was a romantic image: these diggers were 'tough and inventive, loyal to their mates beyond the call of duty, a bit undisciplined (but only in non-essentials), chivalrous, gallant, sardonic'.[26] The words 'digger' and 'Anzac' came to be used interchangeably. During the War itself and for many years thereafter, this was the preferred image – the one that historians and national commentators wrote about and that children were taught about in schools.

This image is not entirely a fiction – such men did exist, their courage was documented, their sacrifice undoubted.[27] In film, the heroism of the Anzacs was represented within weeks of the actual landing,[28] and when they were represented in later films – for instance in *Ginger Mick* (1920), *Fellers* (1930) or *Diggers* (1931) – they were instantly recognisable. During World War Two, the image – in films such as *Forty Thousand Horsemen* (1940) – was used as a rallying call for a new generation of diggers. It survives in popular memory, and continues to surface on screen.[29]

But, where it was once universally accepted, it has over the years become more problematic. So, instead of the assumption that every Australian soldier at all times matched the Anzac ideal of courage and tenacity and loyalty to his mates, it has been increasingly recognised that Bean's image was rather of 'how some men were and many might be'.[30]

Even at the time, there was some acknowledgement of this. After the euphoria of the first few months of the War, Australians learned that war is not a game, and discovered the truism that stress can bring out the worst in people as well as their best, and sometimes both at different times. Though Bean (in his published writings) was more responsible than anyone else for the idealised image, in his private diary he admitted the incompleteness of the ideal. Fear was omnipresent, accepted as a part of life, met with stoicism (as the digger image required) much of the time, but also causing some men to flee from the fighting, so that it was possible to see 'two streams going in opposite directions and not taking the faintest notice of one another'.[31] The fierce determination of the

4.2   *Fellers*. Arthur Tauchert (centre) is now 'Roughie', the
Digger/Anzac, still surrounded by his mates in the desert in Palestine
(Australian National Film and Sound Archive)

Australians in battle impressed the British command, who had not
expected either fortitude or skill from mere colonials. But the corollary
of that was a recklessness with their own lives and a lack of respect for
enemy life:

> up the hill . . . we swarm . . . the lust to kill is on us, we see red. Into one
> trench, out of it, and into another. Oh! The bloody gorgeousness of feeling
> your bayonet go into soft yielding flesh – they run, we after them, no thrust
> one and parry, in goes the bayonet the handiest way.[32]

Men who enjoyed killing made good fighters, but not necessarily good
soldiers, and certainly not good role models for peacetime. The lack of
discipline among the Australian troops was legendary also. Building on
the anti-authoritarianism of earlier versions of the bush myth, it was
defended as a proper disregard for pomposity and elitism: discipline
imposed from above was assumed to be unnecessary among egalitarian
Australians who would always obey any reasonable order from anyone

who had earned the right to give it. But anti-authoritarian attitudes could also be interpreted as simply anti-social. Later, in France, the Australians had an enviable reputation among the civilian population for restraint and generosity, but this was the era of the White Australia policy, when racism was deeply embedded in the Australian psyche, particularly in the working class which provided most of the enlisted men. So, in the early part of the War, while they were training and fighting in Egypt and the Middle East, the Australians saw the local population as inferior and therefore fair game. The most obvious case was the two occasions when rioting in the red light district of Cairo led to casualties and the burning of homes and shops, all treated by the soldiers as a 'bit of fun'.[33] part of their motivation was anger and resentment against the prostitutes and their 'bullies' (pimps): in this case, racism was compounded by a sexism which blamed the women for the high incidence of venereal disease among their customers.[34] The Australian community was shocked when infected troops were repatriated, at the height of a moral panic which was already involving state Health Departments and producing renewed calls for censorship of immorality in films.[35]

Over the years, historians have exposed more and more of this under-belly, but the myth was powerful and resistant to change. Screen representations of the myth (in films such as *Gallipoli* and *The Light-horsemen* and television series such as *1915* and *Anzacs*) have slowly accommodated this 'new' (meaning 'newly public') knowledge, gradually extending the boundaries of the legend to incorporate more variants within accepted definitions.

Gallipoli provided the first tentative steps towards such revision. The central characters – both the two heroes (Frank and Archie) and their mates in the Light Horse (Barney, Billy and snowy – all fit the main parameters of the legend: they enlist early, stick together as mates,[36] and behave admirably under fire. However, there are also flaws beginning to become apparent. First, Frank does not enlist out of patriotism (either Australian or British), but from lack of money and a desire to be with Archie. Then, four of the five (with Snowy a reluctant and disapproving observer) take advantage of the sexual opportunities of the red light district, despite the earlier lecture on the dangers of venereal disease. They all take part, also, in terrorising a shopkeeper – the film's very restrained gesture towards the representation of the Wasser riots.

Though they are all still likeable and (in their own way) admirable, these characters are not the perfect physical and moral specimens of the heroes of films like *A Hero of the Dardanelles* or *Forty Thousand Horsemen*. Within the legend, efforts are being made to reconcile

4.3   Chips Rafferty (on the left of group),
the quintessential Aussie bloke, teaches an old Australian game
to an Egyptian trader in *Forty Thousand Horsemen*
(Australian National Film and Sound Archive)

'innocence and guilt, brutality and chivalry, self and other, the actor and the acted upon':[37] these Australians are depicted as the innocent victims of British stupidity, their lack of discipline reconstituted as high spirits, their violence re-read as bravery, their racism justified by the dishonesty of the locals. And, after *Gallipoli*, the parameters of the legend were stretched still, further, to incorporate groups of men who in earlier times would have been well outside the boundaries of the Anzac myth – shirkers, cowards and those of German descent.

Those who enlisted early (particularly those who were early enough to be in the first landing party at Gallipoli) had a special place in the legend. Those who were slow to enlist were considered to be shirkers, and were liable to receive the shameful 'white feather'. But once they had actually joined up, they could be forgiven. In *Anzacs*, Max Earnshaw is a librarian, a peaceable young man, convinced he is too incompetent to be any use at the front: but he is also the son of a jingoistic government minister, who needs the publicity of his son's enlistment to cover his own limitations, and is also sure that the War will be over before Max can reach active service. The War, of course, does not end in time: but Max proves he is no coward, and eventually becomes a good officer, precisely because he does not arrogantly insist on enlisted men following his orders, when he can recognise that they actually have more experience than he has. Cowardice has been slowly redefined over the years. During the War itself, the only explanation for any man not performing as ordered was assumed to be cowardice. But Dave in *The Lighthorsemen* enlists with every intention of being a good soldier: after all, he can ride like a dream and is the most accurate shot in the troop. When he is finally in an engagement and has the enemy in his rifle sights, he finds himself inexplicably unable to kill a man, even when his inaction may lead to his own death. This endangers the whole troop, who ostracise him, until they realise that he is not afraid. He becomes a field ambulance officer – under fire, in the front of the attack, but without a weapon, and he acquits himself admirably in this role. Neither was shell-shock recognised as a medical condition at the time, but in *Anzacs* Harold Armstrong is invalided out, with 'disturbed action of the heart', and the whole troop is sorry to see him go and recognises that he is ill. Sergeant Macarthur in *Anzacs* freezes during an attack, remaining pinned to the ground in a paroxysm of terror. Mr Armstrong, far from court-martialling him, recommends him for a valour award, and when Mac later confesses to Marty that he does not deserve the medal, Marty replies: 'I wouldn't let one bad night worry you. It might have the wrong date – but it's the right name.' And, indeed, Sergeant Macarthur later dies heroically, defending his mates. In *Anzacs*, Pudden' even deserts, after one horrific engagement leaves him shell-shocked. Mr Armstrong sends the platoon to rescue him from the camp of a group of deserters, holding out in No-man's-land: and Pudden' returns to the platoon, because he has missed the mateship, even though he knows that it means a spell in detention and a return to the front. In all these cases, the person's whole service is judged rather than any single incident, and their right to be included within the legend is never in doubt.

Australia has a large population of German descent, concentrated in several areas (such as the vineyards of the Barossa valley in South Australia, or the wheat farms of the Victorian Mallee). During the War itself, it was generally assumed that these were all enemy sympathisers, but by *Anzacs* it was possible to include someone of German descent among the Australian soldiers. Wilhelm Schmidt is ironically rechristened 'Kaiser' by the troop, and – once he has proven his mettle –

included as a mate, despite his parentage and accent: he is even promoted to Lance Corporal and awarded the Military medal for a particularly brave rescue.

Part of the reason that such – once unthinkable – accommodations can now be made is that the currency of the Anzac myth more generally has been weakened over the years, by challenges such as the movement against Australian participation in the Vietnam War. In more recent times, that myth is once again reviving. It is difficult to tell whether changing screen representations of Anzac are part of the cause or are the result of these more general changes. But it does seem that the gradual incorporation of more Australians within the Anzac myth has helped to strengthen and re-invigorate it, to make it more 'authentic'.

None of this extension of the Anzac myth, however, can hide the fact that it never did have the consensual appeal of the Sentimental Bloke: Anzac was always grounded in division and elitism. Despite the legendary anti-authoritarianism of the Australian forces, one of the strongest divisions remained that of class: the officers were as a rule upper/middle class (Armstrong is referred to throughout *Anzacs* as *Mr* Armstrong, rather than by his rank), and the other ranks were most commonly working class. This cannot be hidden under the oftrepeated claim that these officers respected the troops under them, and would not ask the men to do what they would not do themselves. The officer's decision to go 'over the top' to certain death in *Gallipoli* both illustrates this respect and emphasises the actual difference – the officer *chooses* to do what the men have no choice *but* to do.

But within the legend, anti-authoritarianism is recast as national character, eliding its basis in class divisions. So the attitudes of 'good' Australian officers to the men under them is very different from that of all the British officers – the 'spit and polish' brigade, with British authoritarian attitudes – and the few Australian officers inherited from the peace-time regular army, which recent screen representations depict as chocolate soldiers: in *Anzacs* one new regular-army officer is a stern disciplinarian in camp but panics in battle, placing the platoon at risk until he is knocked out and the sergeant can take over to lead the men.

There is a light-hearted side to this anti-authoritarianism also – one that provides welcome respite from the horrors of war. In *The Light-horsemen*, a British officer, in an effort to restore a semblance of discipline among the Australians, orders that they not wear shorts: later, the men walk past him, still not saluting, but also naked from the waist down. In *Anzacs*, when a British officer tetchily asks, 'Don't you salute in your army?'; Flanagan replies 'No, not a lot', and Cleary adds, 'Well, we

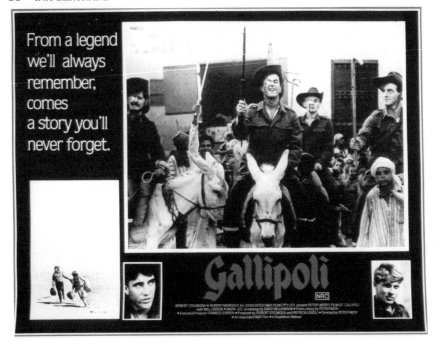

4.4   *Gallipoli*. Four Australian diggers in Cairo parody
the British hierarchical system, to the amusement of the locals
(Australian National Film and Sound Archive)

used to, but we're trying to give it up', as they saunter off. Such humour
further contributes to the displacement of Australian elitism onto Britain.[38]

These elisions discourage the liberal version of the Anzac myth, which
recognises that true mateship crosses class barriers, and that co-operation achieves more than social division: if that version had survived into
peace, it would have led to a strengthened union movement (the ultimate
form of mateship within the working class) and/or the breakdown of
social caste barriers more generally. Instead, the conservative (Returned
Soldiers League) version of the myth won out.[39] The inevitability of this
victory was also represented on screen. In *Anzacs*, the officer's mother
and the enlisted man's mother understand each other, but this is
symbolised by the latter going to work for the former at the big house:
Barbara Hooks suggests that this 'improbable friendship' reeks of
'convenience, coincidence and condescension'.[40]

The real difference between the British and Australian forces – the difference which allows for that displacement of elitism onto Britain – is the fact that the Australian soldiers were volunteers. They chose to go – they made a deliberate decision – they were not forced. The myth then insists that they did not surrender their autonomy by that choice: they continued to exercise choice, even when they followed orders, which therefore must be reasonable and given by qualified officers, who had won their respect. From this perspective it is not surprising that the two conscription referendums were defeated: in addition to the many reasons given in so many articles (such as the reluctance of volunteers to serve alongside conscripts, who might be unreliable in any tight spot)[41] is the powerful pull of the Anzac myth, which was already in place, and for which only volunteers qualified.

There were, of course, men who *had* volunteered, and who still remained forever outside the myth. The racism which fuelled the White Australia policy and the Wasser riots[42] excluded all those of non-British descent. In 1924 Adam Tavlaridi, a Greek-Australian café proprietor, wrote and financed *Daughter of the East (The Boy of the Dardanelles)*, to demonstrate the contribution of the Greek people to the British war effort: it was not successful at the box-office, but it did attempt to make non-British participants in the War visible, even if it still could not place them within the Anzac legend. Similarly permanently outside are the aboriginal soldiers (their contribution recorded only in a few still photographs and an occasional glimpse outside the group of mates in films such as *Gallipoli*) and the homosexuals (still completely invisible).[43]

Women also did not qualify: even the nurses, so essential to the successful waging of the War at any level, were limited to supporting roles, both within the legend and within its screen representations. They could not be 'mates', even (or perhaps especially) when they entered into sexual relations with a soldier. So Ann in *The Lighthorsemen* writes a letter crucial to the success of the Beersheba campaign, but must wait on the sidelines during the battle, and afterwards seek among the wounded for her lover. But the presence of such female characters draws attention to the more general absence of women in the myth. Rose Lucas explains of *Gallipoli*:

> Thus, the film's ostensible cluster of goals – to demonstrate the formation of individual male identity, the primacy of male bonding and the analogous formation of a national identity – are periodically disrupted by manifestations of the denied binary element on which the dominant, apparently homogeneous, masculinised identity is built.[44]

Of course, most women stayed at home, and so were relegated permanently to the margins as sweethearts and mothers:

> The battlefield, the new symbol of sexual definition in imperialist mores,
> was proclaimed the sole preserve of man, and thus, while the men went off
> to war, to decide the fate of nations and to achieve 'fame, glory and
> manhood' (and, incidentally, death, injury and disease), it was the lot of
> modern women, as it had been through history, to deliver up uncondi-
> tionally to the 'Moloch of War' the fruit of their womb.[45]

In films made during the War itself, mothers nobly sacrificed their sons, and sweethearts put on a brave face as their 'boys' sailed away (*A Hero of the Dardanelles* 1915). These depictions enshrined the view of women as victims, willing to sacrifice themselves: but it also placed a heavy burden on men, as Marilyn Lake persuasively argues:

> In the light of the challenge to men's autonomy [and independence which
> marriage and the acceptance of the God's Police role as women's appro-
> priate role] posed, it is tempting to see the celebration of Australian
> masculinity under the banner of Anzac as a mythic reparation to 'hobbled'
> men.[46]

Is it, then, the women left at home or the men of Anzac who benefit most from the revisions of the myth in later years, allowing mothers to be much more ambivalent about sacrificing their sons? In *Gallipoli*, *The Light-horsemen*, *Anzacs* and *1915* all the mothers are clearly distressed, wish to dissuade their sons, and often argue against their husbands' desire for the boy to go, to 'make a man of himself'. Sweethearts in these later representations were fickle: in both *The Lighthorsemen* and *1915* women abandon their men once they are overseas.

There is also, as well as the gender division, a further division being represented here – that between those who served at the front and those who stayed at home. There were 'enemy aliens' interned for the duration, and the subject of hate campaigns, particularly against German nationals or descendants.[47] But there were also those who had a conscientious objection to the War – either as pacifists, or as political dissidents who identified the War as simply a source of profit to capitalists. The Labor movement had a very ambivalent attitude to the War – many working-class men seized the opportunity for travel and adventure, or sincerely believed they were needed by their country and the Empire, but trade union discontent was also strong, culminating in a general strike in

1917.[48] Such unrest was often blamed on the Industrial Workers of the World, an organisation which was pursued mercilessly and its leaders accused of treason, tried and imprisoned.[49] Propaganda against the War was blamed for the drop in recruitment which occurred after the first euphoria was past,[50] leading to the two conscription referenda. Billy Hughes was convinced the country would fall in with his wishes on conscription, was astonished when the first referendum was defeated, and horrified when the result was confirmed a second time.

None of this opposition to the myth appeared in screen representations at the time: only the official line was visible, and that laid the foundation for the victory of the conservative version of what was always an elitist myth. Despite attempts in more recent screen representations to acknowledge at least some of the omissions and elisions, the myth remains powerful, perhaps because it is so hard to represent the flaws in the myth without at the same time being accused of denigrating the sacrifice of the real men. The result is that when the limits of the myth are tested (as in recent campaigns to insist that the women raped in war be recognised in Anzac Day commemorations), there is dismay and confusion (as in the feminist backlash against this move, on the grounds that it results only in co-option).[51]

The debate about 'Australian identity' persists – re-invigorated by arguments over native title, multiculturalism and the prospect of Australia becoming a Republic. No matter how unfashionable it may be in some circles, the Anzac myth remains at the core of this debate, and, while that is so, there will be further screen representations of Australian participation in World War One. However, the consensual myth of the Sentimental Bloke seems to have little chance against the power of the elitist myth of the Anzac.

DRAMATISED SCREEN REPRESENTATIONS OF WORLD WAR ONE

Further information about the films listed here can be found in:
Andrew Pike and Ross Cooper, *Australian Film 1900–1977* (Melbourne: Oxford University Press/Australian Film Institute 1980)
Scott Murray, *Australian Film 1978–1991* (Melbourne: Oxford University Press/Australian Film Commission/Cinema Papers 1995)
Further information about the television programmes listed here can be found in:

Albert Moran, *Moran's Guide to Australian TV Series* (North Ryde: Australian Film and Television School 1993)
+   = commercial video available
+ + = commercial video has been available but is no longer
*   = stills available in National Film and Sound Archive (NFSA), Canberra
**   = short extracts held in NFSA
*** = long extracts held in NFSA
**** = complete film held in NFSA
(access to material held in the NFSA depends on copyright clearance and on the availability of a viewing print)

1914 *The Day*: dir. Alfred Rolfe, p.c. Frazer Films, script by Johnson Weir from poem by Henry Chappell
 A Long, Long Way to Tipperary: dir. George Dean, p.c. Higgins Bros, ph. Ernest Higgins**
1915 *For Australia*: dir. Monte Luke, p.c. J. C. Williamson, ph. Maurice Bertel*
 A Hero of the Dardanelles: dir. Alfred Rolfe, p.c. Australasian Films, sc. Phillip Gell, Loris Brown**
 How We Beat the Emden: dir. Alfred Rolfe, p.c. Australasian Films*
 Within Our Gates, or Deeds That Won Gallipoli: dir. Frank Harvey, p.c. J. C. Williamson Ltd, ph. Monte Luke, sc. W. J. Lincoln
1916 *If the Huns Came to Melbourne*: dir. George Byers Coates, ph. Arthur Higgins
 The Joan of Arc of Loos: dir. George Willoughby, ph. Franklyn Barrett, sc. Herbert Ford***
 The Martyrdom of Nurse Cavell: dir. John Gavin, C. Post Mason, p.c. Australian Famous Feature Company, ph. Lacey Percival, sc. Agnes Gavin*
 Murphy of Anzac: dir. J. E. Matthews, p.c. Frazer Film Exchange*
 Nurse Cavell (Edith Cavell): sc. W. J. Lincoln*
 La Revanche: sc. W. J. Lincoln
1917 *Australia's Peril*: sc. Franklyn Barrett*
 The Murder of Captain Fryatt: dir. John Gavin, p.c. Australian Famous Features Company, ph. Franklyn Barrett, sc. Agnes Gavin
1918 *The Enemy Within*: dir., sc. Roland Stavely, p., ph. Franklyn Barrett.****
 Scars of Love: p.c. Austral Photoplays*
1920 *Ginger Mick*: dir. Raymond Longford, p.c. Southern Cross Feature Film Company, ph. Arthur Higgins, sc. Lottie Lyell, Raymond Longford*

1924 *Daughter of the East (The Boy of the Dardanelles)*: dir. Roy Darling, ph. Tasman Higgins**
      The Digger Earl: dir. Beaumont Smith, ph. Lacey Percival***
      The Spirit of Gallipoli: dir. Keith Gategood, William Green, ph. Jack Fletcher**
1928 *The Exploits of the Emden*: 1926 German original, 1928 Australian sequences, d. p.d Ken Hall***
1930 *Fellers*: dir. Arthur Higgins, Austin Fay, ph. Tasman Higgins*
1931 *Diggers*: dir. F. W. Thring, ph. Arthur Higgins, sc. Pat Hanna and Eric Donaldson****
1933 *Diggers in Blighty*: ph. Arthur Higgins, sc. Pat Hanna****
      Two Minutes Silence: dir. Paulette McDonagh, ph. James Grant*
      Waltzing Matilda: dir. Pat Hanna, ph. Arthur Higgins****
1934 *Splendid Fellows*: dir. Beaumont Smith, ph. George Malcolm****
1940 *Forty Thousand Horsemen*: dir. Charles Chauvel, ph. George Heath + ****
1976 *Power without Glory*: 26 eps, 60 mins, ABC television
1981 *Gallipoli*: dir. Peter Weir, ph. Russell Boyd + ****
1982 *1915*: 7 eps, 60 mins, ABC and Lionheart International, television.
1985 *ANZACS*: 10 eps, 60 mins, Burrowes-Dixon, television + ****
      A Thousand Skies: 6 eps, 60 mins, Seven Network, television****
1986 *A Fortunate Life*: 4 eps, 60 mins, PBL, television + + **
1987 *Land of Hope*: 10 eps, 60 mins, JNP, television****
      The Lighthorsemen: dir. Simon Wincer, ph. Dean Semler + ****
1988 *The Alien Years*: 6 eps, 60 mins, ABC television
      Always Afternoon: 4 eps, 60 mins, SBS television
      The Dirtwater Dynasty: 10 eps, 60 mins, Kennedy Miller, television*

NOTES

1 C. J. Dennis, *The Songs of a Sentimental Bloke* (Sydney: Angus and Robertson, 1914).
2 *The Sentimental Bloke*, Australia 1918, production Southern Cross Feature Film Company, direction Raymond Longford.
3 There is one sequence where the War is indicated – in the uniformed men leaving the theatre after a performance of *Romeo and Juliet*.
4 John Tulloch, *Legends on the Screen: The Narrative Film in Australia 1919–1929* (Sydney: AFI/Currency Press, 1981), ch. 1.
5 The argument summarised here is expanded upon in Ina Bertrand, 'The

Sentimental Bloke: Narrative and social consensus', in Ken Berryman (ed.), *Screening the Past: Aspects of Early Australian Films* (Canberra: National Film and Sound Archive [NFSA], 1995), pp. 97–106.

6   Amanda Lohrey, 'Australian mythologies – Gallipoli: Male innocence as a marketable commodity', *Island Magazine*, nos. 9/10, March 1982, p. 30.

7   Australasian Films produced a regular newsreel during the War, and late in 1915 they purchased footage from a documentary about the Australian Navy, showing the hulk of the German cruiser *Emden*, sunk by the Australian cruiser *Sydney* near the Cocos Islands in the first Australian engagement of the War. A fictional narrative about a naval cadet serving on board the *Sydney* was then built around this footage, and the result was *How We Beat the Emden* (1915), released on 6 December 1915 to great acclaim (Andrew Pike and Ross Cooper, *Australian Film 1900–1977* [Melbourne: Oxford University Press/Australian Film Institute, 1980], p. 7).

8   Anzac is a term shared by Australia and New Zealand. However, this chapter concerns Australia, and from now on the discussion will centre on Australia – with no offence intended to New Zealand, which has its own story to tell.

9   *The Anzac Book* (London: Cassell & Co. 1916).

10   C. E. W. Bean, *Anzac to Amiens: A Shorter History of the Australian Fighting Services in the First World War* (Canberra: Australian War Memorial, 1968), pp. 22–3.

11   *Age*, Melbourne, 3 November 1913, p. 7.

12   *Age*, Melbourne, 4 November 1914, p. 9.

13   *Age*, Melbourne, 9 November 1914, p. 5.

14   B. J. McKinley, 'Three events in Corangamite electorate', *Labor History*, no. 16, May 1969, p. 53.

15   In this he can be compared with a later Australian Prime Minister, Robert Hawke, universally known as 'Bob', and with a similar populist philosophy that crossed boundaries of class and education.

16   See Ina Bertrand and Diane Collins, *Government and Film in Australia* (Sydney: Currency Press, 1981), pp. 43–5.

17   The Australian War Memorial holds footage shot by war cameramen: see http://www.awm.gov.au/sitemap–frames.htm. The National Film and Sound Archive, holds some of the resulting newsreels, issued by companies like Australasian Films: two early examples are *Departure of the Australian Expeditionary Force*, 1914, 5 mins (showing troops boarding a ship carrying kit bags, horses taken on board, a tug pulling the ship out and soldiers waving) and *Patriotic Appeal by Theatricals*, probably 1914 (showing theatre personalities participating in a motor car procession through Martin Place, Sydney, to raise funds for the War). Newsreels such as *Allies Day* (1916), *Australia Prepared* (1918), *Toys for Soldiers' Children* (1918), *The Patriot Spirit* (1918?), all show

the Home Front united in support of the War. In later years, there were also films made to raise funds, but not representing the War directly, such as *Cupid Camouflaged* (1918) or *What Happened to Jean* (1918): see Pike and Cooper, *Australian Film* pp. 105, 110.

18 In addition to factual reporting films, a series of short animated cartoons appeared between 1915 and 1917, based on events reported in the newspapers and encouraging nationalist and anti-German sentiment. The NFSA holds about a dozen of these, most of them under the generic title of *Cartoons of the Moment*, for instance *Cartoons of the Moment: Australia's Prime Minister Delights the Empire*, *A Zeppelin Bombing*, *An Ammunition Explosion and a Giant Gun*. They were produced for the *Australian Gazette*, by well-known cartoonist Harry Julius, and are rather simplistic animated cut-outs. They were short (about 3 minutes), and most cannot be accurately dated with current knowledge.

19 Ruth Megaw, 'The American image: Influence on Australian cinema management 1896–1923', *Journal of the Royal Australian Historical Society*, vol. 54, pt. 2, June 1968, pp. 194–204.

20 Pike and Cooper, *Australian Film*, p. 69.

21 See Bean, *Anzac to Amiens*; also Bill Gammage, *The Story of Gallipoli* (Ringwood: Penguin Books, 1981), p. 7.

22 This phrase has circulated widely, and was quoted by Walter in the last episode of the television miniseries *1915*, as something he read on German propaganda leaflets dropped on the trenches at Gallipoli.

23 See D. A. Kent, '*The Anzac Book* and the Anzac legend: C. E. W. Bean as editor and image-maker', *Historical Studies*, vol. 21, no. 84, April 1989, p. 379.

24 Quoted by Kevin Fewster, 'Ellis Ashmead Bartlett and the making of the Anzac legend', *Journal of Australian Studies*, no. 10, June 1982, p. 20.

25 Kent, '*Anzac Book* and the Anzac legend', p. 377.

26 Will Mandle, *Going It Alone* (London: Allen Lane, 1978), p. 4.

27 The foundation of the myth can be clearly recognised in the reminiscences of the veterans, used as the basis for Alistair Thomson, *Anzac Memories: Living with the Legend* (Oxford: Oxford University Press, 1994).

28 In *A Hero of the Dardanelles* the landing at Gaba Tepe was restaged at Tamarama Bay near Sydney (see Pike and Cooper, p. 71). In *Within Our Gates, or Deeds That Won Gallipoli*, the landing at Gallipoli was staged at Obelisk Bay (see Pike and Cooper, *Australian Film*, pp. 72–3).

29 For instance, one episode of the television series *Michael Willessee's Australians* (60 mins, Roadshow, Coote & Carroll, and Film Australia, broadcast 1988) concerned Gallipoli stretcher-bearer 'Jack Simpson', immortalised in legend as 'Simpson and his donkey'.

30 Kent, '*Anzac Book* and the Anzac legend', p. 379.

31   Bean's diaries, quoted in Kent, 'Anzac Book and the Anzac legend', p. 378.

32   This is one of several similar letters quoted in Bill Gammage, 'ANZAC: Nationhood, brotherhood and sacrifice', in Story of Gallipoli, p. 53.

33   Bill Gammage, The Broken Years (Canberra: ANU, 1974), p. 40. See also Kevin Fewster, 'The Wazza riots', Journal of the Australian War Memorial, no. 4, April 1984, pp. 47–53.

34   See Carmel Shute, 'Heroines and heroes: Sexual mythology in Australia 1914–1918', Hecate, vol. 1, no. 1, January 1975, p. 20.

35   Ina Bertrand, 'Education or exploitation: The exhibition of "social hygiene" films in Australia', Continuum, vol. 12, no. 1, 1997, pp. 31–46.

36   Lohrey ('Australian mythologies', p. 33) considers that the film also undermines pure 'mateship' (which is collective effort against a common enemy), turning it rather into a close one-to-one relationship between Archie and Frank.

37   Lohrey ('Australian mythologies'), p. 30. Lohrey also discusses the application of these concepts to the film Gallipoli.

38   Making some representations, understandably, unpopular in Britain – as described by Jane Freebury, 'Screening Australia: Gallipoli – a study of nationalism on film', Media Information Australia, no. 43, February 1987, pp. 6–7.

39   Lohrey, 'Australian mythologies', p. 29.

40   Age, Melbourne, 25 October 1985, p. 2.

41   Ina Bertrand, 'The Victorian country vote in the conscription referendums of 1916 and 1917: The case of the Wannon electorate', Labour History, no. 26, May 1974, pp. 19–31.

42   Quoted in Bean's diaries (see above) and discussed by various commentators since, for instance Verity Burgmann, 'Racism, socialism and the Labour movement, 1887–1917', Labour History, no. 47, November 1984, pp. 39–54; Kent, 'Anzac Book and the Anzac legend'.

43   An exception is a homosexual character in the miniseries Nancy Wake (1987), but that is a different war (World War Two) and a different story of gender representation.

44   Rose Lucas, 'The gendered battlefield: Sex and death in Gallipoli', in Joy Damousi and Marilyn Lake (eds), Gender and War: Australians at War in the Twentieth Century (Cambridge: Cambridge University Press, 1995), p. 151.

45   Carmel Shute, 'Heroines and heroes', p. 23.

46   Marilyn Lake, 'The politics of respectability: Identifying the masculinist context', Historical Studies, vol. 22, no. 86, April 1986, p. 116.

47   R. J. W. Selleck, ' "The trouble with my looking glass": A study of the attitude of Australians to Germans during the Great War', Journal of Australian Studies, no. 6, June 1980, pp. 2–25. These attitudes were

represented on screen in the miniseries *The Alien Years* and *Always Afternoon* (both 1988).

48   Lucy Taksa, 'The 1917 strike: A case study in working class community networks', *Oral History Association of Australia Journal*, no. 10, 1980, pp. 22–38.

49   P. J. Rushton, 'The trial of the Sydney twelve: The original charge', *Labour History*, no. 25, November 1973, pp. 53–7; Frank Cain, 'The Industrial Workers of the World: Aspects of its suppression in Australia 1916–1919', *Labour History*, no. 42, May 1982, p. 54–62.

50   Murray Perks, 'Labour and the Governor-General's recruiting conference, Melbourne April 1918', *Labour History*, no. 34, May 1978, pp. 28–44.

51   Adrian Howe, 'Anzac mythology and the feminist challenge', in Damousi and Lake, *Gender and War*, pp. 302–10; Adrian Howe, 'Anzac Day – who owns the means of resistance?', *Scarlet Woman*, no. 19, Spring 1984, pp. 22–6.

5

Canadian Film and the First World War

Tim Travers

In 1914, before Canadian troops were in Europe, Canadians were already watching war newsreels produced by private companies. These newsreels often focused on training and parades, and carried titles such as *First All-Canadian Regiment in Training*, *Ottawa Army Field Day* and, later, *Canada Goes Over*. However, in November 1914 the province of Ontario banned all war films, and, early in 1915, the Canadian Department of Militia and Defence directed the censor boards of each province to ban all war films. The Department was concerned that actual war scenes might discourage enlistment. Thus when the Militia Department produced *Canada's Fighting Forces* in December 1915, there were no scenes of warfare itself, and the battle of Second Ypres (April 1915), in which Canadian troops played a central role, was portrayed through animation. In the same vein, a year later, Canada's Chief Press Censor, Lieutenant Colonel Ernest J. Chambers, actually cut out some scenes of the British epic, *Battle of the Somme*, because although Britain was used to seeing wounded men arriving from the battle fronts Canada was not.[1]

This rather negative Canadian attitude to filming the War changed under the direction of a capable, ambitious and wealthy individual from the Maritimes, William Maxwell Aitken, the future Lord Beaverbrook. Aitken was first appointed in late 1914 as an unofficial delegate to the British War Office, and assumed the role of Canada's official press representative. Then, in January 1915, Aitken was appointed Director of the Canadian War Records Office (CWRO), to gather documents on the Canadian war effort in Europe. Aitken soon used this position to also provide Canadian film of the War as both record and propaganda. Then, using his high-level contacts in Britain, Aitken achieved the post of chairman of the British War Office Cinematograph Committee (WOCC) in November 1916. After this date, the film work of the CWRO and the WOCC became very similar, and sometimes identical. Finally, Aitken, by now Lord Beaverbrook, was named Britain's first Minister of Information in February 1918, enabling him to centralise almost all aspects of British film propaganda. Subsequently, the WOCC and, to some extent, the CWRO gave up their roles to the Cinematographic Section of the Ministry of Information (MOI). What is of general significance is that in his positions as CWRO Director, Chair of the WOCC and then Minister of Information, Beaverbrook did a great deal to pioneer film propaganda, and to insist on the value of filming the War for public consumption.[2]

All this was not easily achieved. Aitken found that film propaganda in Britain in 1915 and 1916 was an exceedingly complicated business. It involved an uneasy and competitive mix of film companies, the War Office, GHQ in France, a series of official propaganda committees, financial agreements concerning film distribution with various companies, the cinematographers themselves, problems of censorship, and the ambitions of various individuals, including Aitken himself. Indeed, when a friend wrote to Aitken in late 1916 suggesting simply combining all film-making efforts into a single entity, Aitken replied at that time:

> I do not think you can have the slightest conception of the intricacies of the film arrangements over here, or of the difficulties which we have to contend with on this side of the water.
>
> For a long time, the Canadian Official Films were in the hands of separate committees; all kinds of different contracts were entered into, and the attempt to sort out all these arrangements has in itself taxed the resources of diplomacy here to the utmost. It has now been more or less successfully accomplished . . . Further, we are here under the most rigorous censorship restrictions, and everything that we do is watched, I may say, with jealous care by the Military Authorities . . .[3]

Nevertheless, it was in mid-1916 that Aitken began to organise film affairs from the Canadian point of view. In July 1916, he obtained permission to send the first official Canadian cameraman to the Western Front to secure Canadian footage exclusively. Canadian footage was also filmed by three other British official cameramen, especially G. H. Malins and J. B. McDowell, and then, in 1918, by Walter Buckstone. Once the footage of these cameramen was turned into films or newsreels, there arose the question of distribution in Canada. Here, in his joint role at both CWRO and the WOCC, Beaverbrook arranged to sell the distribution rights of all war films in Canada to Famous Players as the sole distributing agent in Canada. Famous Players was chosen as providing the best deal, but Beaverbrook explained incorrectly to Sir Robert Borden, the Canadian Prime Minister, that Famous Players was an 'entirely Canadian Corporation'. Subsequently, Beaverbrook informed Sir George Perley, the Canadian High Commissioner in London, that exclusive rights of the film *Canadian Victory at Courcelette* had been sold to Famous Players for £4, 400 for two years. The money went first to the WOCC, and then to Canada for Aitken's War Memorial Fund. Famous Players made no profit, but used the films for their own publicity.[4]

Aitken's ultimate plans apparently aimed at taking control of war film propaganda in Britain, and at the same time providing himself with public office. This was all achieved by 1918. However, the Canadian film story in World War One concerned not only Beaverbrook but also filming at the front. The first difficulty was in finding suitable cameramen. Oscar Bovill, originally a British driver in the Artillery, was the first official Canadian cameraman on the Western Front. He was given a commission in the Canadian Expeditionary Force (CEF) on 27 July 1916, and was attached to the CWRO. Initially, Bovill was praised by Aitken for his film of the Canadians at Courcelette (September 1916), 'which exceeded in brilliance the already famous British pictures [of] . . . the first two great offensives on the Somme'. However, Bovill's contributions soon went downhill. He told Beaverbrook in early 1917 that he had two attacks on film, but the light was poor. Then, after leave in England, Bovill claimed he could not go back to France until he had a new camera. Once back in France in March 1917, Bovill complained that GHQ was not allowing him to film in the Somme area. Next, he asked for an assistant to carry his tripod and camera. This elicited a sarcastic response from the CWRO, wondering whether he and the Canadian still photographer, Captain Ivor Castle, were 'developing into an Army Corps'. Concurrent with this was CWRO's attempt to get Bovill to send in weekly reports, and to provide vouchers for expenses. Neither were forthcoming, and Captain Holt-White of the CWRO became irritated with Bovill. In particular, Holt-White suspected Bovill of chasing ladies in Amiens and Boulogne, with 'a fresh attraction at Rouen'. Holt-White noted that 'there seems to have been the most amazing amount of travelling and nights out'. The final straw came with fights between Bovill and Castle over the use of their car – both said, 'No car, no pictures'.[5]

Bovill may still have survived at the front except that he was sending back poor film material. This was particularly the case with the important Canadian Corps offensive at Vimy Ridge in April 1917, where Bovill's film only captured the rear lines and none of the attack itself. Hence Bovill was asked to resign. In June 1917, Beaverbrook prepared a memo for GHQ in which he explained that:

> Bovill's services were dispensed with by the War Office Cine Committee because he brought back a lot of drivel about the Vimy operations. His pictures were absolutely worthless and he had not taken the opportunity to make the slightest effort. What he said was the picture of an attack was merely the movement of troops in the afternoon intended to support the troops in the front line. Consequently, we took his resignation.[6]

Surprisingly, Bovill continued his connection with the CWRO, and was given a second chance at the Topical Budget newsreel. Here, Bovill failed again, and was asked to resign his Canadian commission. Amazingly, he was given yet another chance when he stepped in after an operator's camera failed while filming in London. However, Bovill failed yet again at Topical Budget, but somehow still remained attached to the CWRO in September and October 1917. Finally, Bovill at last resigned his commission on 23 November 1917. Bovill's surprising longevity was partially related to the problem of finding good cameramen. Thus, in May 1917, another potential Canadian cameraman, L. Hodges, was rejected because, while competent as a film projectionist, his previous career, he was poor as a cinematographer. Subsequently, a rather pathetic appeal went out in June 1917 from the CWRO, asking for applications for three Canadian cameramen positions. None applied.[7]

   After Bovill's departure from the front, and because the CWRO had trouble finding cameramen, official British cinematographers actually filmed most of the Canadian footage after mid 1917. Those particularly involved included Malins and McDowell. Hence, after the departure of Bovill, Beaverbrook contacted Captain J. C. Faunthorpe, manager for the WOCC in France, who put McDowell onto filming Canadian operations in mid 1917. In June 1917, Faunthorpe reported: 'I saw McDowell today and told him to hang on to the Canadians until he gets a good film. It is a matter of waiting on the spot until the right thing turns up'. However, this was elusive, and Faunthorpe sounded doubtful: 'I hope [McDowell] will get you a really good film for Canada'. This was still difficult at the end of June 1917, when the Canadians attacked, 'but the zero hour was a bit late and it was a very dark afternoon and rained heavily. Hence *two* operations got nothing. However, we hope for the best . . .'. By mid-July 1917,

McDowell had sent home quite a lot of Canadian film. Even so, wrote Faunthorpe, 'We have not yet succeeded in getting an actual attack. It is hard to get one by daylight'. Nevertheless, 'McDowell is being kept on the Canadian film till he gets what is wanted'. But even during the 1917 Passchendaele offensive, although McDowell shot 1700 feet of film, Faunthorpe admitted that 'he has not got an attack – one cannot get it when zero [hour] is always in the dark. He has run great risks and I hope the stuff will be good'.[8]

By April 1918, McDowell was put in charge of all official cameramen on the Western Front, and was replaced by G. H. Malins and Walter Buckstone to film Canadian material. Malins was not popular with GHQ in France because of the boastful interviews of his exploits that he gave to the press in England, and so in early 1918 the CWRO asked GHQ France to keep a close watch on him. Also on occasion, other companies were used for Canadian content: for example, in April 1917, Gaumont filmed Prime Minister Borden's visit to the Canadian training centre at Witley. Captain Holt-White reported that 'the film is top hole and shows the Prime Minister in the snow and so on'. Holt-White thought it should be shown in the next Canadian newsreel. Similarly, Pathé filmed Our Heroic Canadian Brothers in 1917 and 1918.[9] There were also other cameramen of the semi-official variety. The very first Canadian to film at the front was actually Hilton de Witt Girdwood, who, for commercial purposes, and sponsored by the India Office, filmed Indian troops in France for two months in 1915. Due to censorship and copyright problems with the War Office, his film With the Empire's Fighters was not released until September 1916. Another film-maker, and most ex-asperating, was an American, D. J. Dwyer. In 1916 he managed to attach himself to the CEF and made a film which he did not submit for censorship, and which he intended to circulate in Canada for private profit. At the same time, he was being paid for his expenses. A 1916 draft cable from Aitken to Sam Hughes, then Minister of Militia, acknowledged that 'Dwyer is missing and so far untraced. Stop. War Office insist he must be found'. Next, a CWRO draft to Ottawa in late 1916 read in part, 'It would be an outrage if this [Dwyer] film was allowed to circulate in Canada for private profit . . .'. But Dwyer was resourceful – 'elusive as an eel' – and managed to get his film to Canada, and follow himself without being apprehended. Dwyer refused to obey orders and Aitken declared that no price was 'too high for the riddance of Dwyer. Unless you have had transactions with him, it would be beyond anyone to conceive the sheer impossibility of dealing with him'. The most that could be done was to dismiss Dwyer from the CEF on 17 February 1917.[10]

One other distraction was the appearance on the Western Front of the celebrated American film-maker, D. W. Griffith. The origins of Griffith's eventual film, *Hearts of the World* (1918), is obscure, and initially neither the British Department of Information nor Beaverbrook seemed enthusiastic. But by June 1917, Beaverbrook was promoting Griffith, and had introduced him to Canadian forces at the front. This did not go well, for Griffith announced a love interest in the film, and so the Canadian military felt they would simply be 'supers' for a non-military film. According to Beaverbrook, this had 'a very startling effect on the Canadian military authorities', and the next day the Canadian's would not do anything for Griffith. But Griffith persevered, and in August 1917 Beaverbrook arranged for the Americans to film fake scenes in England, using £853 worth of explosives set off by the Canadian training division at Witley. In September, Beaverbrook wrote to the French asking them to help Griffith film scenes of ruined French towns around Senlis, because this would help political problems in Canada caused by the conscription crisis, especially in French-speaking Quebec. Hence, film showing the suffering of French people was 'a matter of great urgency'. Then by October 1917 Griffith was taking scenes in the 15th Canadian Brigade area. There was eventually, therefore, considerable Canadian support for Griffith's film, although, ironically, Canada's chief censor, Chambers, cut out disturbing combat scenes before the film was screened in Canada.[11]

Censorship was always a problem. From the Canadian point of view, films were initially passed if GHQ and the War Office had approved them, and the Canadian versions were identical. Then, in Canada, if scenes were judged offensive, Chambers simply censored them himself, having legal authority to do so from January 1917. But a problem emerged in summer 1917, when gruesome scenes in a Famous Players film were condemned by Chambers and others. However, Famous Players did not make any cuts because of their contract with Beaverbrook and the CWRO. Beaverbrook argued that the clause forbidding cuts was there for financial reasons, but that he would ask Sir Edward Kemp at the Militia Department to censor the films himself, while he, Beaverbrook would personally attempt to cut out unpleasant scenes. Nevertheless, Beaverbrook pointed out that the films still needed to appeal to the public, while also remaining useful historically. Kemp simply wrote in July that the Canadian films would go in front of Chambers for censorship. However, by October 1917, it seems that Chambers was satisfied with at least the weekly newsreels, and these would not be censored in the future.[12]

Other limitations on filming at the front included the changing demands of the audience. Initially, in 1916, the CWRO thought of feature-length pictures, but in May 1917 Beaverbrook decided that a change was in order, seemingly for a combination of financial reasons and audience reaction. A draft letter on 8 May 1917 from Beaverbrook argued that:

> The truth of the matter is that the present style of film is played out. The public is jaded and we have to tickle its palate with something a little more dramatic in future, if we are to maintain our sales. From this point of view one is naturally compelled to look at the matter from an entirely commercial standpoint.

He continued: 'After all, the films are not supposed to be simply dull records. When one is in this business, one has to consider what the public wants'. Thus Beaverbrook now proposed a weekly newsreel under the title War Office Topical Budget, which would look at events and incidents at the front. In late 1917 this became a twice-weekly newsreel for the rest of the War. Beaverbrook explained the change in mid-May 1917:

> The Budget (newsreel) service of course is undertaken on account of the declining interest in the long story films . . . Until we had exploited the long story films for as long as possible we could not commence on the Budgets until we had accumulated a considerable amount of material.

Sales, however, were feeble, and so Captain Holt-White was appointed in July 1917 to do promotion, while a salesman was hired to handle sales in the US and Canada. These changes helped Budget, and Beaverbrook claimed that Budget was a decisive factor in maintaining morale in early 1918.[13]

The style and form of the documentary/propaganda film owed a great deal to the ideas of Beaverbrook in World War One. His central idea was that propaganda films should appeal to the widest possible audience, rather than aim at elites. For this reason, the films could not be dull, and even sensational items should be included. Beaverbrook also feared that censorship would cut out the most interesting parts of the films. In his CWRO Report to Kemp on 30 March 1918, Beaverbrook believed that film propaganda must be convincing, and must meet the demands of the public. Film was important because it appealed to the emotions 'common to humanity', and it did so 'because it contains that subtle admixture of art, reality, and that swift and dramatic movement, which rivet the eyes and mind past all withdrawing'. Moreover, its appeal was not just to the 'elect', but 'to the mass of the people and the [Canadian] Dominion Government has been the first to realise the potency of the new weapon . . .'. Not all felt as positive as Beaverbrook, and, in August 1917, John Buchan, head of the Department of Information, complained that Canadian publicity produced a general feeling that 'Canada is running the war'. Probably in reaction to this, in September 1917, Beaverbrook prepared a document entitled 'Crusade by Cinema'. In this document, he claimed that the Canadians had partially lifted the veil of secrecy which surrounded the story of the War at the front, and argued that:

> From the first they [the Canadians] grasped the Power of the Picture in Propaganda work. There are a disgruntled few who think the Canadians' cameras and films have been too busy. That is a mistake. The fault is that ours [the British] have not been busy enough.[14]

But what was the reaction in Canada to these films? Judging by some newspaper reports, the reaction was mixed. The Toronto *Telegram* of 12 January 1917 raved about the latest war films:

> Every man, woman and child through the length and breadth of Canada should make a point of seeing the latest war films from the Canadian front . . . As the pictured Battalions of Canada's sturdy sons tramp along the muddy French roads, you can almost hear the rhythmic crunch of their boots on the soil, the snatches of song and cheery whistles . . .

In contrast, a journalist with the Montreal *Daily Star* noted in April 1917 that the latest Famous Players' picture had fizzled in Montreal. Another way of looking at the public reception of the films is to review box office receipts, and here one example is the least successful of the 'big battle' pictures, *The German Retreat and the Battle of Arras*. This was a WOCC film, sent overseas for distribution in July 1917, but contained no Canadian scenes. Although receipts in Canada until 1 November 1917 for this film produced a profit of $2944.84 for the WOCC, a separate set of figures for the Regent Theatre, Ottawa, for the same film and dates, showing full revenue and expenses for Famous Players, resulted in a net loss of $658.80.[15]

It would appear from the last statistic that Beaverbrook's sense of a decline of interest in 'big battle' war films in 1917 may have been justified. But Beaverbrook himself seemed as much interested in profit as anything else, and his files are filled with financial agreements and methods of promoting war films. However, all profits were split between the British Government, Canada's Patriotic Fund and Beaverbrook's Canadian War Memorial Fund. This last was dedicated to perpetuating the memory of Canadian war veterans through oil paintings and monuments, and by September 1917 had raised £10, 000.[16]

But what kind of factual war films were Canadians actually seeing in 1917 and 1918? Here it is only possible to analyse a selection of these films. An early CWRO effort praised by Aitken was *The Battle of Courcelette*. Filmed in September 1916 at the Somme by Bovill, this film was extremely episodic, with little sense of continuity after the first scenes.[17] The Courcelette film is a curious mixture of detachment and involvement, of contrivance and realism. The silence of the film, the static camera, the ruined landscape, the shots of raw technology of tanks and artillery, and dim pictures of soldiers attacking, all reduce the human presence and produce a powerful detachment from reality. In contrast, the march-past of a Canadian battalion, and the close-up of artillery pieces being fired, show us the human face of individuals at the front. Occasionally, and unprompted, men wagons and horses move past the camera, or soldiers stand and watch, or prisoners light cigarettes, and all these chance vignettes give the viewer an abrupt sense of immediacy. Similarly, and unintended, at the very end of the film, as German prisoners are walking along one stumbles and falls. A Canadian guard helps him up, and in this brief scene, the camera suddenly breaks through all artificial barriers and preserves forever a small moment of human life. Indeed, it is these unintended scenes that the historian Arthur Marwick sees as most valuable for the historian.[18]

During 1917 and 1918, a different atmosphere emerges from the films taken for Canadian consumption. The cameramen, McDowell, Malins and Buckstone, now focus on human interest scenes, and there are attempts to follow a single story through a series of scenes. For example, *Canadian Victory at Courcelette and the Advance of the Tanks* (CWRO, 1917) and *Canadian Sections 1: 1917* (CWRO, 1917) show Canadians voting at the front; men eating, smoking and cleaning rifles; and in a tank part men go about their tasks of cleaning and repairing tank engines, while one man draws a maple leaf on a tank and stands back to admire his work. But the cameramen also show long sequences of an observer and his observation balloon, of communication systems between ground and planes, of how to send a message by pigeon, or, in particular, in *Canadian Sections 1*, a long sequence of men carrying heavy shells into trenches. Another method was simply to show long pans of certain scenes such as Albert Cathedral or the ruins of Vimy. Yet once again the unintended breaks through – boy and dog run happily past as aviation panels are set up – or, in the carrying shells sequence, one man struggles to lift his burden, but still manages to casually smoke as he staggers along.[19]

Then by 1918 the CWRO/Ministry of Information (MOI) films generally offer an even more relaxed and casual atmosphere. Thus in *Canadians East of Arras* (CWRO, 1918) men and officers cheerfully ride on Mark V tanks, or jokingly walk just in front of the massive tanks. The same casual attitudes occur in *Scenes in Cambrai 1* (MOI, 1918), a film taken shortly after the Canadians captured the city on 9 October 1918. The city is burning, possibly set on fire by retreating Germans. Canadians casually watch the flames, or simply wander round as spectators. The estaminet Moithy burns, and the camera shifts to a group of officers led by Brigadier General Draper, 3 Canadian Division, who study maps and look around without achieving much. Finally, in *Our Heroic Canadian Brothers* (Pathé, 1918), shots of soldiers casually voting in the general election of 17 December 1917 reveal there was no such thing as privacy in wartime voting. At a pay parade, Canadian soldiers receive their pay and inspect it carefully. Others smile, and walk around with hands in their pockets. Intentionally or not, this scene depicts an extremely relaxed Canadian military culture. An unusual shot in this film is a long, slow 360-degree pan of the ruins of Vimy, impressive in its silence and unspoken critical comment on the works of man. A final interesting sequence shows the Canadian 42nd Battalion marching through the Vimy Ridge craters, an almost endless number of men, viewed in close-up from a static camera, which gives the battalion a sense of dynamism and purpose. The camera then pans slowly over the men as they rest on a hill. In an unintended conclusion many of the men are still smoking as they get up to leave, but while some smile and wave others look sullen and even angry.[20]

These films reveal a lot about Canadians on the Western Front, despite censorship and technical limitations. The films show the relaxed culture of the Canadian military, the portraits and behaviour of individual solders, the reactions of civilians to the Canadian presence and the technology of war. However, these were all factual films. Back in Canada feature films were being made, but these were usually unrelated to the War, and in fact it was not until the post-war era that Canada produced its first full-length feature film that focused entirely on World War One. That film was *Carry on Sergeant!*, released in 1928. The background to the film involved the well-known British cartoonist, Captain Bruce Bairnsfather, whose World War One soldier character 'Ole Bill' was well known. Bairnsfather was recruited by a company called Canadian International Films to 'assist' and promote a film based on 'Ole Bill', but ended up both writing the script and directing the film as well. Canadian International Films was run jointly by two British partners who raised the very large sum of $300,000 from among prominent Canadians. Given Bairnsfather's credentials, the prominent investors, and the largest sum raised to date in Canada for a film production, all portents seemed favourable.[21]

In fact, the idea of this film was not new. The secretary of Gaumont Pictures had previously written to Beaverbrook in October 1917 with the idea of turning 'Ole Bill' into a film, and in 1918 a film version of the play was released, entitled *Carry On!*, which did well in Canada. Meanwhile, Bairnsfather had co-authored the successful London and Broadway play, *The Better 'Ole'*.[22] Thus the concept was well known, but the filming itself in Trenton, Ontario, in 1927 and 1928 was a disaster. Bairnsfather, who became the director, was autocratic, inexperienced and somewhat paranoid. Salaries were far too high, money was wasted, and internal conflicts raged. Bairnsfather spent three months editing the film, which was released as a silent film in November 1928. Although the film shows flashes of genuine talent and emotion, the basic problem seemed to be how to combine comedy and tragedy in a World War One setting. What worked well in a music hall was more problematic in a film that shifted uneasily between humour and mud and blood. This is epitomised by some of the captions which offer humour and sarcasm, even when the scenes call for a serious approach. Thus when the Canadians take over the line from a British battalion in the mud and rain, the caption reads: 'The English made no attempt to stop them'. Similarly, after a scene showing heavy shelling, the film shifts to an estaminet, with the caption: 'If ever you lose an army, go straight to the nearest Estaminet. You'll find it there'. Again, when the Canadian soldiers leave their grim trenches and head for Ypres, the caption sarcastically relates: 'Nobody broke down at the parting'.[23]

How would the Canadian public respond? The film opened in Toronto at the Regent Theatre on 12 November 1928, and received a mixed reaction. Most reviewers praised the film for its realistic war scenes, although the war scenes in *Carry On Sergeant!* were actually far from realistic. However, many reviewers also focused on the moral problem of the hero and his estaminet love affair. Typical was the review of the Toronto *Globe* which praised the film as 'a great war picture, strongly tinged with Canadianism'. Yet, the reviewer did not like the love episode, where the hero yielded 'To the most ordinary sort of temptation in a squalid estaminet . . . surely the clean of heart among Canada's soldiers, who resisted the wiles of the estaminet women, also were valiant in the conflict!' The moral complaints of the reviewer and others may actually have increased viewer interest in the film, but the film did not make money at the Regent and closed after a two-week run. Possibly the film did not do better because it was silent in a period when theatres were shifting to sound. Yet in Toronto, only two theatres were wired for sound at that time, and in fact a two-week run was normal for films at this period. After some editing, the film played in several theatres in Ontario and Quebec, but was finally withdrawn in December 1928. The film which cost the vast sum of $500,000, lost money for the investors, and damaged the Canadian film industry for several years.[24]

Despite renewed interest in Canada during the 1930s in memorialising the War, it was not until 1935 that another World War One film appeared in Canada. The genesis of the lengthy documentary film *Lest We Forget* (1935) lay in the re-discovery in 1932 of 25,000 feet of lost film from the CWRO. A government committee was formed to edit this footage and all available material into a form suitable for general viewing. The film, provisionally entitled *Heritage*, was ready in 1934, but the committee spent much time debating various aspects of the film, and only the emergence of rival American films speeded up the actual release in March 1935. Meanwhile, the Canadian Legion assumed production costs for *Heritage*, which was now retitled as *Lest We Forget*, coincidentally the same title as a 1918 American film about the loss of the *Lusitania*.[25]

Lest We Forget was a fast-paced and striking film, and, despite historical inaccuracies, tended to give an unvarnished mud and blood version of the War.[26] Certain themes emerge from this film. First, the film stresses the cult of the ideal Canadian soldier. As war breaks out, the title declares that Canadian 'Free Men throughout this land kept faith in the hour of trial and in the day of battle remembering the traditions they had been taught . . .'. In the film, Canadian soldiers are stubborn, brave, cheerful and gallant. Even the wounded at Vimy are 'elated over the progress of the attack . . .'. Negative episodes, such as Canadian 2 Division's problems with the craters at St Eloi in 1916, were happily ignored. Instead the caption boasted that the Division's 'great gallantry at St. Eloi was to bring it lasting renown'. Secondly, in keeping with the pacifist mood of the time, the film goes out of its way to emphasise the destruction of the War. For example, after the battle of Courcelette (1916) the ruined village is shown, and the narrator intones: 'dead men lay everywhere: war is not a glorious thing . . . these were once men . . .'. After Vimy (1917), enemy corpses are shown as 'silent witnesses to the toll of war . . .'. The results at Passchendaele (1917) were the 'corpses of men in whose veins had once flowed the sweet red wine of youth [which] lay foul and rotting . . .'. A long sequence shows the funeral of twenty-one soldiers and nurses, killed at a hospital in May 1918: 'Ghastly, pitiless, diabolical, but that too is war'. Thirdly, in keeping with the previous theme, one phrase obviously appealed to the film's editors – 'the tortured earth'. This is used at least four times, evidently as a metaphor for the War's cosmic impact. Finally, the film does condemn Germany and its allies, perhaps reflecting a growing concern with fascism.[27]

The rather harsh image of *Lest We Forget* reflected the intentions of the committee to condemn the futility of war. The film actually opened in Ottawa on 7 March 1935, and somewhat surprisingly produced a good deal of criticism. The problem was that the opening night was a gala social affair, which contrasted rather unhappily with the grim nature of the film. The Ottawa *Citizen* headed their critique 'Dress up to see the slaughter'. This uncorked a hot debate in Ottawa newspapers and letter columns as to whether the film was really anti-war, or was actually a glorification of war. Meanwhile, the *Evening Citizen* offered a general critique of the film and argued that nobody thought of peace, the Ottawa *Citizen* continued to argue that the film would stir up martial ardour, the *Mail and Empire* said that every child should see the film, and the Toronto *Telegram* believed the film would help bring about peace. Finally, *Liberty*, the voice of the Legion, which had promoted the film, found it to be an anti-war picture.[28]

Obviously, opinion was divided about the meaning of the film. Regardless, the general public did not support the film, especially in general release, and *Liberty* was forced to admit that it 'completely failed to appeal in our largest centres'. A rather similar fate met the next film to commemorate the War, *Salute to Valour* (1937), which depicted the pilgrimage to, and unveiling of, the striking Memorial to the Canadians at Vimy Ridge in 1936. Although a visually attractive film, *Salute to Valour* attracted controversy rather than audience interest because it allegedly contained the last official pictures of Edward VIII before his abdication. Although *Lest We Forget* and *Salute to Valour* may not have been terribly successful at the box office, this did not indicate any lack of public interest in World War One. The 1936 Vimy pilgrimage attracted 6,000 Canadian veterans and their families to the memorial, the 1938 Remembrance Day saw the peak of attendance at events across Canada, and the country had finally established suitable financial systems to support the disabled and ageing veterans of World War One. Perhaps the relative lack of success of the two films meant that most Canadians had already formed their own ideal images of the War, and needed no reminding, while others were pacifists and so reacted against the films.[29]

With the outbreak of World War Two, World War One faded into the background, not even commemorated by a complete official history until 1962. After World War Two, interest in the First World War continued to recede and was replaced by controversies over the Second War. But in the 1960s a number of Canadian books about the First World War marked a revival of interest, as in Britain. Yet the overriding Canadian image of the War still embraced the ideal, gallant Canadian soldier amidst the mud and blood of the trenches. Hence, when the next Canadian film about World War One emerged in 1982, *The Kid Who Couldn't Miss*, a negative story about the World War One Canadian flying ace, Billy Bishop, there was a storm of protest. The theme of the film was that Bishop had invented some of his victories, especially the solo raid on the German airfield which earned Bishop his Victoria Cross. The film also created dialogue in which Bishop's mechanic, Walter Bourne, doubted Bishop's claims. As a result of the controversy surrounding the film, some 3,000 letters were written in protest to the National Film Board (NFB), which had sponsored the film, and the Canadian Senate held hearings in 1985 to establish the truth of the matter. During these hearings, Senator Walker articulated what Bishop meant to him and his generation: 'This is a life and death matter to many of us. We admired Billy Bishop, we knew his family, and our colleague, Senator Molson, served with him'.[30]

This debate mirrored some of the earlier pro- and anti-war arguments over *Lest We Forget*. But the difference now was that *The Kid Who Couldn't Miss* concerned a particular individual, and, with the backdrop of the Vietnam War, a new generation was challenging old ideals. Paul Cowan, the NFB director of *The Kid Who Couldn't Miss* indeed considered that heroes were created to help prosecute war, while the NFB Commissioner attempted to deflect criticism by suggesting that a new generation of documentary makers were inventing new ways of describing reality – 'the creative interpretation of Reality'. However, he was forced to admit that *The Kid Who Couldn't Miss* was in fact a docu-drama and not a pure documentary film, while Paul Cowan defended the historical accuracy of the film, and argued that the film was really about the nature of heroism. The final recommendations of the Senate Committee were that the film should be labelled a docu-drama of both reality and fiction, and that there was no evidence that the real Walter Bourne thought Bishop's claims were fraudulent.[31]

With *The Kid Who Couldn't Miss*, the impact of World War One film on Canada comes to an end, unless the American film *Legends of the Fall* (1994) is included as an external influence. Why have films about World

War One largely disappeared in Canada, while interest in the War remains mainly through history books and Remembrance Day services? Perhaps World War Two and its controversies continue to overshadow World War One; perhaps the historian George Stanley is right, Canadians are an unmilitary people, quick to forget war and interested chiefly in civilian pursuits; perhaps Canadians still have a strong image of the ideal of the World War One soldier and do not look for new interpretations; perhaps the significant Canadian role in World War One still awaits a Canadian film-maker who can really capture the powerful and tragic events of that time.[32]

NOTES

1   Film and Video catalogue at the National Archives of Canada, Ottawa (hereafter NAC), which gives details of the many Canadian produced films of the First World War. Peter Morris, *Embattled Shadows: A History of Canadian Cinema, 1895–1939* (Montreal: Queen's University Press, 1978) pp. 58–9; Jeffrey Keshen, *Propaganda and Censorship during Canada's Great War* (Edmonton, Alberta: University of Alberta Press, 1996) pp. 107–8.

2   Roger Smither (ed.), *Imperial War Museum Film Catalogue*, Volume 1. *The First World War Archive* (Westport, Connecticut: Greenwood, 1993), p. x. The British side of the confusing Aitken/Beaverbrook story is also in Nicholas Reeves, *Official British Film Propaganda during the First World War* (Beckenham, Kent, and Surrey Hills, Australia: Croom-Helm, 1986). Luke McKernan argues for the virtual identity of CWRO and WOCC: Luke McKernan, *Topical Budget: The Great British News Film* (London: BFI, 1992), p. 38. Since Aitken became a peer in January 1917, references before that date are to Aitken, after that date to Beaverbrook.

3   Sir Max Aitken, CWRO to J. W. Todd, Board of Pension Commissioners, Ottawa, 22 November 1916, Reel A 1767, Beaverbrook Papers, MG 27, II, G1, NAC (Beaverbrook Papers in NAC hereafter BP).

4   Draft letter from War Office to F. C. Masterman (Wellington House), 16 February 1917, Reel A 1768, BP. Keshan, *Propaganda and Censorship*, pp. 36–7; Reeves, *Official British Film Propaganda*, pp. 61–2. Beaverbrook to Sir Robert Borden, 29 January 1917, Reel A 1767, and Beaverbrook to Sir George Perley, 22 March 1917, Reel A 1768; BP.

5   W. M. Aitken, CWRO *Report* submitted to Sir Robert Borden, Prime Minister, Ottawa, 11 January 1917, P. 6, Reel A 1767, BP. On Bovill's appointment, Colonel in charge of War Records to Adjutant General,

HQ Overseas Military Forces of Canada, 5 June 1917, Reel A 1767, BP. On Bovill's problems, Bovill to Aitken, 15 January 1917; Captain Holt-White to Beaverbrook, 9 March 1917; Bovill to Beaverbrook, 17 March 1917; CWRO to Colonel Manley-Sims (GHQ), 10 April 1917; Lieutenant Colonel A. H. Hutton-Wilson (GHQ, Intelligence), to Colonel Manley-Sims (GHQ), 17 April 1917; Captain Holt-White to Colonel Manley-Sims; Captain Holt-White to Captain Ivor Castle, 16 April 1917; Captain Holt-White to Captain Roberts (Canadian Representative at GHQ), 9 May 1917; Reel A 1767, BP.

6   Beaverbrook, Memo to Captain Holt-White for a letter to Colonel Manley-Sims, 4 June 1917, Reel A 1767, BP.

7   Bovill's career is revealed in a series of CWRO letters in mid-to late 1917: Bovill to Beaverbrook, 1 June 1917; Bovill to Beaverbrook, 28 June 1917; CWRO Memo from Captain Holt-White, 14 August 1917 (Bovill's failure at Topical Budget); Topical Budget to Aitken, 17 August 1917 (re Bovill and the failed camera); Jeapes (Topical Budget) to Beaverbrook, 3 September 1917; Captain Holt-White to HQ Canadian Troops, 26 September 1917; Lieutenant Colonel at CWRO to Adjutant General, 14 October 1917; Lieutenant R. D. Scott (CWRO) to Beaverbrook, 14 November 1917 and 15 November 1917 (asking for Bovill's final resignation); Reel A 1767, BP.

8   J. C. Faunthorpe to Beaverbrook, 6 May 1917, 9 June 1917, 11 June 1917, 29 June 1917, 19 July 1917, 20 August 1917, 9 July 1917; Reel A 1768, BP.

9   McKernan, *Topical Budget*, p. 51; Beaverbrook, CWRO *Report* to Kemp, 30 March 1918, p. 9. CWRO to GHQ France, 11 January 1918, Reel A 1767, BP. Captain Holt-White to Beaverbrook, 17 April 1917, Reel A 1768, BP. Geoffrey H. Malins's book *How I Filmed the War* (London: Herbert Jenkins, 1920) is not very useful for the Canadian story. He does, however, mention filming General Burstall and the Canadians as they are inspected by the King in 1916 (p. 218). For the Pathé film, see IWM 465, Smither, *Imperial War Museum Catalogue*, p. 178.

10 On Girdwood, Stephen Badsey, 'Introduction', in Smither., *Imperial War Museum Film Catalogue*, p. viii. Draft cable, Aitken to Sam Hughes, 6 October 1916, Reel A 1767; CWRO to Major John Bassett, Ottawa, 3 November 1916, Reel A 1764; Beaverbrook to Sir George Perley, 30 March 1917, and Captain Holt-White to Beaverbrook, 10 February 1917, Reel A 1767; BP.

11 T. L. Gilmour, Department of Information, to Beaverbrook, 11 April 1917, and Beaverbrook to Gilmour, 12 April 1917, refusing to let Griffith film at the front, Reel A 1768, BP. Beaverbrook to Sir Reginald Brade, 27 June 1917 (on the love interest problem); Memo to Secretary WOCC, no date, but refers to 15 August 1917, re explosives used; Beaverbrook to P. Marcel (French news film director), 12 September 1917; Stewart, CWRO, to Brigadier Ashton, GOC 15 Canadian Infantry Brigade, 3 October 1917;

Reel A 1768, BP. Reeves, *Official British Film Propaganda*, p. 123–4, on how much Griffith actually filmed in France, but the Ashton letter shows that Griffith did film in that area. Keshen, *Propaganda and Censorship*, p. 108, on Canadian censorship of *Hearts of the World*. The conscription crisis related to conscription being introduced in Canada in 1917, despite earlier pronouncements that it would not be, plus the reluctance of French Canadians to participate in the War.

12   Kemp to CWRO, 4 February 1917; Beaverbrook to Kemp, 7 February 1917; Faunthorpe to Beaverbrook, 20 February 1917; Beaverbrook to Charteris, GHQ, 20 March 1917; Charteris to Beaverbrook, 21 March 1917; Reel A 1768, BP. On specific scenes censored, Colonel, GHQ to Beaverbrook, 5 August 1917, and 'Censored titles for D. W. Griffith', c. November 1917; Reel A 1768, BP. Re gruesome scenes, Beaverbrook to Kemp, 22 June 1917, Kemp to Beaverbrook, 10 July 1917 (censorship by Chambers), and 23 July 1917; Beaverbrook to Kemp, 15 August 1917; Reel A 1768, BP. Re future censorship of newsreels, Major Bristol for Kemp to Beaverbrook, 3 October 1917, Reel A 1768, BP.

13   Major Parkinson, 'Report of the Office of Canadian Records', 'Conclusion', no date, but late 1916, Reel A 1767, BP. Draft, Beaverbrook, CWRO, to Lieutenant Colonel A. H. Hutton-Wilson, GHQ 'I' (d) (the office connected with press and film), 8 May 1917; Draft, Beaverbrook, CWRO, to Hutton-Wilson, 15 May 1917; Reel A 1768, BP. McKernan, *Topical Budget*, pp. 12, 41, 45. On budget sales, Captain Holt-White to Beaverbrook, 3 October 1917; Reel A 1768, BP.

14   Beaverbrook, CWRO *Report* submitted to Kemp, 30 March 1918, p. 9, Reel A 1767, BP. John Buchan to Sir Reginald Brade (War Office), 14 August 1917, Reel A 1768, BP. 'Crusade by cinema. By a movie man', no date, but c. September 1917. The draft was certainly corrected by Beaverbrook, and most likely, from the style, prepared by him; Reel A 1768, BP.

15   *Toronto Telegram*, 12 January 1917, Clipping in Reel A 1768, BP. C. F. Crandall to Beaverbrook, 16 April 1917, Reel A 1768, BP. Financial figures for *Battle of Arras* in Reel A 1768, BP.

16   On split of profits: CWRO to W. H. Griffith, 19 February 1917; Beaverbrook to C. F. Crandall, 5 September 1917; Beaverbrook to Crandall, no date; Reel A 1768, BP. For the results of the Canadian War Memorial Fund, Jonathan F. Vance, *Death so Noble: Memory, Meaning and the First World War* (Vancouver: University of British Columbia Press, 1997), pp. 102ff. and *passim*.

17   CWRO, *The Battle of Courcelette*, 1916, VI 9709, NAC. This film is not listed in the Imperial War Museum catalogue, and contains different material from the 1917 CWRO *Canadian Victory at Courcelette* film, which is listed and described as IWM 466 in the Imperial War Museum catalogue.

18   The importance of unintended scenes for historians was pointed out by
     the historian Arthur Marwick, who labelled them 'unwitting testimony'.
     Arthur Marwick, *War and Social Change in the Twentieth Century*
     (London: Macmillan, 1974, reprinted 1978), pp. 229–30.

19   CWRO, *Canadian Victory at Courcelette* (1917), VI 9801, NAC. *Cana-
     dian Sections I*: (1917), VI 9801, NAC; respectively IWM 466 and IWM
     1188 in the Imperial War Museum catalogue.

20   *Canadians East of Arras* (1918), *Scenes in Cambrai 1* (1918), *Our Heroic
     Canadian Brothers* (1918), VI 9801, NAC. In the Imperial War Museum
     catalogue these films are numbered IWM 316, IWM 339, IWM 465,
     respectively.

21   The 'Carry On Sergeant!' story is well covered in Morris, *Embattled
     Shadows*, pp. 72–80; and Peter Roffman, *The Story of 'Carry On
     Sergeant'* (Toronto: Ontario Film Institute, 1979).

22   T. A. Welsh, Gaumont Pictures, to Beaverbrook, 6 October 1917; T. A.
     Welsh to WOCC, 23 November 1917; Lieutenant R. D. Scott, CWRO, to
     T. A. Welsh, 29 November 1917; Reel A 1768, BP.

23   *Carry On Sergeant* (1928), 99 minutes, Canadian International Films,
     Directed by Bruce Bairnsfather, NAC. The film has been ably restored
     by D. J. Turner.

24   Lawrence Mason, 'Review of Carry On Sergeant!', Toronto *Globe*, 12
     November 1928, p. 16. Interview with D. J. Turner, Ottawa, 30 July 1998.
     Roffman, *Story of Carry On Sergeant!*, pp. 18–19; Morris, *Embattled
     Shadows*, p. 72.

25   Vance, *Death so Noble*, pp. 169ff; Pierre Berton, *Hollywood's Canada:
     The Americanization of Our National Image* (Toronto; McClelland and
     Stewart, 1975), p. 138; Kevin Brownlow, *The War, the West and the
     Wilderness* (New York: Knopf, 1979), p. 27.

26   *Lest We Forget* (1935), Canadian War Museum version, 1 hour and 40
     minutes, produced by The Great War Motion Picture Committee, NAC.

27   Ibid., Thomas Socknat, *Witness against War: Pacifism in Canada,
     1900–1945* (Toronto: University of Toronto Press, 1987), pp. 131ff.,
     160ff., 190, for the 1930s campaign against fascism in Canada.

28   Clippings from: Ottawa *Journal*, 7 March 1935; Ottawa *Citizen*, 7 March
     1935; *Evening Citizen*, 16 March 1935; Ottawa *Citizen*, 21 March 1935;
     Mail and Empire, 26 March 1935; Toronto *Telegram*, no date; *Liberty*, 23
     March 1935; all in *Scrap Book of Archie Shaw* (Ottawa: Canadian
     Government Motion Picture Bureau), RG 20, Volume 1628, NAC.

29   Vance, *Death so Noble*, pp. 170, 216; Montreal *Standard*, 6 March 1937;
     clipping from *Scrap Book of Archie Shaw*. Desmond Morton and Glenn
     Wright, *Winning the Second Battle: Canadian Veterans and the Return
     to Civilian Life, 1915–1930* (Toronto: University of Toronto Press, 1987),
     pp. 220–1.

30   'The Kid Who Couldn't Miss': Senate Standing Committee on Social

Affairs, Science and Technology. Chair: the Honourable Jack Marshall, 33rd Parliament, First Session, 17 October 1985, pp. 3:13, 3:14; Second Session, 30 October 1985, p. 4: 40; Sixth Session, 28 November 1985, pp. 6: 24–7; Canadian Parliamentary Papers.

31   Ibid., Sixth Session, 28 November 1985, pp. 6:9, 6:13, 6:16, 6:37–8, 6:74; Eighth Session, pp. 8:20ff.; Recommendations, p. 40.

32   George F. G. Stanley, *Canada's Soldiers: The Military History of an Unmilitary People* (3rd edition, Toronto: University of Toronto Press, 1974), pp. 1, 340, 444.

6

France: the Silent Memory

Pierre Sorlin

At the beginning of the twentieth century most French politicians assumed that France was a great power: her colonial empire was the second biggest one; she was an international banker; she was funding the (hopeless) attempt at refurbishing the Russian economy; her guns were more efficient than the German ones; her navy was excellent. Her cinematography bore witness to the quality of her industry. If the Americans had been the first to contrive a way of producing an illusion of motion with successive images the French had been able to transform a scientific principle into a commercially lucrative spectacle. In 1914 the French movie companies had subsidiaries all over the planet and one of them, Pathé, was, for a while, the world's leading exporter of films.

France's only worry was her fear of facing Germany alone as she had in 1870. She knew that her independence could only be assured when allied with Russia, or, better still, with Britain. French opinion-makers were often warning their flocks about the danger of the armament race. The socialists counted on the international solidarity of workers to prevent any risk of conflict but they were scared by the emergence, on the Right, of pressure groups which denounced France's culpable pacifism and greeted with enthusiasm the prospect of a war with Germany. In the silent version of Abel Gance's *I Accuse* (1918), when the declaration of war is announced one of the main characters, François, a crude countryman and a hunter, greets the news with pleasure: he will hunt men instead of animals.[1] But this was a naive trick used to signal how primitive François was. Recent research tends to prove that a majority of the French were not willing to confront Germany. Gance was much cleverer, twenty years later, when he evoked the summer of 1914 in *Lost Paradise* (1939): a newly married couple are walking in a peaceful, sunny landscape; suddenly a bell rings and a batch of youngsters singing a patriotic song and following a flag parades in the background; the couple look at each other in total despair: a few people feel enthusiastic but those who are far sighted know that this is the beginning of a nightmare.

THE WAR IMAGINED

The testimony of cinema is interesting from that point of view. That is not to say that films mirror public opinion: there is never any way of finding the relationship, albeit indirect, between what pictures show and what spectators think. The only reasonable thing we can attempt is to analyse what was offered to movie-goers. The Lumière brothers, who were active until 1904, and then Pathé shot lots of newsfilms which did not cost much and appealed to their public. Beside disasters, fires and explosions there were many military scenes, namely parades and cavalry charges. Clearly the army was seen as an intrinsic element of national life but, as a whole, there was only a limited number of pictures which dealt with that subject. There were no attempts at ridiculing, insulting or even designating the Germans or the English as 'the enemy'. In the few cases when a foe was identified, he was a native who opposed French pacification in colonial countries.

During the film shows newsfilms alternated with enacted stories dealing with fanciful aspects of army life. There were short service comedies giving a pitiful representation of the inadequate though occasionally clever French infantryman: awkward privates only interested in fooling their officers and courting nannies were more prone to helping the latter push their prams than in serving their country. There were also heroic deeds, for instance a very candid Pathé film featuring the courageous defence of a small French military unit against anonymous, fancifully dressed assailants superior in number. This theme, recurrently pictured after the 1870 defeat, stressed both the bravery but also the inferiority of the French. In 1906 another company, Gaumont,[2] began to challenge the Americans by promoting what has been called the French comic school: it was a rough draft of what would be quite soon the classical American track-race but unlike its competitors Gaumont located its scenarios in urban districts (not in studios with all-purpose settings) and involved small groups of typical Frenchmen. Gaumont's wide range of pictures presents an extraordinarily soothing, almost idyllic image of France. This is not to say that the French were pacifist in 1914 but merely that French cinema was not much interested in military problems and that there was nothing, in current film production, that was likely to trigger militarism.

The second decade of the century, the years of the armaments race, brought its diplomatic complications which film companies had to take into account. Their films reflected part of these problems while simulta-neously concealing them. The images of the army became much less military than they had been before. War was not expelled from the cinemas but its depiction took a good deal of inspiration from literature and history: Joan of Arc, the Revolution and Napoleon provided imagi-native topics. A new theme entered the field with the presentation of navy or army manoeuvres. The films were more factual than had been the case previously: long files of military units were shot while passing in front of the camera. Reports were devoted to the navy or artillery, and sailors or soldiers were shown performing warlike activities. But, again, there was no aggressiveness in these pictures, no possible foe was mentioned, no emphasis was ever put on the defence of the eastern provinces – those which were facing Germany.

French cinematography, which was then setting the fashion on the world market, would have looked perfectly innocuous and indifferent to the problems of the time had it not been for a curious, rather puzzling movie, *Cursed be the War!* Its director, Alfred Machin, was a prolific film-maker who worked for Pathé, first in the Netherlands, then in Belgium.[3] While in the latter he persuaded the Belgain army to help him shoot a movie against war. It does not come as a surprise that the Belgian Defence Ministry accepted what its French counterpart would have refused. The military doctrine, in France, was that a German offensive could not come from the North, because of Belgian neutrality. The Belgians were less naive; they knew they were under threat and were keen on making the population realise it. For his script, Machin adopted a very simple structure which would often be reused thereafter, in *The Birth of a Nation*, for example, or in various French films like *Ultimatum* (1938): the inhabitants of neighbour-ing nations lived happily; there were permanent contacts between them and many mixed weddings but war destroyed this felicity; men were obliged to fight, at times to kill their brother's-in-law or their best friends. The first half of *Cursed be the War!* depicts two anonymous countries whose citizens have formed lasting relationships, and there is the un-avoidable engagement between an officer from one of the countries and the sister of an officer from the other.

War is declared. Here, we must make a digression: the conflict has no origin in Machin's picture, but the same can be said of most French films dealing with the Great War. Ordinary citizens like those involved in *I Accuse* or *Lost Paradise* may have been unaware of the Balkan imbroglio which resulted in a European conflict, but such was not the case with the protagonists of *Ultimatum* or *From Mayerling to Sarajevo* (1940). The former film takes place in Belgrade and Vienna at the time when Austria was issuing its ultimatum to Serbia. The main characters are general Simovic, head of the Serbian police, another Serbian, commandant Salic, and an Austrian captain, Burgstaller. These men, who cannot ignore what is about to happen, are worried, but what upsets them is not the impending danger, but the situation of Anna, an Austrian who has married Salic; Simovic thinks she might be a spy and Burgstaller would like her to go back to Vienna. As we shall see, the film tackles rather cleverly the problem of patriotic commitment, but it does not describe the atmosphere in the two capital cities in July 1914, and passes over the international crisis which led to the ultimatum. *From Mayerling to Sarajevo* is entirely dedicated to the dramas that plunged the Habsburg Dynasty into mourning. If the Sarajevo murder is reconstructed with perfect accuracy, it seems to bear no relation with the long-lasting antagonism between Austria and Serbia.

The silence of French cinema is all the more disconcerting in that, between the world wars, Germany produced at least two films, *The World War* (1927) and *1914: The Last Days before the World Conflagration* (1931), which tried to illuminate the causes of the hostilities; both attempted, obviously, at exonerating Germany from any responsibility for the conflict; the blame was put on the armaments race, on foreign generals and diplomats, and above all on the premature Russian mobilisation. But that is not the point: the fact remains that German film-makers did their best to make sense of an event fraught with harmful consequences. How can we account for the reserve of French film-makers? Unlike their German colleagues they did not conceive of cinema as a teaching aid: while films were extensively used in German schools they did not appeal to French professors. But, more importantly, it was quite out of the question, for a Frenchman, to raise the problem of war guilt since nobody doubted that the fault lay with Germany and Austria. No film-maker would have dared justify Paris's action – let alone suggest that French policy had not been totally wise in July 1914. The comparison between the German and French cinematographies goes much further than a simple parallel. It throws some light on the attitudes of two countries with respect to the outset of the Great War.

6.1   Death stalks the battlefield, *Cursed be the War* (Michael
Paris Collection)

Speaking from the Belgian, or French, point of view *Cursed be the War!*
neglected the origins of the conflict. Its plot, logically worked through,
reached a predictable and rather dull conclusion, acted out on a vast
plain by two armies. The story was candid, especially in its melodramatic
part, for instance when one of the officers does not hesitate to kill his
future brother-in-law who belongs to the opposite camp. However, it was
the first film in which victory was not easy and dying for one's country
was not a privilege. The ravages of gunfire were impressive, the hand-to-
hand fighting looked savage, clever use of a few airplanes indicated that
sophisticated weapons might play a decisive part in modern conflicts.
Innovative though it was, the movie developed two preconceptions
universally accepted at the time. The first was that a war would consist
of the clash between infantry regiments marching to the beating drums
and the second that, given that premise, hostilities would not last very
long. Cinema was in tune with the expectations of all European headquarters.

CINEMA AT WAR

We have information about neither the release of *Cursed be the War!* nor the response that it got, but a picture as peculiar as that one was not likely to affect spectators strongly. As soon as the War was declared the film companies hurriedly began churning out 'patriotic' movies, that is to say extravagant stories of heroic individuals who captured or killed hundreds of terrorised Huns. Most of these quickies have been lost and they would not deserve a mention were it not for what they tell us about French opinion. Initially, patriotic films were willingly accepted, all the more so that they were sandwiched between much better pictures. However, when it became obvious that the conflict was not moving towards a quick victory and that the Germans were resisting any attempt at breaking through their lines, spectators' feelings evolved. 1916, the year of Verdun and the Somme, was crucial in this respect. People manifested their dislike for movies which offered a scandalously optimistic view of the front line, and the studios stopped producing fanciful tales.

This move back might have been disastrous for exhibition. Although we lack precise figures we may assume that cinema attendance boomed during the War. Theatres, circus and music-halls, which employed numerous people, having been closed, the picture-houses were the only places where people could spend a few hours' leisure, and exhibitors were badly in need of new programmes. The rescue came from Hollywood. Previously American films, valued though they were, had got a limited share of French screenings. *The Cheat* was the sensation of 1916, papers were filled with enthusisastic reviews, and spectators were soon infatuated with Hollywood productions. They followed avidly *The Perils of Pauline* and *The Exploits of Elaine*. Confronted with this sudden fascination, the French producers were obliged to take it into account and Gaumont put up the money for two serials, *Vampires* and *Judex*, which inaugurated a new trend of European cinema, the popular adventure movie.

If it was absent from feature films, war was screened, week after week, in newsreels.[4] At the outset of the conflict most belligerent countries instituted a War Office department of cinematography. France was especially backward in this field. Until the beginning of 1915 private companies shot, as well as they could, short films which, after having been censored by the military, were sold to exhibitors. The procedure took much time and often resulted in damaging cuts. Therefore an agreement was signed between the War Ministry and the producers: the latter would go on filming but according to the directives of the former and under its direct supervision. More than 500 shorts, newsreels or documentaries were made under these conditions. Finally, from January 1917, an Army Cinema Section was entrusted with producing all footage dealing with the War, particularly a weekly newsreel, the *War Annals*, that all picture-houses were obliged to project.

The war newsfilms are of course official documents which provide a biased vision of military life. Little information is given about hot spots. Take the Battle of the Somme which lasted five months and involved the British as well as the French: there were thirty-eight items devoted to these operations out of more than four hundred subjects shot in 1916. A joint offensive was launched by the allies on 1 July and the coverage given to the event was especially dense during the initial month, with twelve items. As it was hoped that this attack would break the German defence and lead to a swift victory, people were anxious to witness what was actually happening. The first report described the preparations with infantrymen massed in the trenches and the initial assault by the artillery. Then came much shorter reports showing German trenches devastated by French guns, long files of prisoners and mountains of arms

6.2   French colonial troops march to war through the streets of Paris (Pathé Newsreel) (Michael Paris Collection)

taken from the enemy. Toward the end of July, emphasis was put on the villages liberated by the offensive; ruined houses, smashed barns, crumbling churches were explored at length; there were burnt carts, wounded men and corpses along the streets while prisoners crossed the screen in batches. In August, all these sequences were edited together in a special issue titled *The French Offensive on the Somme, July 1916*. The picture was released at about the same time as the British *Battle of the Somme*. There are many similarities between these films, each of which stresses the fire-power and perfect readiness of its respective army but shows almost nothing of the combat and does not explain why the offensive did not put an end to the War. However, while the British movie was cleverly advertised, screened in most towns of the United Kingdom and sent abroad, the dissemination of the French movie was extremely limited.

What explains this lack of concern for the exhibition of *The French Offensive*? A tentative answer may be found in a comparison between the Somme and Verdun. There were not many more reports on the latter (forty-two against thirty-eight) but their mood was quite different. During the first weeks of the German attack on Verdun, in February–March 1916, almost nothing was shown in newsreels: the French headquarters did not assume that its men would be able to resist and did not want to reveal too much about the situation. In the spring and summer there were a few very short items dedicated to units rewarded for the part taken in the defence of the city. Then, when the counter-attack started, information flowed quickly; two special issues, *Defence of Verdun* and *The French Revenge at Verdun* were widely distributed throughout the country. The reports on the Somme were very matter-of-fact about the whole affair and stressed the technical aspects of the War. In contrast, the items on Verdun were lyrical and paid tribute to the bravery of the French soldier and, in so doing, they shared in the institution and celebration of what was called 'the Verdun victory'.

France had feared a disaster at Verdun; she was much relieved when the Germans stopped their assault. Is that enough to account for the difference between the Somme and Verdun? I risk an assumption based on circumstantial evidence: the former was a Franco-British operation and could not be considered a French victory. It is striking to see that only two items on the Somme, released in November and December when the Battle was nearly finished, mention the British. There is more: out of some six hundred items shot until March 1917, only fourteen were dedicated to the British army. Meanness? Nationalistic tendency? Or, more likely, ignorance and lack of concern for the ally. Here, again, the cinema provides an interesting testimony about the climate of the period. In the spring of 1917 the atmosphere changed and the British were often named in the *War Annals*. The relationship between London and Paris had obviously evolved and the *War Annals*, now edited with French and English captions, were projected in the United Kingdom.[5] The French began then to acknowledge the efficiency of their ally: many references were made to the British tanks which seem to have made a great impression on the cinematographers. American intervention may also have played its part in the transformation: in 1918 command was unified on the Western Front, and when they showed military actions the *War Annals* labelled them 'allied operations'.

However, even during the last months of the conflict, little place was granted to foreign countries. The French newsreels remained basically centred upon French deeds. Statistically, the most important topic was 'the Orient' in which is included Serbia, Greece and the Middle-East. The Great War has been baptised 'World War' because fighting took place on different fronts across the world and in countries remote from those of the principal combat. But how did people realise that the conflict was not limited to a small part of Europe? The role of the cinema was crucial in this respect. The Western front line was practically stagnant during four years and there was nothing exciting to show in picture-houses about a military life reduced to heavy losses and stalemate. The Orient provided exotic landscapes, thrills, movement and above all the impression that something was happening somewhere, that it was possible to hit the enemy and make him totter. In the gloomy year 1916, while infantrymen were wading through the mud along the Somme, it was comforting to observe the cavalry advancing on Monastir: maybe the destiny of arms would be decided in these faraway countries.

Clearly, this was pure propaganda. Did war films influence public opinion and play a significant part in achieving victory? No one can answer the question with certainty, all we can reveal is what spectators saw. Looking at the French newsreels today, we cannot avoid an impression of disaster, of the geatest calamity a country had ever experienced. When they did not depict the life behind the front line or the French troops in the Orient, most of the newsfilms were presented as 'objective' that is deprived of commentary) photographs exposing immense damage; opening with shots of burnt houses and corpses, they ended with the same kind of images. If fighting was never filmed, long tracking shots among devastated surroundings highlighted the awful human and material cost of the hostilities. This explains, at least partially, why France was so intent on obtaining German reparations, whereas Britain and the United States would have preferred to settle a peace treaty as soon as possible and get rid of the past. Films contributed to forming public opinion and provided the French with a sense of what the Huns owed them.

ALL THAT WAS MISSING

The list of the forty-three French feature films dealing with the Great War looks imposing and suggests an enduring memory of this ordeal. But the conflict, being an excellent pretext for a tearful separation or short but rewarding reunion, was merely a setting for seventeen of these movies, as for instance in *The Deserter* (1939) where a divided family is reconciled when the son comes home on leave for a few hours. At times, the classical love triangle was made more exciting by the fact that one of its members belonged to the opposite camp. Spy stories were also much appreciated; women of easy virtue or seemingly weak young women turned secret agents paid with their lives for trying to fool French officers. There were also four war stories which, taking place in foreign countries, were of little concern for the French. All these movies, sometimes good, more often bad, could have been set in any country and time. If we add to them the pictures in which the conflict was only treated obliquely or simply mentioned in the initial or final sequence, we are eventually faced with a short series of nineteen films really concerned with the War, twelve shot between the two world conflicts, seven from 1945 to our day.

Before trying to analyse these works, let us raise a simple question: what is missing, what topics did they avoid? We are not astonished by the absence of the peace treaty, of the diplomatic and political conse- quences of the War, of the relationship with America, of the birth of new countries in central Europe and of many other issues that spectators might have found of immediate interest. It is well known that veterans had terrible difficulty in re-entering civilian life, all the more when they were disfigured or severly disabled, but the problem was not directly tackled: it was merely seen from a moral point of view in two films we shall examine later, *Peace on the Rhine* (1938) and *The Horizon* (1966). French films were curiously unaware of the upheaval brought by the War; they did not show that the conflict had provided opportunities for, but also challenges to, ordinary citizens, those who had been mobilised and those who had lost their loved ones.

A generally accepted view is that war cast off old prejudices and that full-scale employment had considerable impact on the life of women, who became freer. As early as 1918 a documentary, *The French Woman in War* depicted this big social change. It is true that many women were obliged to work, be it only to maintain their family, but it has been proved that neither was this beneficial to them nor did it last after the conflict. *Devil in the Flesh* (1947), adapted from a famous novel with the same title, was the only movie in which the question was touched on; the romance between a young lady, Marthe, whose husband had been mobilised and an adolescent, François, would have been a banal story of adultery had it not been for the recreation of the atmosphere of Paris during the hostilities; the characters met because they were fed up with the jingoism prevailing around them; they wanted to escape a world where people felt excited by the smell of blood which invaded the city. In normal circumstances Marthe would not have challenged her family, but her relatives, caught up in the patriotic frenzy, did not care about what she was doing. She soon became independent, but solely because she was well off and did not need to find a job in a factory.

Marthe died while having a baby. This was probably a way of avoiding a difficult conclusion with the young woman either divorcing her husband or leaving her lover. But it is tempting to think that, unconsciously, the novel and the film punished her. A look at the ten feature films on the War released during the 1930s makes the hypothesis more probable. Six of them involved a female character. Mrs Lecoeur, in *Intelligence Branch against Kommandantur* (1939), was heroic but her part was very limited. All other women were central to the plot. In *Two Worlds* (1930) an Austrian officer fell for a Russian girl and had to be severly admonished by his father to continue to do his duty. As for the other movies they featured a German actress, Dida Parlo. It may sound fair to have taken a German as the protagonist of French pictures but the part played by Parlo was always ambiguous. We have noted that, in *Ultimatum*, Anna was an Austrian who had married a Serbian and was suspected of being a spy. *Peace on the Rhine* gave Parlo the role of Edwige, a German woman whom a Frenchman, Emile, married in the years that followed the War; the family disapproved of the wedding; Emile had to leave his village; and it was only after Edwige had, symbolically, offered her blood to give Emile's father a transfusion that there was a sign of reconciliation. The Parlo of *Mademoiselle Docteur* (1936) was a flamboyant secret agent who fooled the French and was about to wreck the armistice between Bulgaria and the Allies when she died tragically. Parlo's most famous part was of a German war widow who, in *Grand Illusion* (1937), took in escaped French prisoners, fell for one of them and helped them reach Switzerland:

not surprisingly German spectators felt outraged whereas the French were delighted.

The six portraits found in feature films are consistent. They make the woman a foreigner likely to weaken the patriotism of men and, more generally, to threaten the security of the country. Let us add that in pictures less important to our topic. *Boissiere, Lost Paradise, Mata Hari,* female characters were doomed to death. Feminist theorists assume that men, having lost their preponderance and having let their wives rule the family during the conflict, were keen on restoring their power and metaphorically killed the women.[6] Whereas, during the nineteenth and early twentieth centuries, novels and movies conformed to a patriarchal pattern organised around male characters whose gaze and desire literally produced the female body,[7] some films of the post-war era made culpability intrinsic to the female nature inasmuch as, while looking at them, males were trapped into desire and could no longer fight or rule: put crudely, men were afraid of moral castration. Yet, we must not forget that the wicked lady is a literary stereotype widely used in the nineteenth century and, in a less sophisticated way, we may suppose that a great many veterans wanted their wives to return to their traditional functions. Drawing on the techniques of the documentary to enhance a virtuous conclusion *The French Woman in War* mentioned above described women taking on men's duties but ended by showing that the place of women was in their home where children were awaiting them and men would soon return.

THE TRAGIC 1930S

We have noted that the German cinema was much more open to debate about international issues than its French equivalent. The same can be said about the documentary reconstruction of the conflict. Beside *The World War* Germany released two factual movies, *Douaumont* (1931) and *Tannenberg* (1932), while France was content with producing *Verdun, Visions of History* (1928, with a sound version in 1931). Since Douaumont was one of the forts that defended Verdun, *Verdun* and *Douaumont* provide two contrasting versions of the same event. Today, these films which mix stock-shots, photographs and re-enacted scenes played by veterans would be classified as docu-dramas. These devices, particularly the innovative presence of witnesses, testified to the historical accuracy of the movies and, as far as circumstances are concerned, no objection

6.3   Poster for *Verdun* (Michael Paris Collection)

has to be raised. But if, from a technical point of view, the German and the French pictures are quite similar, they are fairly different in their mood and illuminate two antagonistic memories of the War. Most of the time *Douaumont* focuses on Captain Haupt who had conquered the fort in February 1916, and follows him while he replays, with veterans and extras, what he had done then. Everything seems perfectly clear and, despite a deafening soundtrack, despite the fall of wounded or dead soldiers, looks unemotional, almost cool. It is even so matter-of-fact as to ignore the reasons why the capture of Douaumont was crucial and passes over the fact that the reconquest of the fort by the French marked the end of the battle. In contrast, *Verdun* sounds like a tragedy. The audience is repeatedly told that the fate of France, her very survival was at stake. If witnesses are included in the film much more is said and shown about the dead, those, we are informed, who sacrificed their life for the country. Instead of unfolding chronologically, as *Douaumont* does, *Verdun* jumps from one point to another, from a dramatic anecdote to a more riveting one. It is, I agree, dangerous to draw too many inferences from a comparison between two cinematic works. Nevertheless, the German vision appears logical and dispassionate: here is what we did and why we were stronger. In contrast, the French vision is sorrowful: look at what we had to sacrifice merely to survive.

Although it was shot at a time when no other conflict was in sight, *Verdun* encapsulates the pathetic mood typical of the few French films dealing with the Great War. The tone was given, very early, by *I Accuse*. It is extremely difficult to evaluate this film, for many reasons. To begin with, there were two very different versions, the first shot in 1917–18, before the War had ended, but released in 1919, the second made in 1938, when perceptive people were foreseeing another conflict. The first *I Accuse* was so long that Gance had to cut it by more than a half; nothing has survived of the original version and very few film archives possess the shortened print. But the main problem is that some film buffs praise the picture while others think it is, at best, a curiosity. In both versions Gance combined avant-garde techniques, sophisticated lighting, close-ups, segmentation, flashbacks and dissolves with long, motionless, verbose sequences of melodrama; the pictures constantly switch between opposite modes, between the reality of the protagonist's current troubled life, dreams that console or excite him and dramatised images of what is happening in the world.

Sillhouetted against slaughter the most fictional part of the first *I Accuse*, the imbroglio of a triangular love relationship, holds less and less of the spectators' interest. As for the story of an unfortunate inventor turned mad, told in the second version, it is dull, emphatic and insipid. But the brilliance with which both films sketch out terror and death is stunning. The first version, which takes place during the War, presents a gripping vision of the inhumanity of war. It shows the mud, the half-buried corpses. It evokes powerfully the deadly fear and affected excitement of the men leaving to attack. The finale is especially riveting. Having gone back to his village the protagonist observes that, despite the sacrifice of his comrades, the civilians are still as egotistic and mean as they were before. He tells his fellow-villagers of a dream he has had and, because he is a good narrator, or because of his supernatural power, he conjures up the dead soldiers who come and haunt the village and persuade the inhabitants to change their life. The phantasmagorical images, mostly made with very clever dissolves and the superimposition of skulls above living faces, are suggestive of a purely subjective, self-supporting reading; their emotional effect is compelling enough so as to blur the plot line and make spectators react emotionally or maybe, in the case of veterans, nostalgically. In the second *I Accuse* the protagonist, obsessed by the threat of an impending war and unable to make people understand that they are rushing towards another catastrophe awakens the dead. His vision of his dead comrades-in-arms stumbling towards him across the war cemetery of Verdun, against an agonising soundtrack is a very impressive moment. Unfortunately, after this spellbinding sequence the film returns to its routine, all politicians turn into peace-makers and war is outlawed for ever. Gance wanted to shoot experi-mental films aimed at a limited audience and, simultaneously, give a message to mankind. His objectives were contradictory and his pictures did not make much impact on spectators, the first version because it was too long and complicated, the second because it was too simplistic.

Still, Gance was unquestionably in tune with the atmosphere of the time. The film-makers who made the few anti-war films of the 1930s[8] share in his compassion, in his awareness of the destitution of human beings reduced, in the trenches, to a permanent struggle against fear, putrefaction and despair. *The Wooden Crosses* (1931) stands out among these pictures not because it is better but because it is atypical. This movie, which follows a group of soldiers through various periods of the War, has much in common with the American *All Quiet on the Western Front* or the German *Westfront 1918*, both produced a few months before. Did these works influence the French picture? Or was there a common concern among ex-belligerents which compelled film directors to com-memorate those who had died? It has been noted that many anti-war novels and memoirs were published during the same period and it could

6.4   *J'accuse* (1938), poster (Michael Paris Collection)

be assumed that this literature shaped the perception of the War as utterly wastful of human life – or, conversely, that the anti-war films prompted a few veterans to relate their horrible experience. At any rate, one thing is clear: the producers of the three films mentioned above were intent on using the recently mastered technique of sound reproduction to fully recreate the atmosphere of the front line; most of their soundtrack was irritating and frightening; spectators heard violent, unbearable explosions that reverberated like intrusions in the movie theatre. The outcome was satisfactory: veterans claimed that, for the first time, a picture had given them a vivid impression of what they had gone through in the trenches.

The war movies of the early 1930s that attempted to be thought provoking were intense, burning pictures, full of cries of pain or terror and of soldiers' lasting agonies. Shot with a seemingly cold briskness which reminded the audience that, in a battle, there was no time to mourn dead comrades, these films moved among dead bodies and human remains, thus delineating a domain of experience totally disconnected from ordinary, 'civilised' life. Indirectly they raised a question that they could not answer: how did young men who did not look especially aggressive and were inclined to help each other so quickly become used to killing? While sharing many common features, the three films we have mentioned were also different. *Westfront 1918* was more analytical than reflective; it provided a phenomenological account of the horrors of war and did not try to show what the soldiers saw or thought; its editing process was extremely swift and its succession of contrasting pictures made the public feel very uneasy. *All Quiet on the Western Front* focused on a group of students who were young and inexperienced but also able to think, and it followed the progressive erosion of their hopes and illusions.

Divided into three main parts, *The Wooden Crosses* attempted to reveal differing perspectives of the conflict. The first part, 1914, marked the discovery of dread. Four soldiers guarding a small hill realise that the Germans are about to blow it up; the sequence is heavy with suspense that ends only when the guard is changed. 1916, the longest section of the work, could in turn be divided into two halves. There was first an uncanny moment of rest and peace, a religious celebration behind the front line with the cries of the wounded filling the soundtrack as soon as those present stopped singing *Hail Mary*. It was in this segment that the leading character, a student who had enlisted for the duration, disclosed obliquely and almost in passing his desperate feelings. The mass ended with a call to arms. The second part of 1916 was a long sequence of battle with a night action in a cemetery which caught the appalling character of hand-to-hand combat. 1918 was much shorter, soldiers seemed to be killed at random as if the War had lost any meaning and was merely a deadly game of ninepins.

Despite gripping scenes of attack and a high count of wounded or dead, *The Wooden Crosses* was less violent than the other two movies. It was intent on denouncing the barbarous effects of war and evoking the distress of injured men vainly calling for help. There was some ambiguity in the mass sequence and in the final section which could be interpreted as a question about the significance of 'all that', but it did not adopt a straightforward attitude. However, the best aspect of the movie, one which enthused the public at the time of the release, was the depiction of the camaraderie in the ranks and the soldiers' permanent concern for their fellows. Unwittingly the film answered the question about motivations: these men went on fighting a meaningless combat only because of the strong link that war had created between them.

Such images were too harsh for contemporaries and the trilogy of 1930–1 remained exceptional. The other movies shot during the 1930s were more traditional, by reason of the fact that they had a plot. Most fictions are built on the same pattern: an individual or a group have to face a challenge or must solve a problem; they have to get over several hurdles and if they succeed the ending is happy, if they fail it is sad. In all the films we are considering now, the challenge is not war itself but a side aspect of the conflict. The dilemma of *Ultimatum* is the Austrian Anna: will she stay in Serbia or go back to Vienna? Having been caught by the Germans the three heros of *Grand Illusion* want to run away: what price will liberty cost them? *Peace on the Rhine* has no central character. In 1918 in Alsace the men return home; Edouard has fought in the French army, his brother Emile and his friend Fritz for the Germans; however, the difficult issue of the return of Alsace to France is passed over in silence and replaced by secondary objectives. Will the family accept Emile's German wife? Will Emile and Fritz be able to build, on the Rhine, a monument to the peace between the two countries? The avoidance of complex problems is particularly visible in *Intelligence Branch against Kommandantur*. Some portions of eastern France were occupied by the Germans from 1914 to 1918. The film takes place in one of these districts. All the inhabitants of a village where the enemy is stationed unite to send information to the French. It is, at the same time, a strange anticipation of what will happen after the French defeat of 1940 and an occasion to try to understand why and how a population organises to resist. But the story soon deviates toward a secondary enigma: how do reports get over the

German lines? A police investigation and a complicated tale of twins transform the film into a detective story.

The War and its cruelties are never forgotten; one officer, in *Grand Illusion* sacrifices his life to help his comrades escape and dies painfully. *Intelligence Branch against Kommandantur* opens with the execution of a patriot and there are then several scenes of brutal beatings. In the first sequence of *Peace on the Rhine* an armless soldier leaves the hospital; later the veterans evoke agonising memories of the trenches; Emile and Fritz have to withstand the ploy of warmongers who would erect a monument to revenge. In these works war is not a mere background and some sequences have a documentary value, all the more that they were generally played by veterans. This instrumental approach was much better than silence but it was hardly comprehensive. Given the threat that hung over Europe, film-makers could have pondered the origins of international conflicts. They were content with offering their public the symptoms of tragedy.

AGAINST THE WIND

The fiftieth anniversary of 1914 triggered a renewed interest in the Great War. Films about the period were shot all around the world. These pictures were highly critical; they showed how incompetence, bad judgement and personal ambitions had destroyed thousands of human lives; deflecting cruelly diplomatic or strategic reflections, they incriminated the miscalculations and prejudices of selfish generals.[9] France did not boycott the celebration but her films differed greatly from the others; they condemned the First World War but, instead of blaming those who had provoked the butchery, they put emphasis upon the absurdity of the serial killing. Irony is at its best, or its worst, in *King of Hearts* (1966) which parallels lunatics with soldiers. After the Germans have evacuated a Belgian town in 1918 the residents of an asylum hold a party in which they impersonate the figures of the cards. But, while the British are arriving, the Germans come back and, compared to the perfectly logical game of the lunatics, their sanguinary clash looks totally insane. Running through the picture is a succession of images of madness that leads to the total absurdity of a slaughter in which both sides destroy not only their foes but also their own men.

The mockery is not as crude in *Thomas the Impostor* (1965) and *The Horizon* (1966). The former is the timeless fable of the young lad who would be a hero and pays for such ambition with his life. But the background is the Great War. The photography gives an elegiac feel to the first sequences; Thomas's innocence is disconcertingly at odds with the film's tragic mood. This ambiguous comedy gets slowly darker; horror overwhelms the screen; trees and houses burn; houses tumble down; the world is changed into hell; and there seems to be no other prospect for the young boy than death. *The Horizon* confronts Antonin, a convalescent soldier, with the inhabitants of his native town, most of whom are only marginally involved in the War and are seeking to attain their relatively small-scale dreams. The tone is wry, tragi-comic, non-judgemental, detached without being cynical. Since his parents are rich Antonin could try and run away to Switzerland but he is unable to do anything but go back to the front. Why? Sometimes the camera seems to gaze on him with a blank, cold curiosity: war has made him a different man who cannot reason and judge, who is no longer himself when he is among civilians and who will obey, however terrorised he is by the prospect of impending death. The three movies made for the anniversary of the Great War have their intentionally comic moments; spectators are inclined to laugh at the stupid philistines ready to sacrifice their friend's sons or at the stubborn politician who promises a quick victory. But the initial aspect of black comedy is soon transformed into genuine tragedy. Unlike the other war pictures of the 1960s the French movies do not denounce individual responsibilites but put the blame upon the folly of military institutions and, more generally, the folly of mankind. The same can be said of the few films released in the following decades. *Black and White in Colour* (1976) imagines that the French residing in Congo, who could ignore their German neighbours, stupidly attack them and start a useless, devastating and ridiculous guerilla war. The protagonist of *Life and Nothing But* (1988), an officer who has gone through four years of merciless fighting and no longer believes in anything, would like to take up his pre-war life-style again but he cannot since he has been entrusted with identifying the corpses found everywhere on former battlefields; it is the endlessly revived memory of the conflict which destroys him little by little.

Was this film a metaphor or a summary of the French attitude with regard to the Great War? For, if there were a few interesting films, as a whole French cinema remained silent and abstained from screening the period. Was that an attempt at forgetting, at driving away an unpleasant past? This does not sound credible. On the contrary, there was a huge effort to maintain the memory of the hostilities. Successive governments did not stop issuing messages to recall the sacrifices of the army; poets

and artists were committed to produce texts and paintings; war memorials were erected in the smallest villages; and Armistice Day was
pompously celebrated every year. Maybe that was too much. The state
had monopolised the remembrance of the conflict, it had frozen it and
made it a glorious page of national history. Of course, this is a mere
assumption which I cannot prove. But it is worth raising the question:
does the discretion of the cinema not suggest that the French had left to
the authorities the celebration of the War?

FRENCH FILMS ON THE GREAT WAR

(square brackets indicate that the War is a mere background or is only
treated obliquely in a few sequences.)
1918 *I Accuse* (silent version)
1919 [*Rose-France*]
1920 [*The Crusade*]
1923 [*Koenigsmark*]
1928 [*The Aircrew*]
      Verdun, Visions of History
1930 *Two Worlds*
      [*The Virtuous Sin*]
1931 *The Doomed Battalion*
      [*One Evening, on the Front Line*]
      [*Under the Leather Helmet*]
      Verdun, Memories of History (sound version of the 1928 *Verdun*)
      The Wooden Crosses
1933 [*The Signalless Track*]
1935 [*Koenigsmark*]
      [*Moscow Nights*]
      [*The Woman I Love*] (remake of the 1928 *The Aircrew*)
1936 *Mademoiselle Docteur*
1937 *Grand Illusion*
1938 [*Boissiere*]
      The Hero of the Marne
      I Accuse (sound version)
      [*Marthe Richard in the Service of France*]
      Peace on the Rhine
      [*Sisters in Arms*]
      Ultimatum

1939 [*The Deserter*]
     The Hostages
     Intelligence Branch against Kommandantur
     [*Lost Paradise*]
1940 [*From Mayerling to Sarajevo*]
1947 *Devil in the Flesh*
1950 *Shot at Dawn*
1952 [*Koenigsmark*]
1963 [*Landru*]
1965 [*Mata Hari*]
     Thomas the Impostor
1966 *The Horizon*
     King of Hearts
1976 *Black and White in Colour*
1984 [*Fort Saganne*]
1988 *Life and Nothing but*
1996 *Captain Conan*

NOTES

1   Abel Gance will be often mentioned in this paper. On his work, see Norman King, *Abel Gance: A Politics of Spectacle* (London: BFI, 1984). See also Richard Abel, *French, Cinema: The First Wave, 1915–1929* (Princeton: Princeton University Press, 1984).

2   Let us recall that what remains of Gaumont's productions can be viewed at the Gaumont film-archive, 30 avenue Charles de Gaulle, 92 200, Neuilly.

3   There is still much work to be done to list Machin's films and in detailing how they were produced. See Eric de Kuyper, Marianne Thys, Sabine Lenk and Emmanuelle Toulet, *Alfred Machin cinéaste/filmmaker* (Brussels: Cinémathèque Royale, 1995).

4   Our knowledge of this production has been updated by two recent works. When the Army Cinema Section was disbanded, in 1919, the main part of its material remained in the military film archive where it can still be viewed (ECPA, Fort d'Ivry, 94 250 Ivry sur Seine) but many films were lost. In *Les films militaires français de la première guerre mondiale: Catalogue des films muets d'actualité* (Paris: ECPA, 1997), Françoise Lemaire gives a comprehensive list of the movies produced by the Army Cinema Section or on its behalf, with an abstract and where a copy can be found when it exists. Information about the shooting and

screening of war films is to be found in Laurent Véray's *Les films d'actualité français de la Grande Guerre* (Paris: SIRPA, 1995).

5   A complete series of the newsreel can be seen at the Imperial War Museum in London.

6   Mary Louise Roberts, *Civilization without Sexes: Reconstructing Gender in Postwar France, 1917–1927* (Chicago: University of Chicago Press, 1994).

7   See Laura Mulvey, 'Visual pleasure and narrative cinema', *Screen*, XVI, 4, 1975, pp. 6–18, and Mary Ann Doane, *Femmes Fatales. Feminism, Film Theory, Psychoanalysis* (New York and London: Routledge, 1991).

8   Well described in Andrew Kelly's *Cinema and the Great War* (London: Routledge, 1997).

9   See above, pp. 169–72.

7

The United States' Film Industry and World War One

Leslie Midkiff DeBauche

When the United States entered World War One in April 1917, the film industry seized the opportunity to enlist in the government's efforts to rally the homefront.[1] A number of federal departments and agencies routed educational programmes and propaganda through the variety of channels the film industry made available. Throughout the nineteen months of American involvement in World War One, the government's needs to garner support for the war effort, to conserve food, to raise money and to recruit soldiers were met through the production of short instructional films, the public-speaking activities of movie stars, the civic forum provided by movie theaters and the administrative expertise offered by film industry personnel who had been assigned by their trade association, the National Association of the Motion Picture Industry (NAMPI), to work directly with governmental agencies.

The film industry also had much to gain from working closely with the United States government. In trade journals and in private correspondence, individuals representing all of its branches alluded to this belief. The War posed a direct challenge to the conduct of business as usual: the industry might have been deemed 'nonessential' and shut down for the course of the War, or it could have been subjected to government influence, which could easily have involved altering its product and disrupting distribution channels and timetables. The movies might have been decried as a frivolity not fitting to a nation at war. These threats were successfully countered in part through co-operative association with the government. Even more, the goodwill of both the movie-goer and the federal government which accrued to the American film industry on account of its war work served as a selling point in the 1920s when its major companies began to trade their stock on Wall Street, and it provided a buffer against national censorship when movie stars became embroiled in scandal. In addition, the War itself provided film producers with material for narrative films throughout the 1920s and 1930s.

The actions of the film industry, nearly from the moment war broke out in Europe, followed the precept of practical patriotism: it was appropriate and reasonable to combine allegiance to country and to business. In fact, it was understood that enlisting in the war effort on the home front would likely benefit the film industry's long-range interests. It also reflected the attitude of many individuals working in the movies. I found the term 'practical patriotism' in a 1917 advertisement in the *New York Times* for a feature film called *The Bar Sinister*. As well as showing this movie, the manager of the Broadway Theater was also promoting a sweepstakes to give away a fifty dollar Liberty Bond. The ad ballyhooed this combination of entertainment and support for the country, and it urged theatre managers across the land to do likewise. 'One Bond given away daily in each of America's 16,000 picture theaters would place $5,000,000 a week in Uncle Sam's pocket and give strength to his mighty blows.'[2] Movie-goers were given a timely incentive to buy a ticket, the government gained fifty dollars to help support the war effort, and the theatre manager, who donated the Bond, likely made back his financial investment in addition to gaining useful public relations from his promotion. Cecil DeMille, director-general of the Famous Player Lasky Company, voiced the same sentiment later that summer. He wanted to go to Europe and entertain the troops by projecting movies. He had developed a portable generator for use at the front and only needed permission of his bosses, Jesse Lasky and Adolph Zukor, to embark. DeMille justified his plan by invoking practical patriotism. 'It would serve three great purposes: primarily the great good to the men; secondly, the great good to this firm; and thirdly, the great good to me.'[3] Lasky and Zukor denied DeMille's request. They felt the greatest good would be served if he remained in California directing films for the newly formed company.

The American film industry treated the exigencies of World War One as opportunities and raced to the aid of the federal government. Still, they helped without sidetracking regular production, distribution and exhibition of feature film programmes, and without converting the industry to the creation of only war-related product. In short, the film industry was able to fit its duties to the government within already existing categories of professional behaviour. In this chapter, I will survey the ways that film producers, distributors and exhibitors adapted standard business practices to meet the circumstances of wartime. The effects of the War on the film industry outlasted the nineteen months of US involvement in the conflict. American film assumed a position of pre-eminence in the world market and classical Hollywood cinema became a style other national cinemas emulated or reacted against for decades.

The War also survived as grist for film-makers. This chapter will conclude with a discussion of the way the war-film genre developed between the 1910s and World War Two. The changing narrative focus and thematic concerns of movies made about the Great war provide insight into the complex of influences on film production. D. W. Griffith's *Hearts of the World* (1918), advertised as the 'Sweetest Love Story Ever Told' was one of the most popular films of that year. The War was treated much differently by the mid-1920s when some film titles posed questions like *What Price Glory?*. The antiwar film, *All Quiet on the Western Front*, adapted from Erich Maria Remarque's international best-selling novel, won the third Academy Awards for production and direction in 1929/1930. Yet in 1941, *Sergeant York*'s story of a young soldier's coming to terms with the job of war took the prizes for best actor and editing. Times had changed, the industry had changed, and the generic ways of telling war stories had also changed.

FILM PRODUCTION, 1917–18

American films of World War One were a mixed lot. Movies with war-related narratives included Hate-the-Hun propaganda exemplified by titles like *The Kaiser, the Beast of Berlin* and *The Prussian Cur*. In these films mustachioed German officers, already identified with Erich von Stroheim, tossed babies out of windows, raped young women and murdered innocent civilians. Not all war stories were so virulent. In *The Little American* (1917) Mary Pickford plays Angela, an American born on the Fourth of July. She is in love with her German neighbour. After an ill-fated voyage to Belgium, and many plot twists, she liberates her love from a prisoner of war camp, brings him back to the United States, and presumably marries him.

While there were war films in release over the nineteen months during which the United States was engaged in World War One, the preponderance of movies playing in picture palaces and neighbourhood theatres across the land did not tell stories about the War. Comedy and drama, literary adaptation and original scenario, scripts with war-related narratives and, more frequent, scripts with no narrative relation to the War – all were offered by film producers to the exhibitor, and by the film exhibitors to their local clientele.

Film historian Benjamin Hampton described a three-to-six month production process as the norm for feature-length films. Studios could, if they chose, respond in timely fashion to the pressing issues of their day. Although they were produced and distributed in ever-increasing numbers over the months of US involvement in World War One, War-related narrative and documentary films never dominated other films. Instead, there was a slow yet steady increase in numbers of war-related feature films during 1917 and 1918. Working from the data base of films listed for distribution in the trade journal *Moving Picture World*, one finds eight dramatic features listed in May 1917, eighteen in October 1917, twenty-eight in March 1918, thirty-two in August 1918, and fifty-four in October 1918. This cautious consistency indicated that the production of war-related feature films was the result of decisions to respond tactically to the War through the timely adaptation of film narratives, and, further, that this decision was based at least in part on the testing of this type of film in the marketplace. There had been vociferous opposition to the US entry into the War, and it may have been the case that film producers were waiting to see what the popular consensus would be before committing themselves and their products to any single point of view. It is also the case that the most strident anti-German films appeared late in the War: *My Four Years in Germany* (March 1918), *To Hell with the Kaiser* (June 1918), and *The Prussian Cur* and *Kulture* (both in September 1918).

Still, numbers do not tell the whole story. All films in release were not equal: brighter stars, bigger promotional efforts and more elaborate exhibition differentiated film from film, creating a hierarchy ranging from (top to bottom) the special film to the programme picture. While films with war-related content were always the minority of all films in release, the conclusion does not follow that war-related films were insignificant. Certain of these film stood out. They received more press attention, and their audiences knew they were special. About half of the most prestigious and the most expensive movies released in 1917 and 1918 told war stories. In fact, one of the 'biggest' films of World War One was D. W. Griffith's *Hearts of the World* (1918).

Hearts of the World was the longest running and arguably the most prestigious film produced and released during the entire period of US

THE MOST NOTABLE AUDIENCE THAT
EVER FILLED A THEATRE IN NEW YORK

| CHEERED | APPLAUDED | SHOUTED |
| CRIED | LAUGHED | WEPT WITH JOY |

When the final scene came, 2000 people were on their
feet paying thunderous tribute to the man who had thrilled
them as no other could have done, save a Washington, a
Lincoln, or a Wilson, or some equally great statesman.

D. W. GRIFFITH'S SUPREME TRIUMPH

HEARTS OF THE WORLD

(MANAGEMENT OF WILLIAM ELLIOTT, F. RAY COMSTOCK & MORRIS GEST)

A LOVE STORY OF THE GREAT WAR
EIGHTEEN MONTHS IN THE MAKING

Battle Scenes Taken on the Battlefields of France
Under Auspices of the British and French War Offices

No papier mache scenery, no studio
"props," no supers, no artificialities
of any kind figured in filming this
wonderful new Griffith masterpiece.

The greatest achievement in Mr.
Griffith's entire career, surpassing
even "The Birth of a Nation"
and "Intolerance."

44th ST. THEATRE—MATINEE TO-DAY AND EVERY DAY

| TWICE DAILY
INC. SUN. 2:15 & 8:15 | EVGS. & SAT. MAT.
25c TO $1.50 | OTHER MATINEES
25c TO $1.00 |

"Mr. Griffith Has Proved He is Still the Master-Producer, With No Real Rivals in His Art"

7.1   Press advertisement for *Hearts of the World*
(Leslie Midkiff DeBauche Collection)

participation in the War. This romance between the children of American neighbours living on the Rue de la paix in a French village was a good example of the way in which the War could be incorporated as a plot device in an otherwise conventional, melodramatic love story. An early inter-title introduced it as, 'an old fashioned play with a new fashioned theme'. Griffith also stated the theme in a later intertitle: 'God help the nation that begins another war of conquest or meddling! Brass bands and clanging sabres make very fine music, but let us remember there is another side of war.' *Hearts of the World* showed the other side of the Great War. The marriage plans of Lilian Gish and Robert Harron, the 'Girl' and the 'Boy', were interrupted by war. The Germans advanced on their village, the Boy's mother died, the Girl was mistreated at the hands of the enemy, and in a wonderfully eerie-made scene the Girl, clutching her wedding dress, roamed across a desolate battlefield searching for the Boy. The film's climax came as the Boy fought a German (played by Erich von Stroheim), nearly lost, and was saved by the arrival of French and American troops. The film concluded in 'Happy Times'. 'America—returning home after freeing the world from Autocracy and the horrors of war forever and ever.' Viewers saw shots of American flags, followed by ships at sea, and a flag-draped portrait of President Wilson. *Hearts of the World* ended with a shot of the Boy and the Girl waving flags against a backdrop of bright light. Audiences loved it.

PROGRAMMING THE MOVIE THEATRE, 1917–18

World War One did have an impact on film production. Some of the most prestigious and some of the most memorable films made and released during 1917 and 1918 were feature-length films with war-related narratives. Still the impact of the War on the industry's production of its standard product was not pronounced, and genre is not the sole measure of how the American film industry incorporated the topicality of the War into its entertainment product. Film exhibitors also found ways to make their movie houses necessary to both their local patrons and the federal government. Like film producers, exhibitors accomplished this mission by adapting standard business practice: using their building, as well as the films and live acts on their bills, to woo customers and aid the war effort. As early as 1915, Epes Winthrop Sargent, author of *Picture Theater Advertising* (and a columnist for *Moving Picture World*), had urged managers to promote their theatre's as vigorously as they promoted their entertainment programs. 'Films are but a part of what you have to sell. Advertise all your features.'[4] In choosing films, both feature length and shorts, and in methods adopted to promote such film programmes, theatre managers reacted to the War, even while the strategies already in place for running their businesses remained constant. From Roxy Rothapfel, the trend-setting manager of the Rivoli Theater in New York City, to C. W. Martin at the Temple Theater in McCook, Nebraska, exhibitors' ultimate goal was to make their theatres an integral part of their communities. By participating in the War on the home front film exhibitors were simultaneously creating goodwill for their houses, and they knew it. Like film producers, they were operating well within the boundaries of practical patriotism.

Harold Edel, manager of New York's Strand Theater and a columnist for *Moving Picture World*, advised his readers and fellow-exhibitors to link their theatres to the war effort.

> 'It is up to every exhibitor in the country to bend every effort toward doing his "bit" whenever and wherever possible. The exhibitor is a potent factor in that all important thing, public opinion. I do not mean by this that he should clutter his program with war films and news pictures of soldiers . . .'[5]

Film exhibitors took his advice.

The following examples – which function as advertising designed to attract trade as well as propaganda for the government – show how exhibitors enlisted their theatres in the war effort. While war-related activities taking place in movie theatres informed citizens of governmental needs like food conservation and the purchase of Liberty Bonds, they simultaneously promoted the movie theatre sponsoring them. It is also important to note that home front programming was not necessarily part of a co-ordinated promotional campaign for a war film. Thus, the advertising value of allowing the Marines to set up an enlistment booth in the theatre lobby, and in permitting speakers to lecture about the causes of the War during a film's intermission, lay, first, in attracting customers to a specific theatre. In programming and promoting their theatres during American involvement in World War One theatre managers had a great number of options.

They could, like Frank Maegher, a Boston theatre manager, decorate the exterior of their building with giant American flags and bunting, or, like C. W. Martin in McCook, Nebraska, managers might advertise that they were donating a portion of ticket receipts to the First Liberty Bond

Drive. The manager of Seattle's Clemmer Theater not only offered to donate the entire receipts from 25 June 1917 to the Red Cross, but he also tried to drum up business that day by hiring small boys to walk around town costumed as giant red crosses![6]

As the advertising value of donating money to civic projects was recognised and advocated as good theatre management, so the use of the lobby to attract trade had likewise been recognised. *Moving Picture World* published advertisements for such products as portraits of President Wilson: 'The President's face is done in water color and oils, and the American Flag is worked up beautifully in artistic reproduction of the proper shade of red and blue, giving in all a permanent display for the lobby.' The United States Food Administration also offered a six-color poster, suitable for framing and display in the theatres lobby. The Red Cross provided placards urging patrons to contribute, as well as coin boxes in which to place donations. Harold Edel wrote about how he had mounted a bronze plaque bearing the names of all Strand employees in the service in the lobby of his theatre.[7]

In addition to decoration, theatre managers could also add war-related presentations to their film programmes. Music roused patriotic feelings in yet another example of adapting existing exhibition practice to a timely situation. Sargent's *Picture Theater Advertising* had also noted that music could serve an advertisement for the theatre. Some theatres reported playing the National Anthem at each screening, and the Alhambra in Milwaukee, Wisconsin, instituted the practice of 'Community Singing' of contemporary and topical songs at showings.[8] Prominent local folk, working under the auspices of the Committee for Public Information, made speeches at movie theatres during the War. Called Four Minute Men to invoke the American Revolution and to signal the time limit for their talks, these speakers used material generated in Washington to inform and persuade movie audiences during World War One. Topics included reasons to contribute to the first Liberty Loan, food conservation, ways of maintaining morale on the home front, and why Americans were fighting in the War.[9]

Once the houselights dimmed and the movie-goers' attention was directed to the screen, the theatre manager had a final opportunity to promote his theatre by striking a patriotic chord. An advertisement in *Motion Picture News* read: 'Attention Patriots Do Your Bit. Open or close every show with the Stars and Stripes. 60 feet or longer at only 10 cents a foot.' This patriotism by-the-foot was offered for sale by the American Bioscope Company. Slides were another option. The Excelsior Illustrating Company of New York sold 'a few of the other beautifully

7.2   This cartoon from *Moving Picture World* encouraged the
film industry to cooperate with the US government's fund raising efforts
(Leslie Midkiff DeBauche Collection)

hand-colored patriotic slides, 25 cents'. Or exhibitors could make their
own slides. Joseph Yeager, owner of a chain of theatres in Raton, New
Mexico, showed slides of local men who had enlisted. Exhibitors also
made use of newsreels showing hometown boys at boot camp. Later in
the War 'smiles' films provided yet another way for exhibitors to connect
their theatres to their community, their nation and the War in Europe.
People were invited to stand on a particular street to be photographed by
a cameraman, often employed by the local newspaper. The resulting film
was to be sent to Europe and shown to the soldiers. These films were first
screened in the local movie house, however, providing the exhibitor
another time-honored way to attract trade.[10]

   World War One presented film exhibitors with a set of challenges to
their business, and they responded by attempting to turn those challenges into opportunities. Through advertising movie-goers were encouraged to see the theatre as a necessary, inexpensive and entertaining relief
from the worries and inconveniences of the War, and, conversely, they
were encouraged to consider attendance at the theatre as a way of
participating in the war effort in that contributions to various war fund
drives advanced the national cause.

THE NATIONAL ASSOCIATION OF
THE MOTION PICTURE INDUSTRY ENLISTS

Clearly the film industry's desire to co-operate with the federal government was manifested in their product: films and theatrical entertainment. They also enlisted at the institutional level. Film producers, distributors and exhibitors, and such allied trades as suppliers of theatre fittings and publishers of theatre programmes joined in the US government's war effort on the home front. Combining the desire to help their country with the realisation that such help could further their own business goals, these various members of the film industry were willing to co-operate with government agencies. Only a structure was needed, and this was provided by the newly formed trade group the National Association of the Motion Picture Industry (NAMPI). NAMPI's co-operation with the government gave its members – the film companies, their leaders, their stars and theatre owners – the opportunity to integrate more fully with the many other industries mobilising the home front.

The National Association of the Motion Picture Industry was organised in July 1916 when the existing trade association for producers and distributors, the Motion Picture Board of Trade, proved unable to mediate a dispute between its members and the Motion Picture Exhibitor's League of America. NAMPI took as its mission to enrol representatives from all sectors of the motion picture industry. Its five classes of membership included producers, distributors, exhibitors, actors, insurance companies and advertising agents. Membership on the board of NAMPI ranged across the film industry, including such companies as Universal, Goldwyn, Bell and Howell, Pathé, Vitagraph and *Moving Picture World*, and such individuals as Adolph Zukor, Lee A. Ochs (president of the New York Motion Picture Exhibitors of America), N. C. Cotabish (National Carbon Company), William A. Johnson (editor, *Motion Picture News*), and D. W. Griffith. William Brady, of the production firm World Films, was elected president. It is significant that the board contained men who were gaining power and prestige within the film industry by conducting their business in a particular way; they were expanding, in part, through the acquisition of other companies. While NAMPI wanted a broad representation and a large membership, the make-up of its board of directors also reflected a desire to exercise control over that membership.

The stated goals of NAMPI represented the industry's main concerns: to facilitate discussion among all facets of the industry, to monitor government regulation of its business, to mediate disputes among members, and to serve a public relations function between the industry and the public. NAMPI's more specific goals and worries were manifested in its standing committees, which were focused on membership, finance, publicity, hostile legislation, censorship, taxation, fire-prevention regulations and insurance, foreign trade, copyrights and trademarks, standards and labour issues, among others. When the United States entered World War One, NAMPI added support for governmental initiatives to the list of its functions.[11]

Co-operation between the government and the film industry, represented by NAMPI, began as early as 23 May 1917, when its president, William Brady, acting in response to a request from Secretary of the Treasury McAdoo, called a meeting of representatives from the motion picture industry to discuss ways in which the film community could aid the First Liberty Loan Campaign. One month later *Exhibitor's Trade Review* reported that a War Cooperation Committee had been created 'to handle all matters in which the motion picture can be used to further the interests of the American Government in the world war'.[12] The government had contacted the industry through the one trade association comprising representatives from all its branches; NAMPI had responded to a specific request for help with the First Liberty Loan and had in the process willingly expanded its role.

Once appointed and introduced to Washington, the War Cooperation Committee went to work. Arthur Friend of Famous Players-Lasky was assigned to the Food Administration, where one of his first official acts was to send a memo 'To All Manufacturers and Distributors of Pictures' announcing that he was in Washington, and that he would be 'glad to consult and advise with anyone in the trade in regard to its [USFA's] future activities'. He also pledged to keep exhibitors and others in the industry informed of future plans by publicising the Food Administration's programmes in motion picture trade papers 'at the earliest possible moment'.[13] By 7 September 1917 the first Food Administration – film industry joint effort was underway.

A catalogue of the Food Administration's motion picture activities serves as a template for co-operation of the film industry with the federal government, and illustrates the active involvement of all sectors of the motion picture industry in the government's mission. The aid the film industry rendered took a variety of forms. Film producer Thomas Ince suggested that film and theatrical producers should refrain from using real food in their productions as a conservation measure. More important, the industry arranged for the distribution of Food Administration short-subject films through Universal, Pathé and Mutual newsreel distributors. Arthur Friend also enlisted film exhibitors to participate in the Food Administration's extensive Second Food Pledge Card Drive which took place from 21 to 28 October 1917. The Pledge Drive was a multi-media event. Exhibitors agreed to run a series of slides as part of their entertainment programme which would encourage audience members to conserve food by substituting fish for meat and corn for wheat, for example. In addition, the USFA sent out posters heralding 'Food Will Win the War'; exhibitors were encouraged to frame these and display them in the lobbies of their theatres. The Four Minute Men were scheduled to deliver talks on the need for a 'vast home army for conservation' the week of 21 October.[14]

By January 1918, the Film Division of the Food Administration added film advertisements called 'trailers' to its arsenal of advertising methods and in May short films called picturettes were also being distributed, with stars appearing in both. By this time the film exhibitor was the key purveyor of food conservation propaganda.

Co-operation between the film industry and the United States Treasury Department was also successfully manifested both in money and motion pictures. In June 1917, Lasky employees donated $75,000 to the First Liberty Loan, and in September the New York Times reported, 'A film production designed to help sell the next Liberty Loan was exhibited yesterday morning at the Strand Theater.'[15]

NAMPI named Adolph Zukor, of Famous Players-Lasky, Marcus Loew of Loew Enterprises, Jules E. Bruletour of Eastman Films, Walter Irwin of Vitagraph and George Spoor to its War Cooperation Committee which was assigned to the Treasury Department. While information regarding the activities of the Food Administration as it worked through the motion picture industry must be gleaned from archival documents, film industry co-operation with the Treasury Department can be found in the news, entertainment, rotogravure, and even the comics sections, of the nation's newspapers. The Treasury Department employed plenty of 'live interest' – movie stars – in its propaganda. The most popular actors and actresses in the business, including Mary Pickford, Douglas Fairbanks, Charlie Chaplin, Marguerite Clark and Marie Dressler, travelled the country giving speeches urging their fellow-citizens to contribute to Liberty Loan drives. They made short films, like Chaplin's The Bond and Mary Pickford's 100% American, designed to be shown in movie theatres to coincide with Bond campaigns. The Treasury Department also produced slides which were distributed to movie theatres in support of buying bonds. In October 1917, in fact, some 17,500 sets of slides, three slides to a set, were distributed to as many theatres. For the third Liberty Loan, NAMPI released 17,200 trailers, 17,200 sets of posters and a 'splendid patriotic film contributed by Douglas Fairbanks'.[16]

The film industry, co-ordinated by the War Cooperation Committee, went 'over the top' to promote the sale of Liberty Bonds. Many of the specific examples cited here were reported in the *New York Times*, the *Chicago Tribune*, the *Milwaukee Journal* and the *Minneapolis Tribune*, as well as other local newspapers. Movie stars, film companies and movie theatres all benefited from the image building that accompanied their war work. NAMPI also assigned film industry personnel to other departments in the federal government.

NAMPI assigned members of its War Cooperation Committee to the War Department, the Navy Department, the Department of Agriculture, the Department of the Interior and the Aircraft Division. Film industry personnel worked with the Committee on Training Camp Activities, the Shipping Board, the American Red Cross and the Commercial Economy Board. In August 1918, a committee of NAMPI was formed to aid Fuel Administrator Garfield find ways to help the film industry conserve fuel and to educate the public about ways to save fuel. On a less-grand scale, motion picture exhibitors aided the United States Army's 'pit and shell' drive. *Forward*, the paper of the Wisconsin Council of Defense, reported particularly good results among Midwestern theatre managers: 'One house in Indiana obtained four barrels of peach stones at one afternoon matinee.'[17]

The United States Army's pit and shell drive, the United States Food Administration, the Treasury Department and the Red Cross, among other agencies, benefited from the co-operation of the film industry during World War One. The film industry benefited too. The National Association of the Motion Picture Industry facilitated government–industry relations and increased its own membership during 1917 and 1918. Stars and other industry personnel, working through NAMPI, became identified by their war work as well as their movie making and achieved wider recognition and a brighter image.

Over the course of the War, NAMPI defeated most state and all federal attempts at censorship through its lobbying efforts and through a voluntary agreement allowing the National Board of Review to screen and approve all films for release. Stars, producing companies, NAMPI and local exhibitors, all received press coverage as they participated in the war effort. The film industry and the reformer were, for however brief a period of time, on the same side. As the image of the film industry improved, its potential for attracting a wider audience increased. War

One offered the film industry a greater number of selling points in advertising its product. Movie-going offered not only entertainment – important enough in this time of stress – but included in the price of admission a war tax that went directly to the government. The theatre functioned as a rallying point for the community. It was the place to be informed and inspired by the government's Four Minute Men, the place to be reminded about specific food conservation tactics, and the place to contribute to the Red Cross. In their advertising, exhibitors plugged these reasons for coming to the theatre as heartily as they promoted the feature film being shown. Film-producing companies also sent current movies overseas to be shown to soldiers.

Trade associations were primarily protective alliances which also helped to standardise business practices and foster good public relations with the consumer.[18] The National Association of the Motion Picture Industry followed these general guidelines and functioned with special effectiveness during the months from April 1917 until November 1918. As a result, both the government and the film industry benefited.

THE AMERICAN FILM INDUSTRY AT THE END OF THE WAR

As film historian Janet Staiger points out, 'If there was a "golden age" of the studio, it was in full operation by 1917'.[19] It was not only the studio system's mode of production which had been established but also the foundations for the structure of the film industry, at least until 1948, were also set. Economic power was vested in the large integrated, or soon-to-be integrated, companies within all branches of the film industry. The traces of the future oligopoly were present. Pre-war trends, such as independent production, decreases in the number of small theatres and increases in the number of theatres in chains, continued and accelerated over the months of American involvement in World War One. The industry emerged from the War a big business, its stock bought and sold on Wall Street.

It had also become a reputable business. One of the abiding benefits for the film industry of its participation in the war effort on the home front was an enhanced public image, an effect that was felt in both tangible and intangible ways. The most prominent movie stars like Chaplin and Pickford, as well as lesser lights, had the opportunity for increased public exposure. They travelled the country speaking on behalf of Liberty Bonds; they appeared in picturettes for Herbert Hoover's

United States Food Administration; they were regularly in the photo-gravure sections of newspapers working in their gardens, knitting for soldiers and donating ambulances to the Red Cross. These photo opportunities helped weave film personalities even more tightly into the fabric of popular culture. They became home-front heroes and heroines, and the goodwill they garnered almost certainly added to the audiences for their films. These activities also helped forestall potential criticism when their private lives got messy. When Pickford and Fairbanks divorced their mates to marry each other in March 1920, the public which had responded so generously to their Bond Drives revelled in their union.

William Gibbs McAdoo, Secretary of the Treasury, Director-General of the Railroad Administration and son-in-law of President Wilson, had met Pickford, Chaplin and Douglas Fairbanks during their work on the Third Liberty Loan. He would serve as counsel to United Artists, formed in 1919. The film industry also won the aid of Republicans. Will Hays, Republican Party chairman, and postmaster general in Warren Harding's administration, would join the film industry in 1922 as its point man – heading the Motion Picture Producer and Distributors Association. His task was to quell any federal censorship of the movies. Hays did his job well, with the industry instituting its own self-regulation.

Thus, World War One provided the film industry with the opportunity to enhance its goodwill with its market – the American public – and to win the goodwill of those in positions of power in the government. When Woodrow Wilson embarked for France to attend the Peace Conference, he carried fifteen movies with him for entertainment. 'The Famous Players-Lasky Corporation received a wire from Washington November 28 to supply the motion pictures . . .' The work of Douglas Fairbanks, Mary Pickford, D. W. Griffith and Dorothy Gish, among others, sailed with the American delegation on board the *George Washington*.[20]

WAR NARRATIVES: MOVIES IN THE 1920S AND 1930S

Throughout the 1920s, and up until World War Two, the Great War was used as narrative fodder in a variety of films. We can also see the foundations of the combat film genre established in a set of films about World War One made in the middle years of the decade. These films, including *The Big Parade* (1925), *What Price Glory?* (1926) and *Wings* (1927), told very different stories, featuring a new sort of hero than had

7.3   Press advertisement for *Wings* (Leslie Midkiff DeBauche Collection)

been seen in the war films made in 1917 and 1918. When the War became the stuff of so-pervasive and popular a medium as the Hollywood film, narrative conventions and industrial practice joined history and politics in shaping the image and meaning of World War One.

After the Armistice, the War found its way into a variety of genres whose films told contemporary stories. Threaded through the narratives and *mise-en-scènes* of two-reel comedies, westerns and big-budget dramas were reminders – as if the audience had ever really forgotten – that the Great War had been fought, and its effects were still felt. *Rolling Stone*, a Billy West comedy released in 1919, revolves around a jailbird

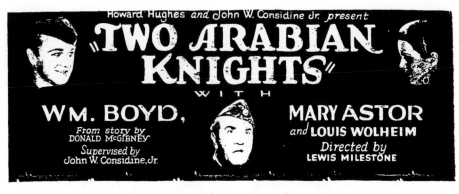

Raising the Roof
at the PARAMOUNT
New York City

"Paramount audiences thrown into high state of glee."
N.Y. Times

"A laugh in every twenty feet of film."
N.Y. American

"The perfect comedy with funniest pair of soldiers that ever graced a film."
N.Y. Tribune

"Destined to enjoy long life and a happy one."
Eve. World

"At Paramount they're laughing loud, lustily and lingerlingly."
Daily News

"Hilariously funny. Superior comedy."
N.Y. Post

"One of funniest comedies since Chaplin's 'The Kid.' Line forms to the right for this one."
N.Y. Telegraph

"A comedy which you could not afford to miss."
N.Y. Telegram

FUNNIEST of all *Doughboy* **Comedies** with the war left out — 'the laughs left in — and the thrills piled on —

7.4   The Great War also became the stuff of comedy in the late 1920s.
Advertisement for *Two Arabian Knights*
(Leslie Midkiff DeBauche Collection)

who falls in love with the warden's daughter. Near the end we see Billy's two babies, in their cradle, dressed in military uniforms. Billy reads a newspaper, its headline – 'Wilson Sees End of War'. Another two-reel comedy, *The Detectress, c.* 1919 featured Gale Henry traversing 'Dirty Alley'. An inter-title explains, 'Dirty Alley was as peaceful as no mans land on a busy day.' Still another example is the 1928 short comedy *Vacation Waves*. In it, Edward Everett Horton, a train conductor who has just been shot in the backside, yells, 'War is over but if you shoot me again, I'll start another one.'

Comedy was not the only genre to incorporate references to the War into narratives and *mise-en-scène*. *The Stolen Ranch*, a 1926 western directed by William Wellman, shows two army buddies, Frank and Breezey, who survive the 'inferno' of the Western Front. The War cemented their friendship, and that relationship was the 'net profit taken from Flanders Fields'. Frank suffers from shell-shock, and Breezey must protect him from sudden loud noises which trigger flashbacks to battle. The two return home to find that Frank's ranch has been taken over by bad guys – presumably slackers who did not fight in the War. *The mise-en-scène includes flashbacks to battlefields where the two friends fought. Its iconography includes coils of barbed wire, airplanes flying overhead, bombs exploding, trenches and skeletal trees – a visual shorthand that had, by 1926, come to signify the Great War.*

Of the films touching in some way on the diverse experiences of World War One, those receiving the most critical attention in the 1920s, and those which served to influence the war-related films that would come in the 1930s and during World War Two, were movies that showed the experiences of the doughboy and the flyer in combat. Pictures like King Vidor's *The Big Parade* (Metro Goldwyn Mayer, 1925) and Raoul Walsh's *What Price Glory?* (Fox, 1926) replaced D. W. Griffith's *Hearts of the World* as the quintessential World War One war film in the 1920s. Building on foundations of narrative and *mise-en-scène* set in Charlie Chaplin's *Shoulder Arms* (First National, 1918), they focused on the ordinary soldier, his bleak and muddy life in the trenches (air combat movies like *Wings* [Paramount, 1927] would dominate the last years of the decade) and scenes showing basic training, mail call and soldiers going over the top or out on dawn patrol. While reiterating certain narrative characteristics – for example, sequences depicting life before and after the War – typical of the war-related pictures released during the War, the war films of the 1920s also displayed striking innovations. They were told from the soldier's point of view and foregrounded battle over any other wartime experience.

The function of women also changed dramatically. Combat films made in the 1920s eliminated or significantly reduced the role of women as causal agents in their narratives. In the war films of the 1910s the love story was central to the war story. Women were seen on the battlefield, and, more significantly, the War invaded their villages and homes. Both a domestic threat and a national threat were posed by the Great War. The worst thing Germans do, in the logic of these movies, is rape, or threaten to rape, the film's heroine, and, as in the propaganda posters of the era, soldiers enlist and fight to keep women safe. In the 1920s, however, characters like Melisande and Charmaine, or Mary, Clara Bow's character in *Wings*, still appeared in *The Big Parade* and *What Price Glory?*, but a clear divide was created between the 'love story' and the war scenes. Now, mothers and sweethearts lived on a distant home front where they wrote letters and were, most often, faithful; if overseas, they either drove ambulances or served as nurses. They might also be French villagers providing love and comfort behind the lines. Still, in most films made in the mid-1920s, war was defined as combat, and women were well out of the fray.

Realism was the main selling point in advertising these films, and it was a standard to which they were held by film reviewers. When *The Big Parade* opened in Boston the reviewer for the *Boston Transcript* praised the film and damned its cinematic predecessors. 'To watch it unroll is to realize anew all the shallow bombast, all the flatulency and all the saccharinity with which previous picture-makers have encumbered the trade of war.' Instead, he placed Vidor's film within the newer literary tradition of 'tough' stories about realistic doughboys, 'soldiers nearer convention than Dos Passos's, less professional than Kipling's, and somewhat less pungent than Stallings's own marines in *What Price Glory?*'[21] New conventions for realism affecting story, intertitles, costume make up, setting and theme, among other aspects of film form, were being set and applied across theatre, literature and film. Women did not figure in this aesthetic of realism.

Thus, it is significant that the most influential war films of the 1920s and the novels and plays they resembled were written by a relatively small number of men who had served in the military during World War One. The review of the play *What Price Glory?* in the *Women Citizen* concluded by linking verisimilitude with authorial experience: 'Laurence Stallings, who, with Maxwell Anderson, wrote it, was a captain of marines, and lost a leg and won years of pain as a result of Belleau Wood. He ought to know.'[22] Stallings provided the story for *The Big Parade* – in which a young soldier loses a leg in a battle like Belleau

Wood. John Monk Saunders, Second Lieutenant in the Signal Corps Aviation Section, contributed the story for *Wings*, *The Legion of the Condemned* (Paramount, 1928) and *The Dawn Patrol* (First National, 1930; 1938). Maxwell Anderson, co-author of *What Price Glory?* adapted Erich Maria Remarque's *All Quiet on the Western Front* for the screen. The stories these men told, based on their experiences in the War, were transformed into scenarios by other men and women, veterans not of combat but Hollywood. The result was a change in the conventions governing the way war stories were told – women and romance were removed to the subplot.

The combat films of the 1920s were also different in tone from 1917–18 movies with war-related plots. *The Big Parade*, *What Price Glory?* and *Wings* were perceived, at least by movie critics, as being ambivalent in their attitude toward war. Even a perfunctory glance at titles like *The Big Parade* and *What Price Glory?* finds an irony absent from *The Little American* or *Hearts of the World*. Jim Apperson, the young rich man who enlists in 'the big parade' – the War – after being surcharged with enthusiasm by the rousing martial music he hears in a recruitment parade, comes limping home at war's end. He has lost a leg; his two buddies – a riveter and a bartender – are both dead. Jim's fiancée has taken up with his brother, who stayed home. The price paid by Apperson for a dubious glory is indeed high, and he knows it. An inter-title late in the film fairly shouts, 'What the hell do we get out of this war? Parades— who the hell cares?'

What Price Glory? was released as a roadshow in the year following *The Big Parade*. It tells of two career soldiers, Quirt and Flagg, who spend most of their time, and much of the movie, competing for the affections of women in China, the Philippines and, finally, in France. Although its ads promised that 'Women Love It's [sic] Daring—Its Romance and Its Uproarious Humor', the film also had, in addition to its quizzical title, a 'tragic note'.[23] This included what the reviewer for the *New York Times* called the 'Trench of Death' – a shell explodes in a trench and buries all the men positioned there. The scene closes on an image of bayonets spiking up through the rubble. The film's thematic terrain is equally bleak. After one of the young soldiers, an artist who spends much of his onscreen time writing home to his mother, dies in Flagg's arms, an inter-title describes a setting fraught with poignant irony: 'And all night long that wounded spiner in a tree screams for mercy. You talk about honor and courage and a man bleeds to death in a tree over your head.' Soon after, Quirt screams – in inter-title – 'What Price Glory Now?'

These influential films, plays and novels voiced a belief, broadly felt in

American culture by the mid-1920s, that the government's wartime propaganda had been false. Stories of atrocities perpetrated in Belgium by bestial German combatants were unfounded, and the more high-toned metaphorical description of this War as the Great Crusade of Civilization against Autocracy was at odds with the soldiers' experience. Before the 1920s, war – at least at the movies – had been a necessary evil undergone in order to save the honour and chastity of women, to make the world safe for democracy, and to end all wars. In the 1920s, it was not so clear why men went 'over there'.

The war films of the 1930s and early 1940s, including *All Quiet on the Western Front* (Universal, 1930), *Hells Angels* (United Artists, 1930), *The Dawn Patrol* (1938), *The Fighting 69th* (Warner Brothers, 1940) and *Sergeant York* (Warner Brothers, 1941), show, at first a honing of the narrative conventions relating to the hero, the role of women and the themes set in the 1920s. Still, as the country moved closer to World War Two certain films began, as they had in the 1910s, to portray the redemptive possibilities of war.

The mode of production operating in the United States film industry in the 1930s is best described as producer unit. Within each studio, units comprising a producer, directors, technical staff, writers and actors, would work together on movies. Genre films were the norm in the studio system of the 1930s. Units worked together, over time, and honed both their visual style and generic conventions. Public disillusionment and the inclusion of war veterans in the production process help to explain the rather significant changes from the war film as historical spectacle made while the United States was at war to the war film as combat and coming-of-age tale in the 1920s. From the 1920s through the early 1940s I believe that genre was shaped more by the business of movie making than by ideology. As America verged on World War Two, the film industry again reframed its war stories to show what good could come out of war – even a war which had lost its lustre and whose aims had apparently failed. Young men could find God, could reaffirm democratic principles, and could experience a noble self-sacrificing love in the company of their comrades. Female characters did not fit in the trenches or in an airplane's cockpit: their romantic function only served to create division among friends and distractions from the soldier's job. Two men love the same woman in *Wings*, and a woman tries to come between brothers in *Hells Angels* – better to write them out of the story.

CONCLUSION: PRACTICAL PATRIOTISM

Over the course of the Great War the film industry refined its product, and in the 1920s it set an international standard for film-making. It also continued along a path of corporate growth toward oligopoly which helped to ensure its profitability in the succeeding decade. There was no government-initiated censorship of the films, and, in fact, key figures in the government, like Will Hays, went to work for the film industry in the 1920s. The War did not divert the development of the craft or the business of film-making from its pre-war course.

While movies about the Great War never dominated the release schedules of film distributors, they did become a staple throughout the late 1910s, 1920s and 1930s, even though both their function and their form changed over time. Before the United States entered the conflict in April 1917, films told stories of the need for preparedness as well as the need to refrain from mixing in the problems of Europe. After American entry movies like *The Little American* and *Hearts of the World* showed movie-goers bestial Huns, endangered women, and brave, young, patriotic American men. Increasingly during the 1920s those films defined by the industry and the critical establishment as war films portrayed soldiers in combat – in the trenches and in the air. Here war was not depicted as a noble enterprise. In fact, in films like *The Big Parade, What Price Glory?* and *Wings*, it replaced the Hun as enemy. Still, the Great War on the screen did offer young men the opportunity to come of age and to act in noble ways. The films of the early 1930s, beginning with *All Quiet on the Western Front*, continue trends begun in the 1920s, especially the narrative focus on combat, and they deepen the cynicism about the War's aims and its results. Until, that is, World War Two looms large.

War films have been the most durable legacy of the participation of the United States' film industry in World War One. These movies were made by individuals working with and within the narrative conventions and modes of production sanctioned by that film industry. The films discussed here were neither idiosyncratic nor anomalous as they told war stories. Instead, the films of World War One made in the 1910s 1920s and 1930s fit comfortably within the boundaries set by popular culture for depicting the War. The genre that developed always was, and remains, dynamic, responsive to creative film-makers, new technology, industrial practice and the influence of popular writers and historians.

NOTES

1   Much of this chapter is taken from my book *Reel Patriotism: The Movies and World War One* (Madison: University of Wisconsin Press, 1997). For more detailed analysis and explanatory case studies of selected films of World War One, please see this text.
2   Advertisement for *The Bar Sinister*, *New York Times*, 3 June 1917, sec. X.
3   Cecil DeMille to Jesse Lasky, 14 August 1917, box 240, folder 1, DeMille Collection, Brigham Young University Archives.
4   Epes Winthrop Sargent, *Picture Theater Advertising* (New York: Chalmers, 1915), p. 27.
5   Harold Edel, 'How it is done at the Strand', *Moving Picture World*, 34. 12, 22 December 1917, p. 1769.
6   'Live wire exhibitors', *Motion Picture News*, 5 May 1917, p. 2823. Epes Winthrop Sargent, 'Advertising for exhibitors', *Moving Picture World*, 33.5, 4 August 1917, p. 789; 'Seattle film men aid Red Cross drive', *Moving Picture World*, 33.2, 14 July 1917, p. 273.
7   Advertisement, *Moving Picture World*, 32.4, 28 April 1917, p. 630; United States Food Administration letter, 2 October 1917, National Archives, record group 4, 12 HC-A4, box 505; 'Fairbanks starts Red Cross fund', *Moving Picture World*, 33.1, 7 July 1917, p. 64; 'Strand places dedicatory tablet', *Moving Picture World*, 35.10, 9 March 1918, p. 272.
8   'Baltimore makes anthem obligatory', *Moving Picture World*, 35.2, 12 January 1918, p. 272; Advertisement, *Milwaukee Journal*, 14 July 1918, sec. 2.
9   For more information about the Four Minute Men see Bertram Nelson, 'The Four Minute Men', in Monteville Flowers (ed), *What Every American Should Know about the War*, (New York: Doran, 1918).
10 Advertisement, *Motion Picture News*, 28 April 1917, p. 2629; Advertisement, *Motion Picture News*, 5 May 1917, p. 2876 Epes Winthrop Sargent, 'Advertising for exhibitors', *Moving Picture World*, 35.9, 2 March 1918, p. 1235–6.
11 'Film men form temporary organization', *Moving Picture World*, 29.4, 22 July 1916, p. 612.
12 'Industry oversubscribes 2 1/2 million to Liberty Loan', *Exhibitor's Trade Review*, 23 June 1917, p. 173.
13 Arthur Friend, memo 8 August 1917, United States Food Administration Collection, record group 4, 12 HC-A4, box 504.
14 Maxcy Robson Dickson, *The Food Front in World War One* (Washington, DC: American Council on Public Affairs, 1944), p. 131; United States Food Administration letter to exhibitors, 2 October 1917, United

States Food Administration Collection, record group 4, 12 HC-A4, box 504; William Clinton Mullendore, *History of the United States Food Administration, 191701919* (Stanford: Stanford University Press, 1941), p. 87.

15 'Movies boom Liberty', *New York Times*, 19 September 1917.

16 'War achievements of the motion picture industry set forth in brief to federal officials by National Association', *Exhibitors Trade Review*, 20 July 1918, p. 552.

17 'Motion picture industry aids pit and shell drive', *Forward*, 2.9, 3 October 1918, p. 6.

18 Janet Staiger, 'Standardization and differentiation: The reinforcement and dispersion of Hollywood's practices', in David Bordwell, Janet Staiger and Kristin Thompson, *The Classical Hollywood Cinema: Film Style and Mode of Production to 1960* (New York: Columbia University Press, 1985), p. 104.

19 Staiger, 'Central producer system', in Bordwell, Staiger and Thompson, *Classical Hollywood Cinema*, p. 142.

20 'Paramounts and artcrafts to entertain peace party', *Moving Picture World*, 38.11, 14 December 1918, p. 1188.

21 'Watching the War from an orchestra chair', *Literary Digest*, 99.10, 6 March 1926, p. 38–42.

22 Review of *What Price Glory? The Woman Citizen*, 18 October 1924, p. 11.

23 Advertisements for *What Price Glory Motion Picture News*, 28 October 1927, p. 1333.

8

The Representation of the Great War in Italian Cinema

Giovanni Nobili Vitelleschi
[Translated by Liz Hart]

Italy became involved in the European War in 1915, but after the success of Giovanni Pastrone's *Cabiria* (1914), for a series of converging reasons, there was a crisis in national film production which led to the decline of the historical epic genre, which had made Italian cinema famous throughout the world.

In spite of this, a number of films were produced about the European War during the conflict. One of the first films which took the war as its central theme and which was filmed in real time was *Sempre nel cor la Patria!*, 1915 (*My Country is Always in My Heart*), directed by Carmine Gallone, produced by Cines and starring Leda Gys. The film, which was released barely three months after Italy's entry into the War, told the story of an Italian girl who, after marrying an Austrian, chooses to return to her native land when she learns that the country is at war. '[T]he reveille sounds', declares the caption. Realising that her husband is about to embark on a mission against Italy, the girl sets about thwarting the plan and, having succeeded, falls a victim to the Austrians, thereby heroically sacrificing herself for her country. In order to simulate Cadore, the site of fierce battles during the War, Gallone's company went to the Abruzzo between Avezzano and Tagliacozzo, which at the beginning of 1915 had been almost totally destroyed by earthquakes. In this way, the houses ruined by the earthquake could be used as *mise-en-scène* for the houses destroyed by the fighting. In Italy, *Sempre nel cor la Patria!* had an extraordinary success and on its release was acclaimed by a delirious public; in France, where it was equally successful, it was released under the title *Pro Patria*.[1]

Moreover, the film gave the green light for a whole series of pseudo-patriotic war films which, between September and December 1915, obtained a censorship permit and were immediately released. *Sempre nel cor la Patria!* was like a starter's pistol, noted Vittorio Martinelli. Italian cinema, in a manner of speaking, armed itself and desperately threw itself into the patriotic genre.

Between the end of 1915 and the early months of 1916, like a whirlwind came tens upon tens of films whose protagonists were the infantry, the officers, the Alpini and the Bersaglieri.[2] They were, on the whole, works of no outstanding merit, partly because of the speed with which they were completed, but today they are of interest as social history and as an insight into the way of thinking, because they allow us to see how the War was portrayed – even through already codified generic inflections – to the public. After Gallone's film, there was a proliferation of patriotic genre films – including *Patria!*, 1915 (*Our Country*); *Patria Mia!*, 1915 (*My Country*), directed by Giuseppe De Liguoro; *La Patria che redime*, 1915 (*Our Redeeming Country*), directed by Guglielmo Zorzo, and *Viva la Patria!*, 1915 (*Hurrah for Our Country*), director unknown.

Besides the obvious (*Sempre nel cor la patria!*) really popular Italian films about the War were few in 1915. Amongst the better known are: *Cretinetti e le aereomobili nemiche*, 1915 (*Cretinetti and the Enemy Planes*), directed by Andrew Deed; *Il sogno patriottico di Cinessino*, 1915 *Cinessino's Patriotic Dream*), directed by Gennaro Righelli; and *Il sottomarino n. 27*, 1915 (*Submarine 27*), directed by Nino Oxilia.

The film *Cretinetti e le aereomobili nemiche*, which belongs to the comic genre, shows the character Cretinetti (Andre Deed), together with his wife and his wedding guests, terrified by enemy bombing and getting up to all sorts of tricks. The film foregrounds Cretinetti's attempts to consummate his marriage despite the hazards of the War. *Cretinetti e le aereomobili nemiche*, because of its unrestrained rhythm and its spectacular nature, is still one of the best works of the time and only serves to confirm that the representation of war remained after all an 'object' distant from real space and time, where the war is sublimated into a comic farce. In Righelli's film *Il sogno patriottico di Cinessino* contemporary advertising tells us that the young protagonist dreamed of 'daring deeds and heroic battles only to wake up safe in the arms of his mother'. The glory of war is simply a dream. In relation to the preceding two films, it can be said that they belong to a genre which was at the time unknown – one in which war is seen as something unreal, a product of the imagination, a dream. In the last of the series, *Il sottomarino n. 27* by Oxilia, the subject matter did not meet with critical approval which considered it 'unstructured, fragmented and incoherent'.[3] The film, however, starred Ruggero Ruggeri, considered the best Italian actor of stage and screen at the time, and thus enjoyed a certain popularity.

Even in 1915 a reviewer wrote of Italian war films: 'The real war is diametrically different from that portrayed by the un-warlike fantasies of some of these masters of mise-en-scene who know nothing of war only of parades'.[4]

It is worth noting, however, that the distinctive feature of these films is that of adopting the particular perspective that the cinema historian Gian Piero Brunetta has defined as the 'inverted telescope', that is, the heavy reliance on the categories of 'distance' and 'absence' rather than on the more predictable ones of 'presence' and 'nearness' (to the War), a distance which is both required and guaranteed moreover by military censorship and politics.

The years 1916–17 provide a series of films which show how Italian censorship attempted to shift the subject of war, obscuring the more brutal images, in favour of a more sanitised view. This is what one censor, anxious at having to show some images which might in some way disturb the spectator, said: 'the scenes in the trenches with bodies gruesomely positioned should be removed' and 'all the frames in which you see bodies laid on the ground should go'.

The most well-known works of 1916 were: *Come mori Miss Cavell*, 1916 (*How Miss Cavell Died*), directed by Amleto Palermi; *Kri Kri contro i gas asfissianti*, 1916 (*Kri Kri against the Poison Gas*), director unknown; *Amor di Barbaro* (or *Vae Victis*), 1916 (*Love of a Barbarian*), directed by Amelto Palermi; *La guerra e la moda*, 1916 (*War Fashion*), directed by Raffaele Cosentino; *Turbine rosso*, 1916 (*Red Hurricane*), directed by Oreste Gherardini; and obviously the famous *Maciste alpino*, 1916 (*Maciste, Alpine Soldier*), directed by Luigi Maggi and Luigi Romano Borgnetto, supervised by Giovanni Pastrone and played by the star, Bartolomeo Pagano.

The film *Come mori Miss Cavell* recounts the true story of the English nurse, Edith Cavell, who was captured by the Germans and shot on 12 October 1915. The film takes its inspiration from this event, which resulted in a wave of disgust at German behaviour, throughout the world. At the same time as Palermi's film was being produced, a similar film was released in England, entitled *Nurse and Martyr*, directed by

Percy Morgan and starring Cora Lee. Contemporary critics were unanimous in emphasising that the production company Augusta Film's idea of translating the drama of the English heroine to the screen was an excellent one, above all in showing to the public, 'one of the major infamies with which the German state had tainted itself'.[5] Even from a purely aesthetic point of view the critical response was favourable.

If this film gains its inspiration from a real event, then *Kri Kri contro i gas asfissianti* shows us instead the War through comic stereotypes, which were at the time very popular. In the film, Kri Kri is a soldier in the trenches who has to face and deal with the enemy gas attacks. With his native cunning, Kri Kri manages to redirect the gas against the enemy and destroy them instead.

Amor di Babaro gives us a fairly real image of the horrors of war and the huge losses which France had to suffer during the German invasion. The content of the film was often ascribed to the English writer, Annie Vivanti, even if the latter had more than once disclaimed all knowledge of the film.

Even fashion was represented in the war films: in the film *La guerra e la moda*, for example, the pre-war fashions are juxtaposed with the actual needs of a nation at war. When the film was on general release, it was defined as a 'cinematic eccentricity'.

A typical example of indirect anti-enemy propaganda, in that it relates to the resistance of the Serbs against the oppression of the Central Empire, is the film *Turbine rosso*. The advertising of the time went thus:

> the Serbian army routed by the enemy, which ravages, tortures and executes, re-groups in the mountains turning towards that other shore of the Adriatic; there those strong and generous hearts will find a land sacred to the freedom of oppressed peoples: Italy.

The actual historical event from which the film took its inspiration was filmed by the great documentarist, Luca Comerio in *Prodigiosa opera della Marina italiani in aiuto dell'esercito serbo*, 1916 (*The Prodigious Effort of the Italian Navy in Helping the Serb Army*), even if the Ministry of Internal Affairs' censorship office imposed some severe cuts.

Finally, *Maciste alpino* is the work which, in mixing the genres then in fashion in Italian cinema more than any other, represents (and synthesises) the war films produced in the period 1915–18. The character of Maciste, who was the protagonist of Giovanni Pastrone's *Cabiria*, was promoted to popular heroic status and would become, right up to the early sixties, the protagonist of many herculean epics always based on

8.1   *Maciste, the Alpine Soldier* (Giovanni Vitelleschi Collection)

the original character of Maciste. However, the type of hero which the film suggests is closer to a metahistorical character, rather than one identifiable as a real person of the present. Moreover, the war in which Maciste is the central figure is refigured almost as a private affair between him and the enemy soldier, the Austrian 'Fritz', according to the dictates of an ideology based upon individual action. '[A] sedentary life is not the one made for Maciste', which carries with it a de-politicised language and is based on the play of words, so restoring to war the human face of a game.

This is also due to the fact that the film achieves a type of spectacle which is rigorously functional to the logistics of war and which is realised through the obscuring of the more raw and realistic images:

> the carnage and the battalions sent uselessly to the slaughter. The equally useless acts of heroism are removed in favour of the representation of a victorious and exhilarating war, during which the problem of the enemy is apparently resolved without the need for hundreds of thousands dead, but simply with two well-aimed fists or a powerful kick up the arse.[6]

The film, because of its heterogeneous stylistic codes (adventure, romance, conflict, etc.) and its attention to visual effects (applicable to all scenes of mountain climbing carried out by the Alpini with weapons and animals, and the sequence of the crossing of the cliffs by walking across a tightrope stretched over the void) was, in fact, a modern precursor in that it anticipated the triumphal Fascist approach to the making of films about the Great War.

A film which was much criticised for giving a false impression of the War is *Eichi di squillo e trofei di vittoria*, 1916 (*Trumpet Echoes and the Trophies of Victory*) directed by Emilio Roncarolo. Both contemporary reviews and public responded negatively to the film's release, because:

> after a year and a half of war, public taste has been educated and can no longer tolerate that greedy speculators try to present our war under a false perspective in order to satisfy their insatiable thirst for disproportionate profit.[7]

The director of the film was accused by the reviewers of defaming the efforts of the Italian troops in the war.

Farulli si arrulo, 1916 (*Farulli Enlists*), directed by Alberto Traversa, is of the comic war genre. The film was at the time described as 'comic eccentricity', and was conceived by the script writer, Giannino Antona-Traveri for the popular actor, Ugo Farulli.

From the same director and same production company came the propaganda film, *Il soldato d'Italia*, 1916 (*The Soldier of Italy*), which was often shown as part of the film programmes selected for the armed forces during the War, and which attempted to revive a team spirit and a sense of patriotism in the soldiers, a matter of great importance given the heavy casualties suffered by the army in the bloody battles of 1916.

A film which shows how volunteers were used to help the wounded was *Mater purissima*, 1916 (*Mother Most Chaste*), by an unrecorded director from the production company Ora Nostra, and starring the 'diva' Hesperia. The film was made to support the incapacitated, the wounded and the families of conscripts, and illustrates the work done by the civilian support groups behind the scenes and during the War, an attempt to show that the nation was united in the war effort.

In some ways, Italian cinema seems to have returned to those genres which had made it universally famous – the historic epics, the adventures of Maciste and sophisticated comedies. In terms of war films produced in 1917, there were only six, and these, excluding the famous *La guerra e il sogno di Momi*, 1917 (*Momi's Dream and the War*), remain almost totally unknown.

A film which showed how all the state services were working towards the war effort was *La posta in guerra*, 1917 (*The Post at War*), directed by Luca Comerio, produced by the film section of the Royal Regiment of Rome and starring Hesperia. The film shows how the postal service worked during the War, starting with an ordinary letter which leaves home and finally arrives at the front to the trenches. Hesperia, a star of the silent cinema, plays the role of an adoptive war mother who, having received and replied to letters sent by soldiers from the front, encourages them to bravely defend their country.

It is worth mentioning that there were at least two films based on the navy: *La spirale della morte*, 1917 (*The Spiral of Death*), directed by Filippo Costamagna; and the spectacular *Il Tank della morte*, 1917 (*The Tank of Death*), directed by Telmaco Ruggeri. The Turin *Gazetta del Popolo*, 26 August 1918, said this about the film's opening:

> For the first time, the public will see one of those monstrous and terrible machines in full action, a spectacle never seen before, and will experience the sensation of this new form of warfare, which played such a large part in the recent English and French victories.

The most important film of 1917, however, was the famous *La guerra e il sogno di Momi*, directed by Segundo De Chomon, produced by Itala Film

and starring Guido Petrungaro. In the film, little Momi, having enthusiastically read his father's letter from the front, falls asleep and dreams
of a war fought by two puppets (Trik and Trak) and armies of lead
soldiers. Moreover, in the dream, after having accomplished various
heroic feats, Momi manages to save his father, who has in reality returned
home and so can hug his son when he wakes up. The structure of the film
owes much to the earlier feature *Il sogno patriottico di Cinessino*. Its
major value is that it manages to fuse, with considerable mastery, scenes
of reality and spectacular fantasy. The censors insisted that the adjective
'victorious' should be added to *Pax*, the last word of the final caption.
Even in *La guerra e il sogno di Momi*, as in many other films, the War is
located in another space between reality (his father's letter from the front
and return home on leave) and the fantasy (Momi's dream), and it is
sublimated at the level of the conflict between the lead soldiers.

During the year 1918, film production did not appear to be suffering
from the economic crisis which had been ongoing for some time; in fact,
the stars' contracts were increasingly extravagant and new production
houses were emerging, but, in reality, Italian cinema had failed to renew
and develop its own cinematic language and therefore to maintain the
prestigious international position it had achieved before 1914.[8]

However, one of the most interesting Italian films about the First
World War was made in this year, that is *Il canto della fede*, 1918 (*The
Song of Faith*), directed by Filippo Butera, produced by Cleo-Film and
starring Mary-Cleo Tarlarini. The film, through the love story of a
wounded officer and a Red Cross nurse, wants to emphasise that behind
the lines there is a network of support for the wounded. *Il canto della
fede*, moreover, tries to justify, through solidarity with front-line troops,
the role of civilians mobilised to produce patriotic conferences and
immersed in organising hospitals ('At X, through the initiative of some
noble women, a hospital has been opened', a caption from the film tells
us). As the cinema historian, Gian Piero Brunetta has rightly observed,
one of the basic foundations on which the work rests is a matriarchal
one, rather than the more predictable patriotism: 'the woman or the
mother and therefore the family are the guarantors and repositories of
familial values and all the initiatives intended to alleviate the suffering of
the soldiers'.[9] Completed on the eve of the Armistice, which took place on
4 November 1918, *Il canto della fede* obtained a censorship permit at the
end of the same month, but because of its now outdated content, as the
War was now over, its circulation was limited.

Another late film given a censorship permit in December 1918 was *Gli
invasori*, 1918 (*The Invaders*) directed by Gian Paolo Rosimo. The film,

based on the story of the same name by writer Annie Vivanti, was commissioned by the Ministry of Propaganda, which, once the War was over, would have suspended payment, because of the now irrelevant subject matter. However, the star and the director edited everything that had been filmed and put together some 736 metres of film which was never released.

The great star of the Italian silent film, Francesca Bertini, is the protagonist of the sentimental patriotic *Mariute*, directed by Eduardo Bencivenga and produced by Bertini/Caesar. The film, commissioned by the Instituto Nazionale delle Assicurazioni, tells the story of a mother of three children, Mariute, a peasant from Fruili, who, while her husband is at war, is raped by three Austrian soldiers. However, the intervention of her father-in-law, who takes up his gun and shoots the men, avenges the young woman's suffering. It is worth noting that the film ends with the actress encouraging the spectators to buy bonds issued by the Instituto Nazionale delle Assicurazioni, and so help the nation's war effort.

Cowardice and desertion are the themes of *La maschera e il barbaro*, 1918 (*The Mask and the Barbarian*), directed by Paolo Trinchera. The film shows how a weak youth can be tempted to desert, simply by the persuasions of some enemy secret agents, but, after his sister has taken his place, he goes from remorse to making amends for what he has done, and finally redeems himself by dying heroically.

Last of the Italian films made during the conflict is the film produced by the Italian Admiralty and consisting of three episodes, *Trittico italico*, 1918 (*Italian Triptych*): Episode 1, *L'insulto* (*The Insult*), director unknown, starring Diomira Jacobini; Episode 2, *Supremo grido!* (*The Supreme Shout*), director unknown, starring Diana Karenna (This episode takes place on an Italian ship, which is boarded by an Austrian submarine crew. A woman passenger, in spite of the Captain's intervention, is shot on board by the enemy.); and Episode 3, *Combattimento aereo* (*Air Battle*), which makes use of documentary footage of the Italian Air Force's bombing of Cattaro.

EPILOGUE: POST-WAR FILMS AND THE RISE OF FASCISM

Films made between 1919 and 1922 mostly dealt with the aftermath of war and the readjustment problems of the returning veteran, such as *Il soldato cieco* (*The Blind Soldier*) and *L'uomo che vide la morte* (*The Soldier Who Saw Death*).

However, the rise of Fascism after 1922 saw increasing use of the image of the Great War in the collective memory where it was used as the historical antecedent of the fighting spirit of the Fascist party. Here it is important to remember that many Fascists were war veterans, as was Mussolini himself. Furthermore, the myth of the Great War and the bond which linked it to the black shirts was introduced into school books and historical texts. This group of films present the Great War as matrix and antecedent of Fascism, and echoes the theorists of the regime, Gentile and Volpe. Often in these films, the figure of the veteran acts as the link between the epochs, and the father-son relationship recurs to emphasise the Italian warrior tradition.

NOTES

1   For a complete list of Italian films of World War One, see my paper, 'World War One in the Italian cinema: 1915–1940', delivered at the conference, 'Film and the First World War' at XV International IAMH-IST Conference, held in Amsterdam from 5 to 11 July 1993.

2   V. Martinelli, 'Il cinema italiano in armi', in *Sperduti nel buio:, Il cinema italiano e il su tempo (1905–1930)* (Bologna: Capelli Editore, 1992), p. 40.

3   A. Kardac in *La Cinematografia italiana ed estera*, Torino, 3 August 1915.

4   P. Cacace, in *La Cine-Fono*, October 1915; quoted in G. P. Brunetta, *La storia del cinema italiano, 1895–1940* vol. 1 (Milan: Editori Riuniti, 1979), p. 383.

5   Pier da Castello in *La Rivista Cinematografica*, Torino, 22/30 September 1916.

6   Gran Piero Brunetta, 'L'immagine della prima guerra mondiale attraverso il cinema', in Mario Isnenghi (ed.), *Operai e contadini nella grande guerra* (Bologna: Capelli Editorie, 1992), p. 59.

7   Giuseppe Zuccarello in *La vita cinematgrafica*, Torino, 22/30 November 1916.

8   Cfr. Aldo Berardini, 'L'avventura internazionale del primo cinema italiano', in Riccardo Redi (ed.), *Cinema italiano muto* (Roma: CNC Edizioni, 1973), pp. 56–73.

9   G.P. Brunetta, *Storia del cinema italiano*, p. 192.

9

A War Forgotten: the Great War in Russian and Soviet Cinema

Denise J. Youngblood

Historians of Russia who admire Paul Fussell's and Samuel Hynes's work on the European cult of the First World War and seek to replicate it with reference to Russian culture are faced with a most perplexing problem. Despite the massive loss of Russian life on the War's Eastern Front – casualty figures are usually given at two million or more – World War One was 'the war that wasn't' in terms of post-war Russian cultural production. The resistance to mythologising the War began *during* the War itself: the meticulous research of Hubertus Jahn yielded only a slim (though excellent) volume on the patriotic culture of the Great War in Russia.[1]

War did not end in Russia after the Bolshevik Revolution in October 1917, of course – nor even after the 1918 Treaty of Brest-Litovsk. World war and revolution evolved into even greater calamity: a brutal civil war and a variety of foreign 'interventions', including war with neighbouring Poland, that lasted to the end of 1920. It was the events of 1917–20, loosely dubbed 'The Revolution', that became the stuff of mythmaking in art, theatre, literature and the movies. For Soviet Russians, in marked contrast to the Germans, French, or British, the Great War became a mere prelude to the cataclysm that followed. There is, in fact, only one important Soviet World War One film: Boris Barnet's 1933 picture *Borderlands* (*Okraina*; released in the US as *Patriots*, in France as *Le Faubourg*). The purpose of this essay is, therefore, to trace the representation of the 'war forgotten' in Russian and Soviet culture, focusing on a detailed examination of its major artifact, *Borderlands*, and to speculate on the meaning of this culture of absence.

THE GREAT WAR AND RUSSIAN CINEMA

Although the first movies were shown in Russia in spring 1896, Russian film production did not begin until 1908.[2] The new industry grew rapidly, and by 1913 film distribution and exhibition were well developed in the cities of European Russia. That year, on the eve of war, 129 films were produced, with increasing emphasis on the full-length 'feature' film (that is, films about an hour in running time).[3] There were some 1,400 movie theatres in the empire, with 130 in the capital of St Petersburg alone. (Moscow, the film-making capital and Russia's second-largest city, had sixty-seven theatres in 1913.)[4]

By summer 1914, although foreign films still controlled the market and remained very popular, demand for well-made Russian films was increasing, and more and more Russians were entering the business. For these native producers, war broke out at an opportune moment. With the empire's borders closed, trade became difficult even with Russian allies – and trade with Germany ended entirely, cutting off the supply of German movies (which had been extremely popular) as well as German production equipment and supplies. The leading Russian studio, Khanzhonkov, doubled its working capital in the first months of the War, and by 1916 Russian studios were producing 500 films a year, most of them full length.[5] In 1916, there were 4,000 movie theatres, more than double the 1913 number.[6]

One of the more interesting facets of the industry during the War was the absence of patriotic films from the repertory, particularly as war dragged on. From 1 August 1914 to the end of the year, nearly half of films made (50 of 103) concerned the War, but in 1916 the figure was only 13 titles out of a total of 500.[7] This startling fact reflects in large part the extreme disaffection of the public from the government and the war effort – as well as the government's inability to organise cinematic propaganda.

Despite Nicholas II's well-known personal interest in film and photography and the creation of the so-called Skobelev Committee to direct the tsarist government's film propaganda efforts, Russia did not succeed in tapping film's potential for propaganda effectively.[8] Producers made films on patriotic themes if they felt like it, and they felt like it only as long as such themes would attract paying customers to the movie theatres. Aleksandr Khanzhonkov, head of Russia's largest studio, recounted in his memoirs that, in October 1914, he 'had to give in' to pressure to make a movie supporting the war effort, despite the fact that he was 'not a supporter of tendentious war films, lacking in art and unconvincing'.[9] The result was *The King, the Law, and Freedom* (*Korol zakon i svoboda*), based on a play by the popular writer Leonid Andreev. (This movie apparently was better received critically than the play itself, in part because Khanzhonkov recreated a dramatic flood of the fields of Belgium, something that could obviously not be staged in a traditional theatre.)

Very few 'patriotic' films survive, but, based on their titles and descriptions, we can imagine that they were, as Khanzhonkov suggested, 'lacking in art and unconvincing'. As Peter Kenez dryly notes, 'the Germans in Russian films committed extraordinary atrocities even before they had time to do so in real life'.[10] The film *By Fire and Blood* (*Ognem i kroviu*, 1914), to name one of many examples, also went by the alternate and more descriptive title, *The Atrocities of the German Major Preisker* (*Zverstva nemetskogo maiora Preiskera*).[11] The best of the extant specimens of wartime patriotism in cinema are the over-the-top melodrama *Glory to Us, Death to the Enemy* (*Slava nam – smert vragam*, 1914) and the charming animated *The Lily of Belgium* (*Liliia Belgii*, 1915). They give us some clues to the style of these early efforts at film propaganda.

Glory to Us, Death to the Enemy was directed by the gifted Evgenii Bauer, though it certainly falls below the aesthetic and dramatic standards of his finest work. It stars Dora Chitorina as a woman who joins the Red Cross to avenge herself upon the Germans for the death of her husband, played by the Russian screen idol Ivan Mozzhukhin ('Mosjoukine' in his later French incarnation).[12] The idea of the nurse as avenging angel might strike those familiar with the conventions of Western cinema of this period as strange, but the strong, independent, and even murderous female was a recurring motif in pre-revolutionary Russian film melodrama.[13]

The Lily of Belgium, in contrast, is very different: a propaganda film suitable for children created through the 'insect animation' of Wladyslaw Starewicz, who made a number of very appealing films with his 'insect puppets'.[14] In this film the 'rape of Belgium' is portrayed through a battle between gentle, winged insects and loathsome German beetles. A battered lily escapes the treacherous onslaught of the beetles. By 1916, however, no producer felt that he 'had to give in' to any demands the government might make for patriotic films. Audiences were no longer feeling particularly patriotic, and studios returned to the production of the superb contemporary melodramas, historical costume dramas and literary adaptations that drew spectators to the movie theatres in droves.

EARLY SOVIET CINEMA

In late 1917, the Russian film industry collapsed along with the rest of the Russian economy and society. It was reborn as the 'Soviet' film industry in 1918, when the Moscow and Petrograd workers' councils (*sovety*) established film committees. On 27 August 1919, what remained of the once-flourishing pre-revolutionary Russian cinema was nationalised and placed under the jurisdiction of the Commissariat of Enlightenment, or education ministry, a sure signal of Bolshevik views on the didactic potential of the movies.[15]

Over the course of the silent era in the Soviet Union (that is, from 1918 to 1935), nearly 200 feature films were made on revolutionary topics, about 15 per cent of the total.[16] (This number does not include the purely propagandistic shorts called *agitki* produced during the Civil War). Most of these revolutionary features included some reference to World War One, but by no stretch could they be labelled 'war films' in the sense that European and American directors were making films about the world war that focused on the trials of soldiers at the front and in the trenches. Indeed, no sector of cultural production made any but cursory reference to the Great War common, the most notable exception being Mikhail Sholokhov's 1928 novel *The Quiet Don* (*Tikhi Don*, translated into English in 1934 as *And Quiet Flows the Don*). 'Great' was an appellation reserved for the October Revolution, as in the oft-used '*Velikii Oktiabr*' ('Great October'), and World War One became merely the entr' acte to the drama of the Revolution.

A classic example of the extremely tangential role the Great War played in the revolutionary film can be seen in Sergei Eisenstein's *October* (*Oktiaber*, 1928). Although soldiers and sailors are everywhere to be seen in this famous film, it is as revolutionaries, with the exception of the very brief fraternisation scene early on. Russian and German soldiers embrace, brother to brother, until shrapnel fire drives them back into the trenches. The Provisional Government is determined to carry on the losing cause that only the effete officer class still embraces.

Vsevolod Pudovkin's 1927 masterpiece *The End of St. Petersburg* (*Konets Sankt-Peterburga*) provides a slightly more detailed example of the typical function of World War One in the revolutionary genre. The purpose of *The End of St. Petersburg* is, first and last, to chart the rise of class consciousness and class tensions in the empire's capital city, focusing on the conflicts between the workers in the Lebedev munitions factory and its nefarious manager and owners. A secondary theme is the close connection between the 'military-industrial complex' and the tsarist government.

Depictions of the War itself occupy only about ten minutes of the entire film – with a few standard, though well-shot, scenes of soldiers in the trenches. The pandemonium of battle is contrasted with the pandemonium of the stock exchange as Lebedev shares rise dramatically in value because of the firm's exclusive government munitions contract. A title informs us that the purpose of the War is to divert attention away from the revolutionary movement, and we see how cleverly the imperial government manipulates the masses to patriotic fervour (an irony that was overlooked by Soviet censors and critics in 1927).

The only important Soviet film of the 1920s in which World War One battle time occupies significant screen time is Aleksandr Dovzhenko's 1929 *Arsenal*, made for the Ukrainian film studio. *Arsenal*'s prologue, about fifteen minutes or one quarter of the film's length, directly depicts the War.[17] Although Dovzhenko's film directly concerns an interpretation of the Civil War in Ukraine, specifically the conflict between the Bolsheviks and Ukrainian nationalists, the Great War prologue deserves some attention.

Arsenal's opening, establishing shot is a low-angle shot of tangled barbed wire – no soldiers to be seen. The second shot shows a woman standing alone in a bare room. The third shot returns to the front. Then the first title reads: 'A mother had three sons.' This is followed by four highly abstract shots of the front, then the title 'There was a war.' The woman is seen walking though a desolate village, and then she is confronted by a soldier. Title: 'The mother had no sons.'

Unlike *The End of St. Petersburg*, the War is never personalised. There is no war 'story' in the prologue, however, and the character of the mother remains undeveloped. Dovzhenko presents a rapid montage of images, from the impoverished village to the tsar sitting at his desk making inane entries in his diary to the battlefields. The prologue ends with a striking montage of a shell-shocked soldier cut with a medium close-up of a smiling corpse, a travelling shot of soldiers on a train, and a striking, silhouetted tableau of a soldier being executed, apparently by his own officer. The transition to the Civil War part of the film is seamless: 'These are soldiers returning from the front.' This highly stylised and ambiguous film confused viewers, as did most of Dovzhenko's work. Criticism focused mainly on aesthetic issues, however, and a critique of his presentation of Ukrainian nationalism, rather than on the unusual and provocative emphasis on the Great War.[18]

BORDERLANDS

Soviet directors in the 1920s, like their counterparts in the war years, showed no particular interest in making Great War films. No one could expect the Soviet government to encourage nostalgia for the causes of the old regime, nor was the pacifist message of the anti-war film particularly useful to the needs of the state. Given the enormous changes in the cultural climate in the USSR in the late twenties and early thirties, to wit, the Cultural Revolution of 1928–31, with its emphasis on promoting the goals of the Five Year Plans, there was no reason to expect these attitudes to change. If anything, the virtual abandonment of 'internationalist' policies to focus on the domestic front made cinematic examinations of the World War less likely than ever before. In any event, the young Soviet director Boris Barnet seemed a most unlikely candidate to make any film about the First World War, let alone a great one.

Known primarily as a director of adventure serials and comedies, Barnet was born in 1902 to a middle-class family of English origin on his father's side. Barnet had spent the Great War as a student in the Moscow Arts Academy, studying architecture and then painting.[19] After the Bolshevik Revolution in the fall of 1917, the Barnet family business, a printing company, was appropriated, leaving Boris to fend for himself from a very early age. Barnet worked as a set painter in the theatre before enlisting in the Red Army in 1920, where he served as a medic in the Civil War that followed the Revolution. After demobilisation in 1922, he became a professional boxer before being 'discovered' the following year by avant-garde director Lev Kuleshov and his talented actress-wife Aleksandra Khokhlova. They cast him as 'Cowboy Jeddy' in their first major film *The Extraordinary Adventures of Mr. West in the Land of the Bolsheviks* (1924).

Barnet, who later developed a reputation as a rather quarrelsome personality, left the troupe in a huff after an argument with Kuleshov over the stunt work in *Mr. West* and returned to boxing, serving as an instructor for Glavvosh, the central military school. Barnet continued to dream of a movie career, however, and wrote a screenplay that he submitted to the Mezhrabpom studio. Although this scenario was rejected, one of the studio's leading writers, Valentin Turkin, invited Barnet to join him in writing an adaptation of the popular *Mess Mend* novelettes by Marietta Shaginian. Their work became the basis for one of the most popular adventure serials in Soviet cinema, retitled *Miss Mend*. Mezhrabpom was apparently so impressed with Barnet that not only was he cast in a leading role in the picture but also he joined Fedor Otsep as co-director, the beginning of his career with the relatively well-funded, quasi-private studio.[20]

After three *Miss Mend* films, Barnet went on to direct two trenchant social comedies, *The Girl with the Hatbox* (*Devushka s korobkoi*, 1927) and *The House on Trubnaia Square* (*Dom na Trubnoi*, 1928) as well as the largely unsuccessful revolutionary saga *Moscow in October* (*Moskva v Oktiabre*, 1927), commissioned (like *October* and *The End of St. Petersburg*) as part of the celebrations for the tenth anniversary of the Revolution. By 1928 Barnet was in political trouble for his allegedly 'Western' style of entertainment film, and he lay low for a few years, directing only one more silent film, *The Ice Breaks* (*Ledolom*, 1931), which was not well received by the critics.[21] Although his once bright career was faltering badly, Barnet got another chance at the Mezhrabpom studio, and in 1932 he began work on his first sound feature, *Borderlands*.

Borderlands was to be based on the novella of the same name by Konstantin Finn, but, as usual with Barnet, the Finn story had nearly vanished by the time the screenplay was ready for production. Barnet added numerous new characters and made major changes to the depiction of the main characters, Greshin and his daughter Manka.[22] Barnet assembled an impressive crew, including Sergei Kozlovskii as set designer, M. Kirillov and M. Spiridonov as cinematographers, and L. Obolenskii and N. Ozornov as sound engineers. In the leading roles, the cast included established screen notables like Aleksandr Chistiakov, Sergei Komarov and Elena Kuzmina, as well as bright newcomers like Nikolai Bogoliubov and Nikolai Kriuchkov.

Borderlands is set in a small provincial town in Russia, a town that the opening title informs us could be 'anywhere' (the outdoor scenes were filmed in Tver).[23] The film follows the fortunes of two lower middle-class families, the Greshins and the Kadkins. The Greshins appear to be somewhat better off than the Kadkins. Aleksandr Petrovich (Sergei Komarov) is a typical petty-bourgeois cobbler with his own shop; his German boarder, Robert Karlovich (Robert Erdman), is also shabbily genteel; his feckless young daughter Manka (Elena Kuzmina) has spending money and nice clothes. The Kadkins, in contrast, are definitely proletarians, who work for wages at the town's boot factory. Aleksandr Chistiakov, who played the brutish father in Pudovkin's 1926 classic *The Mother* (*Mat*) as well as other 'proletarian' roles, here has the highly sympathetic part of Petr Ivanovich, the pater familias who loses both his sons to war.

The film begins on the first day of the War, and Barnet skilfully introduces both families and shows their reactions with minimal dialogue, through rapid crosscutting rather than linear narration. Kadkin and his boys, hearing the siren, realise that something is terribly wrong, which is confirmed at the factory as workers are urged to set aside their differences with management for the benefit of the nation. Greshin and Robert Karlovich, the German boarder, long-time friends, read the news together and almost immediately begin quarrelling. To their father's great despair, both of the younger Kadkins, Kolia (Nikolai Bogoliubov) and Senka (Nikolai Kriuchkov), enlist. Robert Karlovich leaves the Greshin home in a cloud of rancour, warmed only by Manka's smile.

The second part of the film cuts back and forth between the battle front and the home front. Kolia and Senka languish with their comrades in the trenches, their boredom lifted by their crude horseplay as well as by the sporadic shelling. When the time comes for actual battle, Senka refuses to charge and cowers in the bunker, weeping about his toothache. An officer drags him, crying and screaming, out of the trench into no-man's land, where he is almost immediately shot and killed. Kolia glances back briefly – soldiers are stepping over his brother's body – but forges ahead. As the battle continues, Kolia disarms and rescues a young German soldier, and they share a brief moment of joy at their survival from the mortar attack.

At home, the boot factory, bolstered by a military contract is humming. Able-bodied workers are in such short supply that old Kadkin has to train a very young child as an apprentice, and the German prisoners of war are encouraged to work in town. One of these Germans is the boy Kolia rescued from the battle, Mueller 'the Third' (since there are three Muellers in his company). One day, sitting dejectedly on a bench, he attracts the attentions of Manka, Greshin's daughter. Robert Karlovich had taught her a little German, Mueller has picked up some Russian, and the flirtatious Manka is attracted to him. Dressing up like an adult, with a long gown, heels, parasol, and crudely applied rouge on her cheeks, Manka sneaks out of the house to find Mueller. She eventually invites him back to her bedroom for tea but knocks over the table, waking up her father, who is, not surprisingly, quite angry, especially because the male interloper is a German POW. Attracted by the commotion, a crowd

9.1   Senka in battle, *Borderlands* (Museum of Modern Art, New York)

gathers outside the Greshin home, among them Kadkin, who, upon learning that Mueller is a shoemaker, gives him work.

Mueller's happiness is shortlived. Kadkin learns that Senka has been killed, and a former friend (V. Uralskii), now an embittered disabled veteran who is angry that Kadkin is sheltering a POW, brings a gang of thugs to beat Mueller up. The men set upon Mueller savagely, kicking and

9.2   Mueller 'the Third' and Manka, *Borderlands* (Museum of
Modern Art, New York)

punching until he is bloody and unconscious. Manka hears the shouting
and rushes in, fearlessly, to rescue Mueller. Her bravery stirs Kadkin
from his grief and he throws the girl aside and clears the gang out. As a
result of this altercation, however, the POWs will henceforth be confined
to barracks, and a weeping Manka helps the military police take the
battered Mueller back to the camp.

   The action of the third and final part of the movie takes place in 1917,
between the February and October revolutions. Russian soldiers in the
trenches learn that the Tsar has abdicated; in the town, an assembly has
gathered to hear their local socialist declare himself the representative of
the Provisional Government, to the loud strains of the 'Marseillaise'. (This
man, played by M. Zharov, is variously identified in sources as representing a student, a Menshevik, or a 'socialist-revolutionary-democrat'.)
Quick cutting back to the trenches show an old soldier (M. Ianshin)
ruminating about what all this will mean for ordinary folks, interspersed
with romantic shots of the Russian landscape, unscathed by war and,
ominously, shots of the machines in the boot factory, churning out more

9.3   Kadkin's stand off with the 'patriots', *Borderlands*
(Museum of Modern Art, New York)

boots for the war effort. Clearly the rank-and-files hopes that the
Revolution means an end to the War are doomed to disappointment.

Kolia Kadkin has beaten the odds and survived into the War's fourth
year. His regiment receives an order to attack, and, once again, chaos
erupts on the screen. After a hard-pitched battle, during which Kolia
fights for his life in hand-to-hand combat, all is quiet. The Russian
survivors lie exhausted in their trench. A badly wounded German soldier
crawls toward them, piteously begging (in German) that they spare his
life. Without understanding his words, they understand his meaning: like
the Russians, this German does not want to fight.

Kolia impetuously climbs out of the trench, waving a white flag of truce
on his bayonet. Alone, against the scarred landscape, he walks slowly
toward the German side. He is met by a single German soldier. They
shake hands, and the troops spill over the embankments in a sponta-
neous and joyous moment of fraternisation. But ending the War is not so
simple: a cut back to the town shows the Provisional Government official,
with the leering boot factory owner (A. Ermakov) at his side, ranting

9.4   Kolia waves the White Flag, *Borderlands*
(Museum of Modern Art, New York)

against Bolshevik incitements to desertion and fraternisation. This short
scene is followed by another quick cut back to the front: Kolia is to be
executed by firing squad. The officer in charge slaps him, whereupon
Kolia laughs and knocks him to the ground. The officer orders the squad
to fire, and they do so.

As he lies dying, Kolia manages to whisper to his old peasant soldier friend not to let the 'bosses' (nachalniki) get their guns. His friend sorrowfully tells him that they've received news that some soldiers have taken 'something called the winter palace'. Kolia smiles faintly and dies. In town, Manka too has decided to rebel: when her father orders her to play draughts with him, she angrily sweeps the board to the floor. Meanwhile, Kolia's father, the newly defiant Kadkin, is seen arresting the local head of the Provisional Government. The film closes with a montage of the townspeople marching, led by Kadkin and Manka, with the German POW Mueller joining them in a later shot, intercut with shots of the old soldier kneeling by Kolia's body, urging him to get up. Kolia's dead face seems to wear a slight smile.

The tendentiousness of *Borderlands* is obvious, more obvious than its genuine iconoclasm. Based on plot summary alone, this sounds like a predictable Soviet film. Barnet understood on the basis of painful experience that there were certain essential messages, social and political, that he needed to convey. The heroes in *Borderlands* are all workers; the chief villains are the bourgeoisie (the exploitative factory owner), the socialist intelligentsia (the ubiquitous and upwardly mobile patriotic agitator), and the tsarist officer corps (the snivelling coward who orders Kolia's death while he is lying in the dust where Kolya knocked him). The type casting for the main characters is perfect, especially Nikolai Bogoliubov's tall, strong and ruggedly handsome Kolia as the model of the New Soviet Man.

The film's attitude towards the Provisional Government is also 'correct': betraying the desires of the people to end an increasingly meaningless conflict, the Provisional Government committed itself to continuing the War. We see Greshin, Manka's father, replacing the portrait of Nicholas II in his house with one of Aleksandr Kerenskii, the eventual head of the government, a pointed analogy. (In Finn's original story, Greshin was an intelligent skeptic, not a mindless patriot.) And the Provisional Government is more or less accurately represented as an implacable foe of the Bolsheviks and friend of what we would call today the 'military-industrial complex'.

Finally, socialist internationalism and class solidarity are emphasised over nationalist patriotism, again and again. (This message was becoming a suspect one, given the rise to power of the Fascists in Europe.) A German intellectual like Robert Karlovich might be a German chauvinist, but young Mueller was just a shoemaker. Russian officers, members of the Provisional Government, and war profiteers, might want to continue the War, but ordinary German and Russian soldiers, men of the factory and the soil, did not.

Yet *Borderlands* received mixed reviews, and, as time went on, it became obvious that this film would not be allowed to enter the pantheon of Soviet film classics, therefore further discouraging other Soviet directors from undertaking an exploration of the Great War on film. By 1933, the Cultural Revolution in cinema had more or less ended, and the journal *Cinema* (*Kino*) held sway, a very different situation from the relative diversity in the film press in the decade preceding. Although *Cinema* initially praised *Borderlands* for its technical achievements, a few months later the 'line' had changed. The Leningrad critic and scenarist Mikhail Bleiman, for example, complained that Barnet's understanding of ideological issues was thin at best (and insinuated that the worst might be too awful to mention).[24]

Bleiman was an intelligent critic, although not always an honourable one, and his suspicions about *Borderlands*' political platform were well placed. Barnet's tale only seems straightforward, and the complex relationship between content and form presents a direct challenge to the newly articulated aesthetic strictures of the doctrine of 'Socialist Realism'. Although Socialist Realism was not formally accepted as the official Party policy on aesthetics until 1934, it was well entrenched by 1930.[25] Art needed to present 'life as it should be' in a form that was intelligible to the 'millions'.

Kadkin and his older son Kolia are certainly noble representatives of two generations of the working class. Both manage to control their emotions to do the right thing. Kadkin recognises that Mueller, although a German, is not representative of the evil that claimed Senka's life. Kolia neither shrinks from his execution nor accepts it passively, as he shows when he very calmly knocks the threatening officer to the ground. Apart from these two iconographic portraits, however, we see a much more complicated view of class and class behaviour: most of the 'little people' in the film, especially Greshin (who was actually a Germanophile in Finn's story) are swept up in the jingoism of the War and resent Manka and Kadkin for their evenhanded attitude toward the German POWs. Furthermore, Senka's death is a perfect example of the kind of brutal realism that inspirationalist Socialist Realism intentionally ignored: his fear as he is dragged whimpering to his death is visceral and very difficult to watch.

The depiction of women in this film is also idiosyncratic. Female characters are typically (and naturally) tangential in the war-film genre, so it is not surprising that there are only two recognisable women in *Borderlands* beyond those in the crowd scenes. Manka is, of course, a bona fide protagonist, but there is the curious recurring motif of 'the lady with the little dog', borrowing from the title of Chekhov's famous story. We first see this woman, her heavily made up face like a mask, sitting on a bench, near the beginning of the picture. The irrepressible Senka sidles up to her, knocks her dog off the bench, and attempts unsuccessfully to comfort her. She slaps him away. We next see her bidding Senka fond farewell at the train station as the soldiers prepare to leave for the front. As she and Senka embrace, the camera moves down to show us her little dog being strangled on his leash, as she lifts her arm to her lover, completely unaware of her pet. Finally, she appears as one of the women who glare disapprovingly at Mueller and then at Manka's flirtations with Mueller. Such murky symbolism was definitely frowned on – and, indeed, it detracts from the film's anti-war message.

Manka herself provides another challenge to the unambiguous depiction of character that Socialist Realism required in order to appeal to the lowest-common denominator. In Finn's original version, Manka was a thirty-six year old spinster who ends up marrying the German POW, while Barnet's Manka is a young teen.[26] This presented a glaringly obvious casting problem in that Kuzmina, who was then twenty-four, was playing a child of fourteen or fifteen, still in pig-tails and short skirts. Although Kuzmina was a fine actress, she nonetheless looked – as Mary Pickford did in similar cinematic situations – like an adult impersonating a child, not entirely a pleasant sight. This makes her flirtatious behaviour with Mueller seem not so much innocent as peculiar. As Mueller remarks in German at one point, 'You remind me of my sister, only shorter.' Furthermore, Manka's reasons for joining the revolutionaries at the end of the film appear to be mainly based on her desire to get back at her father for preventing her from fraternising with Germans like Robert Karlovich and Mueller. She displays no class consciousness whatsoever.

In stylistic terms as well, *Borderlands* displays a high degree of individualism and originality, qualities not prized in Soviet society in the early 1930s. The narrative is completely dependent on cross-cutting, which becomes increasingly rapid and sophisticated as the story progresses. The montage is associational as well as relational; for example, Barnet frequently comments on the progress of the War by cutting to the activity on the boot factory floor – or by cutting from the speechifying of the war-mongers back to the trenches. (This becomes a bit treacly near the end of the film as Barnet intercuts shots of Mother Russia with those of the kindly old peasant soldier who has befriended Kolya.)

In pictorial terms, Barnet's visualisations of battle are quite remarkable given the technical limitations of Soviet cinema at the time, relying a great deal on an avant-garde understanding of the possibilities of the medium. A good example is the use of extreme close-up and fast motion cinematography as the soldiers go flying over the trenches. (The design of the battle scenes is reminiscent of those in *The End of St. Petersburg*, not surprising given that Sergei Kozlovskii was art director on both films.)

Barnet's extremely effective utilisation of sound montage exemplifies Eisenstein, Pudovkin and Aleksandrov's theory of sound in their famous treatise 'Zaiavka'.[27] *Borderlands'* battle scenes are filled with sound: explosions, sirens, whistles, which are deliberately asynchronous with the visual effects. Barnet also employs sound as transition, cutting on sound, as when Greshin's smashing of Robert Karlovich's framed photograph becomes the thunk of boots on the factory floor.

Finally, the quirky humour of the film, though characteristic of Barnet's style, is unexpected for a war picture. This is most evident in the scenes with Mueller, who looks like a dazed teenager most of the time. In his first meeting with Manka, for example, he doesn't notice that his abrupt departure from the bench they are sharing turns the bench into a see-saw, and she lurches to the ground.) A talking horse that comments on the foolishness of patriotism near the beginning of the film is a particularly extreme example of the unexpected touches of humour, but there are many others.

All these factors combined to make a memorable picture, one of the most interesting early sound films as well as an important picture about the Great War. Although it is arguably not as fine an example as Lewis Milestone's *All Quiet on the Western Front* or G. W. Pabst's *Westfront 1918*, Barnet had neither the liberty, the resources, nor the technology that his counterparts in the West had. In the context of Soviet cinema in the 1930s, therefore, *Borderlands'* achievements are considerable, while at the same time revealing how politically problematic any Soviet film about the Great War was likely to be.

INSTEAD OF A CONCLUSION

Historians have not yet invented a language to describe the culture of absence. We are accustomed to gathering data, organising and presenting evidence, and coming up with noteworthy conclusions. But how do we make the case that the *absence* of artifacts – in this circumstance an entire cinematic genre – is also important? It seems to me nonetheless that it is.

Much of the recent work on the history of Russian and Soviet cinema, my own included, has sought to emphasise the continuities, rather than the disjunctures, between the pre- and post-revolutionary cinemas.[28] To a certain extent, we can also see major similarities between Soviet and Western cinema in the 1930s and after, especially in the musical comedies of directors like Grigorii Aleksandrov and Ivan Pyrev.[29] The Russian failure, therefore, to produce a significant patriotic culture *during* the Great War – and the Soviet failure to memorialise it must be taken as significant factors distinguishing Russia from Europe. Absence provides important indirect reinforcement for assumptions that we make about Russian and Soviet society: society's lack of moral investment in the Great War and the much more devastating impact of the Civil War on all sectors of society, as well as the obvious conclusion that the Soviet government did not want to pay for movies that would romanticise or glamorise the tsarist past in any way. Nor was the government interested in encouraging pacificism and international-ism at a time when Stalin was beginning a campaign to promote Great Russian nationalism on the domestic front.

So what is the value of *Borderlands* in this historical context? In part, it is a film without a genre, an isolated artifact, at least at home. It does, however, fit securely within the genre of anti-war war films made *outside* the borders of the USSR, as other essays in this volume show, and this internationalism dovetails perfectly with its message. *Borderlands* reveals, therefore, the continuing contacts, tenuous though they may be, with the one truly international language of the troubled thirties – the movies.

FILMOGRAPHY
EXTANT TITLES, 1914–16[30]

1914 *By Fire and Blood* (*Ognem i kroviu*)
      Christmas in the Trenches (*Rozhdestvo v okopakh*)
      Glory to Us, Death to the Enemy (*Slava nam–smert vragam*)
      The King, the Law, and Freedom (*Korol, zakon i svoboda*)
1915 *A Daughter of Tormented Poland* (*Doch isterzannoi Polshi*)
      The Lily of Belgium (*Liliia Belgii*)
1916 *Lumbering Russia Has Stirred to Defend the Sacred Cause* (*Vsko-lykhnulas Rus sermiazhnaia i grudii tala za sviatoe delo*)
      The Poor Devil Died in an Army Hospital (*Umer bedniaga v bolnitse voennoi*)
      Vova at War (*Vova na voine*)

POST-WAR

1933 *Borderlands* (*Okraina*)

This list is based on a review of titles in Tsivian, *Silent Witnesses*.

NOTES

My thanks to Peter Kenez, Frank Manchel, Richard Taylor and Josephine Woll for their helpful remarks on an earlier draft of this essay, and to the Film Stills Archive of the Museum of Modern Art, New York, for the illustrations.

1   Hubertus Jahn, *Patriotic Culture in Russia during World War I* (Ithaca, NY. Cornell University Press, 1995). Chapter 3 focuses on film.
2   The first full-length study of the early Russian film industry in English is my forthcoming book *The Magic Mirror: Movies and Modernity in Russia, 1908–1918* (Madison, WI: University of Wisconsin Press, 1999). Other sources include Yuri Tsivian et al., *Silent Witnesses: Russian Films, 1908–1919* (Pordenone and London: Edizone Biblioteca Dell Imagine/BFI, 1989); Tsivian, *Early Cinema in Russia and Its Cultural Reception*, trans. Alan Bodger, ed. Richard Taylor (London: Routledge, 1994); and Jay Leyda, *Kino: A History of the Russian and Soviet Film* (London: George Allen & Unwin, 1960), chaps 1–4. In Russian see S. Ginzburg, *Kinematografiia dorevoliutsionnoi Rossii* (Moscow: Iskusst-vo, 1963).
3   N. A. Lebedev, *Ocherk istorii kino SSSR*, vol. 1, *Nemoe kino* (Moscow: Iskusstvo, 1947), p. 5.
4   Ibid., p. 33.
5   Ibid., p. 35; Ginzburg, *Kinematografiia*, p. 157.
6   Ginzburg, *Kinematografiia*, p. 158.
7   Ibid., pp. 191–2.
8   See Peter Kenez's brief discussion in 'Russian patriotic films', in Karel Dibbets and Bert Hogen Kam? (eds), *Film and the First World War*, (Amsterdam: Amsterdam University Press, 1995), pp. 40–1.
9   Tsivian et al., *Silent Witnesses*, p. 224.
10 Kenez, 'Russian patriotic films', p. 40.
11 Tsivian et al., *Silent Witnesses*, p. 234.
12 Ibid., p. 236. The film no longer has titles, which makes watching it a surrealistic experience.
13 This subject is treated in Youngblood, *Magic Mirror*, chaps 5–6.

14   Starewicz's work is discussed in more detail in ibid., 'Intermission'.

15   See Youngblood, *Soviet Cinema in the Silent Era, 1918–1935* (Ann Arbor, MI: UMI Research Press, 1985; rpt Austin, TX: University of Texas Press, 1991), ch. 1 for a discussion of the industry's rebirth.

16   Youngblood, *Soviet Cinema*, appendix 2.

17   The only complete analysis of *Arsenal* in English may be found in Vance Kepley, Jr., *In the Service of the State: The Cinema of Alexander Dovzhenko* (Madison, WI: University of Wisconsin Press, 1986), ch. 5. In Russian, see Iu. I. Solntseva and L. I. Pazhitnova, comps, *Arsenal* (Moscow: Iskusstvo, 1977). My translation of the titles comes from the Russian original rather than the print available in the US.

18   For a favorable review, see G. Lenobl, 'Poezd sovremennosti', *Kino*, no. 3 (1929), p. 3; for a critical review, see B. Alpers, '*Arsenal* dovzhenko', *Sovetskii ekran*, no. 16 (1929), p. 5.

19   This synopsis of Barnet's early career is drawn from Youngblood, *Movies for the Masses: Popular Cinema and Soviet Society in the 1920s* (Cambridge: CUP, 1992), Ch. 7, which is devoted to a study of the director's silent *oeuvre*. Also see Francois Albera and Roland Cosandey (eds), *Boris Barnet: Ecrits, documents, etudes, filmographie* (Locarno: Editions Du Festival Internationale du Film, 1985); Mark Kushnirov, *Zhizn i filmy Borisa Barneta* (Moscow: Iskusstvo, 1977); Bernard Eisenschitz, 'A fickle man, or, Portrait of Boris Barnet as Soviet director', in Richard Taylor and Ian Christie (eds), *Inside the Film Factory: New Approaches to Russian and Soviet Cinema* (London, Routledge, 1991), ch. 8, pp. 137–69.

20   'Mezhrabpom' was an acronym for International Workers' Relief, headed by Willi Munzenberg, and supported by German Communists.

21   Silent films were made in the Soviet Union as late as 1935.

22   Kushnirov, *Zhizn i filmy*, pp. 110–15.

23   Ibid., p. 117.

24   Bleiman et al., 'Bez chetkogo ideinogo zamysla (ob *Okraine*)', *Kino*, no. 23 (1933), p. 2. Other reactions from the Soviet film press are translated into French in Albera and Cosandey, *Boris Barnet*, pp. 132–44. The politics of the Soviet film press are extensively discussed in Youngblood, *Soviet Cinema*, passim.

25   See Youngblood, *Soviet Cinema*, chs 8 and 9.

26   Kushnirov, *Zhizn i filmy*, pp. 112–13, says that Kuzmina insisted Barnet rewrite the role as an ingénue part. Kuzmina asserted in an interview with Bernard Eisenschitz that it was Barnet's idea and that she was uncomfortable with the change (Eisenschitz, 'A fickle man', pp. 152–3. Kuzmina and Barnet were briefly married after the making of this film.

27   Translated in Richard Taylor and Ian Christie, (eds), *The Film Factory: Russian and Soviet Cinema in Documents, 1896–1939* (Cambridge, MA: Harvard University Press, 1988), pp. 234–5.

28   This is a motivating principle behind anthologies co-edited by Taylor
     and Christie like *The Film Factory* and *Inside the Film Factory*, and
     Taylor and Derek Spring (eds), *Stalinism and Soviet Cinema* (London:
     Rovtledge, 1993).
29   As examples of Richard Taylor's work on the entertainment cinema of
     the 1930s, see 'The illusion of happiness and the happiness of illusion:
     Grigorii Aleksandrov's *The Circus*', *Slavonic and East European Re-
     view*, 74, no. 4 (October 1996), pp. 601–20; and 'Singing on the Steppe for
     Stalin: Ivan Pyr'ev and the Kolkhoz musical in Soviet cinema', *Slavic
     Review*, 58, no 1. (Spring 1999), pp. 143–59.

10

Between Parochialism and Universalism: World War One in Polish Cinematography

Ewa Mazierska

The First World War has provided a common theme for Polish films with some forty feature films dealing with the subject. However, hardly any films which can be described as 'Polish' were actually made during the War. The first Polish film dealing with the War to be preserved, *Miracle on the Vistula* (Cud nad Wisla), directed by Ryszard Boleslawski, was made in 1921. In this study reference will only be made to those films which are typical in their representation of the War and those which are regarded as the most interesting or significant in their analysis of Polish history. This section will explore the reciprocal relationship between film and outside reality: firstly, the reality of World War One which the films attempted to portray and, secondly, the political and cultural reality of the period in which they were produced. This second reality strongly influenced the mode of representation of the War, either by using it as an instrument of political propaganda or as a tool of more subtle ideological evangelism.

The division of films into those made before and after the Second World War reflects a dichotomy which plays a crucial role in the analysis, because of the dramatic change in the Polish political climate. Firstly, from being an enemy of Soviet Russia, Poland became its political, economic and military ally. Secondly, it became a part of the communist bloc where the State financed and censored all film production and criticism of Bolshevism or even, more generally, of Russia became unacceptable.

However, it must be emphasised that post-1945 cinematography rarely used the First World War as a tool of pro-communist propaganda. There was, in fact, only one example of this – *Soldier of Victory* (*Zolnierz zwyciestwa*), made by Wanda Jakubowska in 1953, the year in which Social Realism, reached its peak in Polish art. More commonly, film-makers conformed to the rules of censorship by avoiding the question of Polish-Bolshevik relations during World War One and by concentrating on less contentious subjects, such as the experience of Polish soldiers serving in the Austro-Hungarian army.

From 1960 until the 1980s, directors dealing with the War ignored all overtly political questions and instead examined the psychological impact of the War on the Polish people. This is understandable in the light of the deaths of over five million Poles during World War Two, the Holocaust, the complete destruction of many Polish cities and cultural monuments and the introduction of a Russian-controlled regime. The notion that war could bring anything good to Poland had been destroyed and it was perceived as a crime against humanity rather than as a method to solve international disputes.

HISTORICAL BACKGROUND

In order to understand Polish films about the First World War, something must first be said about this period of Polish history and the state of cinema in post-1918 Poland. Before the War Poland had not existed for over 100 years as a separate state, being divided between three powerful countries which were adversaries during the War: Germany and Austro-Hungary on one side and Russia on the other. Polish territory was a buffer between them and its strategic location encouraged Poles to hope that their struggle for independence could be advanced during the conflict. This was exploited by both sides in their propaganda, each encouraging Poles to fight loyally for the partitioning power, by promising freedom and independence after the War. Austria alluded to the history of common conflict against the Turks in Vienna in the twelfth century and Russia to the battle of Grunwald when Poles and Russians united to defeat the Teutonic Knights. However, no treaties were advanced by either side and Russia's allies, France and Britain, regarded the 'Polish question' as an internal problem for Russia. The only exception was a statement from the Bolsheviks, recognising the Polish struggle for independence and, in the event of victory, the promise to create an independent state.

This manipulative approach by the annexors and their allies towards the Polish question did not change throughout the War. Poles gained small concessions from each side: for example, in the summer of 1916, in the wake of the loss of any hope of a separate peace with Russia, Germany and Austro-Hungary created a Polish buffer state on the territory of Congress (Russian) Poland. However, this neither matched Polish ambitions for independence, nor balanced the human and material losses Poles suffered: in the first year of the War more than one million Poles were mobilised into the armies of the partitioning powers, and by the end of the War this had risen to more than two millions. The actions of the military authorities, especially the Germans, towards the civilian population in the occupied territories, was also ruthless, seizing raw materials, livestock and food.

During the War Poles adopted political positions very much according to their class background and geographical location. For example, most Conservatives sided with the partitioning powers, while left-wing Socialists took a pacifist position. However, the major divisions were either pro-Russian or pro-Austrian, led by Roman Dmowski and Jozef Pilsudski respectively.

Pilsudski's goal was to unify Austrian and Russian Poland under the Habsburgs, creating an Austro-Hungarian-Polish state.[1] Volunteer Polish armies (known as Pilsudski's Legions), comprising Poles from Galicia and volunteers from Russian Poland, were established on the Austro-Hungarian side in August 1914. (This part of my article paper is indebted to Jozef Buszko's book *Historia Polski 1864–1948* [Warszawa, Panstwowe Wydawnictwo Naukowe], 1987; and 'Poland: The Polish question during World War 1; independence restored', in *Encyclopaedia Britannica*, Chicago and London, William Benton, 1970.)

Dmowski's objective was to unify all the Polish territories under Russian protection and give them considerable autonomy within the Russian state. By the end of 1914 the Pulawski Legion, as a counterbalance to Pilsudski's Legions, was established. However, after suffering great losses in its first year, it played little part during the rest of the War.

In the end Poland did regain independence, following the defeat of the Central Powers, the Bolshevik Revolution and the recognition of Polish aspirations to create a united and independent State by the governments of the USA, Great Britain, France and Italy. It must also be noted that for Poles World War One did not end in 1918, as fighting for its borders continued for another two years against both Germany and Russia. After the War the Polish state was in a very precarious position, founded on the unification of three distinct parts, each with a different level of political and economic development as well as very different cultural traditions and ethnic composition. In 1921 ethnic minorities (including Jews) comprised over 30 per cent of the total population, and in Eastern regions Poles made up less than 40 per cent. Moreover, Poland had suffered serious devastation during the War, causing widespread unemployment, poverty and hyperinflation. The euphoria of regaining independence was tempered by the disappointments of living standards falling well below peoples' expectations.

This situation led to widespread mistrust of democratic structures and to strong popular support for ultra right-wing, nationalistic movements. During the inter-war period Poland experienced, amongst other events, the murder of its first president, Gabriel Narutowicz, in 1922 by a right-wing fanatic and a *coup d'état*, led by Jozef Pilsudski in 1926. The power of parliament was first limited. Then it was dissolved in 1930 and the most prominent members of the opposition arrested. Pilsudski's dictatorship lasted virtually till his death in 1935.

The political situation in the 1920s and 1930s affected national culture in a very significant way. For example, the first half of the 1930s was marked by a substantial restriction in the freedom of speech, manifesting itself in censorship of the press and cinema and self-censorship by the artists. The most distrusted ideology was communism, which the authorities regarded as the major threat to Polish social order and even independence.

THE FIRST WORLD WAR IN FILMS MADE BEFORE 1939

The War was an event of overtly political character, which resulted in Poland regaining independence. Consequently, using it as a setting and referring to the nations which played an important part in post-war affairs seemed to be ideal material for political propaganda. Indeed, although it was very difficult to prove at the time (and is even more difficult now from the perspective of from sixty to seventy years), the proposition that First World War films were made to satisfy the Polish authorities is strengthened by observing a strong concordance between the way the War was portrayed and what was going on in the political salons of Warsaw and Cracow. I refer especially to the fact that the vast majority of films made in the late 1920s and 1930s seem to have a distinctive missionary zeal – their aim to boost national pride and advocate a nationalistic, even xenophobic, vision of Poland. Moreover, they tended to conform to Pilsudski's position of Russia being the main threat to Polish independence and strongly promote the myth of Pilsudski as the saviour of the Polish nation.

Politics alone, however, does not completely explain the way the War is portrayed in films of this period. An equally important factor is the state and character of Polish cinema during the inter-war period. At the time cinema, as in many other European countries, was the main form of entertainment for the less well off. The bulk of the audiences were working class, comprising mainly factory workers and domestic servants, who expected films with sentimental, uncomplicated plots and happy endings, and a cast of famous, glamorous actors – movies which would help them to forget the harsh reality. Comedies, melodramas, action movies, made according to the strict rules of their genres, were the most popular forms. In contrast, realism (understood as historical accuracy) was only a minor consideration or, indeed, was regarded as an obstacle in appealing to a wide audience. A typical film of the period was marked by low budget, technical limitations, stereotyped characters performing exaggerated gestures and speaking words full of pathos.[2] There were no superproductions amongst them and only a handful included any battle scenes. The majority of films represented the War from the point of view of the civilians who couldn't fight because of their age or gender, but were nevertheless exposed to the hardship of war.

It must be emphasised that providing the working classes with an escape from everyday reality did not exclude promoting nationalism or praising Pilsudski. On the contrary, nationalistic ideas which blamed the economic and political crises on 'the others', mainly Jews, were well received amongst the archetypal cinema-goers of the 1930s. Similarly, in spite of his anti-democratic views, autocratic rule and reforms, which badly affected the living standards of the poorest section of society, Pilsudski was very popular amongst the working classes, partly due to his achievements during the War.

The very choice of film subjects fulfilled the primary aim of denigrating Russia and praising Pilsudski. Those made in the 1920s and 1930s concentrated on Polish-Russian relations. There was little reference to the fact that there was a wider conflict or that Pilsudski's Legions were part of the Austro-Hungarian army. The exalted status of Pilsudski's Legions and of Pilsudski's himself is exaggerated by the omission of any reference to the Pulawski Legion which represented the pro-Russian perspective and by ignoring all other Polish politicians involved in the War, such as Roman Dmowski or Ignacy Paderewski.

The majority of films about World War One, made in the inter-war period, are so similar and stereotyped in their pattern of narrative, representation of characters, visual style and – most importantly – ideology, that it may be argued that they form a single genre of their own. I refer here to such films as *Miracle on the Vistula* (*Cud nad Wisla*; 1921), *Heroes of Siberia* (*Bohaterowie Sybiru*; 1936), *Dodek on the Frontier* (Dodek na froncie; 1935), *Madmen* (*Szalency*; 1928), *Year 1914* (*Rok 1914*; 1932), *Florian* (1936) and *Grave of the Unknown Soldier* (*Mogila nieznanego zolnierza*; 1927). Particularly important is their uniform representation of Poland's enemies and Pilsudski's Legions, their attitude to landowners, the Catholic Church, women and ethnic minorities, and their vision of an independent Poland.

Not all the films mentioned have every characteristic, but such features can be found in the majority and some films contain most of them. One such archetypal film, made in the inter-war period, is *Florian* (1936) directed by Leonard Buczkowski, one of the most successful mainstream directors of the 1930s, who also managed to complete several films in the post-1945 era. This film will be described in detail, concentrating on its typical features and with reference to other examples only to supplement the portrayal of the War or to emphasise important shifts from the model attitude.

Florian spans the period from 1916 to the end of the War. This enables the conduct of the three armies, which invaded Polish territory, Russian, German and Bolshevik, to be analysed and accordingly to portray Polish heroism and martyrdom in a broader context. The inclusion of the end of the hostilities also allowed reference to be made to Poland after the War.

The plot centres around the fate of 'Florian', an old church bell in a small town in Congress Poland. The bell is cherished by the local inhabitants, who regard it as a symbol of their Polishness, which in the film equates with Roman Catholicism. They hide the bell first from the Russians, then from the Germans, who both pursued a ruthless policy for requisitioning raw materials, and wanted to melt the bell down to make guns and ammunition. The Poles risked severe punishment and yet they succeeded – Florian remained safe and no one was persecuted for hiding it. The end of the War and Polish independence is celebrated by rehanging the bell in the church tower.

The main characters in *Florian* are members of the Wereszczynski family who are genteel, but impoverished, landed gentry. It is worth mentioning that, in the nineteenth century, it was this section of Polish

society – and not the rich aristocrats, burgeoisie or tradespeople – which
was regarded as the bastion of Polishness. According to this stereotype
of patriotism, the senior member of the family, Melchior, has a heroic
past, having fought in the 1863 'January Uprising' against Russian
authority. All the other adult men in the family fight in Pilsudski's
Legion, continuing the Polish struggle for independence, of which the
War was its final stage.

Wereszczynski's patriotism is further emphasised by showing that
even the women, the old men and the boys in the family who had to stay
at home do all they can to help their motherland. Melchior Wereszczynski's grandsons mastermind and carry out the rescue of the bell.
Moreover, two of them eventually succeed in joining Pilsudski's Legions.
The main evidence of the patriotism of a female member of the Wereszczynski family, named Bronka, is her attitude to Alfred, a rich
aristocrat who at the beginning of the War decides to stay at home
with his mother who could not bear to be left alone. Although Bronka
does not actually persuade Alfred to leave his mother and fight, she
makes it clear that she regards fighting for the motherland as a higher
moral duty than looking after one's own family. As a result, Alfred, who
is in love with Bronka, leaves his mother and joins Pilsudski's Legions.

Florian is based on the novel *Florian from Wielka Hlusza* (*Florian z
Wielkiej Hluszy*) by Maria Rodziewiczowna, a popular Polish author of
the inter-war years. Her books celebrate the life of the Polish landed
gentry, praising the Roman Catholic Church as a bastion of Polishness,
often with a xenophobic, anti-semitic tone. The film also promotes the
idea of cultural exclusiveness and sees alien cultures as a danger to
Polish independence and welfare. This attitude is illustrated by a Silesian
soldier, who comes to the town with the German army. Although he
represents the enemy, he helps the Polish inhabitants in different ways
and even starts a courtship with Bronka's servant. Like everyone else in
the town, he wants Poland to be independent and promises to fight for it.
On his departure Bronka comments: 'Foreign uniform, but Polish soul'.
These words can be interpreted as a metaphor of the circumstances of
many Poles during the War. At the same time they conform with the post-
war, nationalist, right-wing propaganda that after the War all Poles
should overcome their regional differences and try to build a single Polish
identity.

Both the landowners and their servants shown in the film are deeply
patriotic. In the society portrayed by Buczkowski the dream of an
independent Poland serves as a cohesive force, a source of co-operation
and friendship between aristocrats and ordinary people. Yet, it is also

suggested that there is a deep cultural division between the landowners and the working class. For example, officers fall in love with the daughters of aristocrats, while ordinary soldiers seduce the housemaids. This social order is never challenged or questioned; it seems perfectly natural to everyone who is a part of it.

One of the characters of *Florian* is a business man who deals with both German and Russian authorities and provides the Germans with a map of the lake where the young Poles had hidden the bell. Although the ethnic background of the man is not disclosed in the film, the fact that he is a trader (a typical Jewish occupation and therefore despised by Poles), that his name is foreign (Horehlad) and he remains aloof from the town community suggests that he is a Jew. Horehlad is an immediate cause of trouble for the Poles. He shoots a German officer who refused to pay him for guiding him to Florian's hiding place and then escapes. Consequently, Melchior Wereszczynski is taken hostage by the Germans. They threaten to execute him if the killer is not found quickly. Only seconds before Melchior's execution, Horehlad is found by the Poles and denounced to the Germans. This act is portrayed as a manifestation of Polish solidarity – they denounce 'the other' in order to save 'one of our own'. It is worth mentioning that the mid-1930s, when *Florian* was made, are regarded as a high point of Polish nationalism and anti-semitism and the film ideally catches and strengthens the popular mood.

The character of Bronka is shaped according to the cultural stereotype of 'Polish mother' which on the one hand praises a Polish woman as guardian of national traditions and the family and on the other denies her the right to an independent life and sexual freedom. Bronka not only encourages the man who loves her to fight in the Pilsudski's Legions, but supports him even after he is disfigured when fighting against the Russians. She is also able to resist the pressure of a German officer who tries to seduce her. Furthermore, while the men are off fighting, she takes her turn tending the fields and running the household. One of the most poignant scenes in the film shows Bronka and her grandfather ploughing their fields with a single horse.

The local priest, although he does not take part in any military action, plays an important role in the Polish community. He welcomes and encourages the idea of saving the bell and does not divulge the name of the 'saboteurs' when interrogated by the German and Russian authorities. Moreover, when Melchior Wereszczynski is arrested and threatened with execution, he assumes the role of the counsellor to his family. He encourages the Wereszczynskis not to lose hope as God never abandons those who have faith in him and always looks after Poles.

Indeed, his words seem to have the power of prophecy – Melchior is rescued at the last moment.

There are many scenes which show the moral superiority of Poles over all other nations portrayed in the film. For example, they are the only ones with a strong national identity who fight not for personal advantage but for the welfare of their country. Even those who are too young to join Pilsudski's Legions try to play their part in helping the motherland by rescuing the bell. Germans and Russians, in contrast were either forced to fight or driven by the prospect of self-advancement. Their morale is low, shown by their frivolity, preferably in the company of young Polish women. They have no sense of loyalty or fair play and they betray their overwhelming allies whenever it serves their immediate benefit. Whenever they win, it is thanks to either their military strength or simple, but dirty, tricks. Poles, on the contrary, use their intelligence to gain the upper hand. For example, in order to rescue Florian, the young Wereszczynskis hatch a meticulous and cunning plan, which involves diverting the attention of the occupiers by pretending that a great fire had started in the town. A mark of their high ideals is the behaviour of Gawel Wereszczynski, who surrenders to the Germans as the killer in order to save his grandfather's life.

Although the Russian and German armies are shown at their worst as ruthless, cynical exploiters, the Bolsheviks are portrayed as even lower – as irrational destroyers and murderers. One discovers in the film that they set fire to whole villages, rape Polish women and shoot innocent civilians. In contrast to the German army and members of the Tzar's army, who act as individuals, the Bolsheviks are shown as anonymous, faceless, without even a voice. We learn about them only through their cruel deeds, the worst of which is breaking into Wereszczynki's house and killing the youngest member of his family. The fact that he is the only Pole killed during the film underlines the cruelty of Bolsheviks.

As previously mentioned, *Florian* can be regarded as a model of World War One films made in the inter-war period and sharing features with many other movies. Firstly, its criticism of all sides of the War with the exception of Pilsudski's Legions, but reserving special condemnation for the Bolsheviks, was the norm in Polish cinematography of the inter-war period: *Madmen, Miracle on the Vistula, Heroes of Siberia* and many other films conformed to this pattern. Their makers usually depict the Red Army as a faceless mass, blindly following their leaders and indulging in destruction. There was little attempt to understand the goals of the October Revolution. The only film which offered some insight into the life of the Bolsheviks and presented some of them as individuals was *Grave of the Unknown Soldier*, directed by Ryszard Ordynski. This film conceded that the October Revolution attracted many kinds of people, affecting them in different ways. Some regarded it as a chance to save the world, others used it as a tool of revenge and destruction, some were altruistic, others were evil. Yet even this early film concentrates on the destructive forces and admits that the good Bolsheviks were marginalised by the bad ones.

The best indication of the ruthless cruelty of the Revolutionaries is the fact that they have no pity either for their enemies or even for their own folk. 'Ordinary' Russians from Ordynski's film dread the Bolsheviks more than their old oppressor – the aristocrats and foreign armies. Furthermore, the communal spirit, which was meant to play a crucial role in the victory of the Revolution, is denounced as a submission to terror. It is also worth mentioning that the portrayal of the Bolshevik women as asexual and more cruel than their male comrades was a notion commonly promoted by right-wing politicians and press.

In addition to *Florian*, glorification of Pilsudski's Legions as the only true, Polish army and Pilsudski as a leader of the Polish nation can be found in such films as *Year 1914*, directed by Henryk Szaro, *Dodek on the Frontier* and *Heroes of Siberia*, both directed by Michal Waszynski, and *Madmen*, directed by Leonard Buczkowski. *Heroes of Siberia*, which deals with the true story of Polish prisoners of war, who in 1918 crossed Siberia in order to join the Polish army, is worth particular mention because in this film the legend of Pilsudski is promoted more extravagantly than in most films of the period. Pilsudski is portrayed not only as a commander of the Legions and a prominent politician but also as a figure with semi-divine qualities. The soldiers refer to him in reverential, semi-religious tones, his image constantly fills their imagination. This is often represented by the use of nondiegetic material – the soldiers' discussions of their motherland, their families or their future are intercut with the images of Pilsudski's stylized profile. The sanctification of Pilsudski is reminiscent of the way Stalin was portrayed in Russian Social Realist films of the 1930s and 1940s. It is worth mentioning that the film's premiere coincided with the peak of Pilsudski's myth, which followed his death and burial in Krakow's Wawel Castle, alongside the Polish kings.

Films such as *Heroes of Siberia*, *Year 1914*, *Madmen* and *Grave of the Unknown Soldier* typically put the War into the context of the Polish struggle for independence, which lasted for over a hundred years and emphasised the continuity of Polish culture. Many of their protagonists are descended from the insurrectionists of the 'January Uprising' of 1863 who fought against Russian authority. They are very religious, cherishing the traditions of Polish romanticism. In *Heroes of Siberia* even small children are taught about Frédéric Chopin and the nineteenth-century national poet-prophet, Tadeusz Mickiewicz.

With the exception of the unfaithful and hedonistic wife in the *Grave of the Unknown Soldier* all Polish women are moulded according to the sterotyped 'Polish mother', as used in *Florian*. Examples include Hanka in *Year 1914*, the lieutenant's wife in *Heroes of Siberia* or the officer's wife in *Dodek on the Frontier*. Similarly, Catholic priests are always represented as subtle leaders and the counsellors of ordinary people.

The narrative devices, used in *Florian*, are also typical of the genre. For example, the motif of the 'rescue at the last moment' of the Polish character persecuted by the enemy can be found in *Year 1914*, *Grave of the Unknown Soldier*, *Dodek on the Frontier* and *Madmen*. This dramatic construction (although it diminishes the realism) is a perfect way to show Polish bravery and cunning and the power of religious faith as salvation which comes in answer to a prayer or after visiting a church. Another device, applied in *Florian* and used extensively in many other films of the 1920s and 1930s, such as *Grave of the Unknown Soldier*, *Dodek on the Frontier* and *Madmen*, is to include a scene from the end of the War. For example, *Heroes of Siberia* includes the post-war ceremony of commemorating the 'heroes', who sacrificed their lives for an independent Poland, organised by those of their comrades who survived the march across Siberia and managed to reach their motherland. In *Madmen* the survivors from Pilsudski's Legions sing patriotic songs on the grave of their comrade. Juxtaposing the War with post-war reality shows that the fight for independence during the War was not in vain as it enabled the next generations to live in an independent nation.

I will argue that the films analysed in this chapter use the portrayal of World War One as vehicles to glorify a vision of Poland which is xenophobic, class-ridden and patriarchal. 'The promised land' fought for by the characters in *Florian*, *Heroes of Siberia*, *Year 1914* and many others is culturally homogenous, with one language – Polish – and one religion – Roman Catholicism. Poles remain apart from ethnic and religious minorities (Jews, Russians, Germans, Bielorussians, Ukrainians, etc.), treat them with distrust and try to marginalise them. Society is divided strictly into classes, but class conflict is avoided, because the lower classes recognise the superiority of the landowners and are happy to serve them. The landowning classes and Church hierarchy observe the customs and provide guidance for the rest of the nation. Women are cherished and deeply respected, but at the price of conforming to the

traditional female roles of mother, wife and guardian of patriotic traditions. To look for happiness outside the family, the Polish community and
their own social class is forbidden.

There are several factors which can help to illuminate this vision.
Firstly, the knowledge that Poland began its independent existence with
an inferiority complex and a deep distrust of its annexors partially
justifies the nationalism extolled in the films. The xenophobic content
can also be explained by a desire to create a single nation of Poles out of
disparate regions. Recollecting that the First World War was only the
final step on the long road to independence, marked by a series of
uprisings against the oppressors, also serves this goal by emphasising
the continuity of Polish history.

The flattering portrayal of Catholic priests was likewise an indicator
that Poland always existed as one nation, united by a common religion.
Moreover, the Roman Catholic Church played an important role in
preserving the Polish language and cultural traditions during more than
one hundred years of partition. The conciliatory portrayal of class
relations and almost unanimous condemnation of the Bolsheviks, on
the contrary, served to thwart the revolutionary desires of the working-
class audiences.

The only film-maker working in the inter-war period who applied a
different perspective was Jozef Lejtes, director of *Day after Day* (*Z dnia na
dzien*; 1928) and *Wild Fields* (*Dzikie pola*; 1932). The first film, in its
examination of the psychological consequences of the War, displays an
ideology close to Existentialism and a poetic tone, which can be compared
with the masterpiece of Mikhail Kalatozov, *The Cranes are Flying* (1957).
Day after Day tells the story of a Polish soldier, who after the war finds his
wife married to his friend and – unwilling to destroy her happiness –
departs for ever. *Wild Fields* refers to an even more dramatic even – the rape
of a young Polish woman by soldiers from a squadron of the White army.

Lejtes portrays all his characters, irrespective of their nationality and
military status, as casualties of the War. They seem not to be responsible
for other peoples' unhappiness – the War in which they are involved is the
ultimate cause of all misery. For example, the wife in *Day after Day* is not
responsible for her betrayal – she married another man because she was
told that her husband was dead. If the War had not happened, the couple
would have remained together. Similarly, although the rape, shown in *Wild
Fields*, is a deplorable act, the Russian soldiers who committed it are also
victims deserving compassion – they are demoralised by prolonged fighting, constant defeats, fear and hunger. Lejtes suggests that in peaceful
conditions they would behave very differently.

The pacifist tone, present in Lejtes's films, particularly in *Wild Fields*, expressed the views of the liberal Polish intelligentsia. However, in the same way that the voice of this social group was marginalised by the right-wing, nationalist authorities, so Lejtes was marginalised by the film industry. Evidence of this includes the problems he suffered with censorship during the production of *Wild Fields*.[3]

Interestingly, *Wild Fields* is also atypical of the films portraying World War One because of its sophisticated form – inventive, aesthetic images (photographed by German cinematographer, Franz Weihmayer) capturing lesser known features of the Polish landscape, original music, influenced by Polish folklore and editing inspired by Russian Montage.

WORLD WAR ONE IN FILMS MADE AFTER 1945

The Second World War changed Poland dramatically – with the nation again suffering serious devastation and even greater loss of life than during 1914–18 – five million people died and over 90 per cent of the Jewish population were exterminated. Moreover, the social and political system changed, moving from a market economy democracy to a communist system, where the state possessed and controlled the means of production, both material and cultural. Similarly, from being an enemy of Soviet Russia, Poland became its political, economic and military satellite.

The new political situation significantly influenced the status of cinematography. It became much less dependent on the tastes of ordinary audiences as profit was no longer the main motive for film-makers. As a result, the artistic quality of Polish cinema flourished – films made by such directors as Andrzej Wajda, Andrzej Munk, Jerzy Kawalerowicz, or Krzysztof Kieslowski became recognised abroad as masterpieces, a status which was never achieved by the film-makers of the inter-war period. However, the relative financial and artistic freedom of film-makers was achieved at the price of conforming to the communist ideology.

Political pressure on the film-makers and artists in general changed significantly during the communist period. It reached its zenith in the first half of the 1950s, which coincided with Stalinism and Social Realism. I would argue that after this period state intervention in artistic production in Poland was relatively minor, only discouraging film-makers from taking up certain themes, rather than controlling and censoring every aspect of film production.

10.1   *Lessons of a Dead Language* (National Film Archive, Warsaw)

Films about World War One, as with the whole cinematography after 1945, represent on average a much higher artistic standard than films of the earlier period. Recognition of this were the international awards given to such films as *Nights and Days* (*Noce i dnie*; 1975), *Austeria* (1982) and *Lesson of Dead Language* (*Lekcja martwego jezyka*; 1979). They also have a more personal style or at least from a contemporary perspective they seem to be more varied, though I cannot exclude that in fifty to seventy years time they will look more similar to each other than they look now. They cover a wider range of events and contain more historical and cultural details than their predecessors and have more complex characters and story lines. Paradoxically, they seem to be also less overtly political or propagandist and more subtle in promoting certain ideas or ideologies. Of the few common themes which can be connected with the political situation of post-World War Two Poland the most notable is pacifism. Other common characteristics include less interest in Polish-Russian affairs and avoidance of the question of Polish-Bolshevik relations. Instead, more emphasis is put on Polish-Austro-Hungarian or Polish-German affairs. The relative de-ideologisation of the First World War in post-1945 cinema can be partly explained by the simple fact of historical distance. After World War Two, World War One was perceived as a remote incident, without direct relevance to the lives of contemporary Poles.

10.2   *Nights and Days* (National Film Archive, Warsaw)

The only exception to the rule of avoiding controversial political themes is *Soldier of Victory* (*Zolnierz zwyciestwa*; 1953), directed by Wanda Jakubowska. This long (over four hours) and monumental film is a biography of one of the most famous Polish communist revolutionaries, General Karol Swierczewski, known also as Walter. A national hero in the 1950s, nowadays Swierczewski is regarded as a highly controversial figure, responsible for many military failures and atrocities, including the extermination during World War Two of hundreds of soldiers of the Home Army.

Jakubowska covers all important events of Swierczewski's life, from his childhood during the Revolution of 1905 to his tragic death in 1948, through World War One and the Bolshevik Revolution of 1917, the Russian Civil War of 1918–20, the Spanish Civil War and World War Two. In most of the events portrayed his role is hugely exaggerated. This applies particularly to the First World War and the Bolshevik Revolution where Swierczewski is represented as the second most important figure (after Stalin) in defeating the enemies of both Russia and Poland.

All events are shown from the particular ideological perspective of

Stalinism. In effect the World Wars and the Spanish Civil War are all regarded exclusively as a class war with workers and the bourgouisie fighting on opposing sides of the barricade. According to Jakubowska, during World War One Polish workers had the same objectives as workers from Russia or Germany and Polish landlords and factory owners the same as their counterparts from other countries. Also, typical of the era of its production, the film promotes the concept of constant 'vigilance' against conspiracy, warning against an international network of spies of the secret society of industrialists from Germany, Britain and the USA. As a result of applying a social realistic perspective, which reduces all wars to class conflict, the problem of establishing the Polish state, included in all films about World War One, made in the 1920s and 1930s, is ignored in Jakubowska's film.

As a consequence of the large number of actors and extras employed, extensive settings, numerous episodes, the long production time and high cost, *Soldier of Victory* can be regarded as a superproduction, the first in the history of Polish cinematography and one of only a handful made to date. The effect of Jakubowska's work is disquieting. It is hardly possible not to be appalled by the ideology of the film and to accept its numerous omissions, simplifications and 'modifications' of Polish history. For example, in the section concerning the First World War Pilsudski is completely ignored and secondary historical figures are portrayed as key politicians. Yet, it must be admitted that in spite of its historical inaccuracy or perhaps because of it, *Soldier of Victory* was a powerful tool of Stalinist propaganda. Moreover, due to its skilful montage which ignores chronology and holds in play several different scenes of action, its good acting and dashing production, especially of battle scenes, it succeeded dramatically and artistically. Recently, when the film was re-released by Polish television, some critics compared it to the films of Leni Riefenstahl.

Amongst the films in which the portrayal of World War One coincides with the promotion of pacifism, the most artistically accomplished are *Lesson of Dead Language* (*Lekcja martwego jezyka*; 1979) and *Austeria* (1982). The first, directed by Janusz Majewski, is set in the last months of the War, in the small Galician town of Turka, which lay just behind the front. People of different nationalities and cultural identities live there in relative harmony: Hungarians, Poles, Austrians, Jews and even Gypsies. Amongst them is a young lieutenant of the Austrian army, Alfred Kiekeritz – a Pole with an Austrian identity, sent to Turka because of worsening tuberculosis. He can be regarded as a true child of his time, marked by decadence, aestheticism and symbolism. He is sophisticated and well read, loves Mallarmé's poetry and disdains mundane, everyday tasks.

Kiekeritz's principal fascination is in death – this is reflected in his admiration for Mallarmé's poetry. He is fully aware of his own impending end, but tries to gain some kind of immortality by collecting *objets d'art* which he sends to his mother in Graz. The only piece he keeps is a small statue of Diana, found in a ruined estate in the Ukraine. Diana, goddess of hunting, symbolises his dream of being a hunter, soldier and killer. Although Kiekeritz has commanded a firing squad many times, executing soldiers from the Russian army, he never fired himself. He regards this as a weakness in his character and a missed opportunity to experience the most fascinating and intense pleasure of life. His chance comes while out stag hunting, when he encounters a Russian deserter, whom he kills. Several hours later he himself dies. The same day the end of the War is proclaimed.

The story of Kiekeritz can serve as a metaphor for what happened to culture as a whole. He failed to reach his potential, weakened by prolonged illness and brutalised by the War in the same way as his world was destroyed by 'the prolonged illness' of decadence and self-indulgence and then the 'sudden illness' of the War. The last words of Kiekeritz – 'Death is not fascinating – it is absurd' – obviously convey a pacifist message, strengthened by the construction of narrative and iconography. There is nothing heroic or glorious in Majewski's portrayal of the War, no signs of battlefields and victories, but only images of wounded, suffering soldiers, sent in hospital trains back to their countries and of corrupted civilians, trying to profit from the War.

In contrast to films made in the 1920s and 1930s which portrayed the end of World War One as the beginning of 'new life', a fresh start for millions of Poles who suffered a century of oppression, this film does not have any optimistic conclusions. Similarly, the whole question of Polish independence, which was a central theme for the previous generations of film-makers, hardly appears in this film. There is no one to fight for a free Poland as there is no single group of people with a distinct national identity. What brings them together or separates them is not their nationality or language, but their social background and intellectual interests.

This kind of cosmopolitism which is represented in *Lesson of Dead Language* was in tune with communist ideology, which emphasised the importance of class at the expense of nationality or ethnicity. However, this explanation is inaccurate or at best simplistic. *Lesson of Dead Language* appears to be a film without propagandists pretensions, which was meant to convey a personal vision and encourage a multitude of interpretations.

Kaiser's Deserters (C. K. Dezerterzy; 1985), made by the director of *Lesson of Dead Language*, Janusz Majewski, conveys similar values and messages as the earlier film, but using a different genre – comedy. Based on the novel by Kazimierz Sejda, which has been compared with *The Good Soldier Schweik* by Jaroslav Hasek, the film is set in the barracks of the Austro-Hungarian army at the end of the War. The barracks are populated by soldiers of the different nationalities forming the Austro-Hungarian state: Poles, Hungarians, Czechs, Jews and even Italians. They are indifferent towards the Austro-Hungarian state and the War – their favorite pastime is organising parties, visiting the neighbouring brothel and making jokes about their superiors. The best measure of their low morale is their decision to desert the army.

The core of the plot is the conflict between the multinational group of ordinary soldiers, led by a Pole, Kania, and the new Austrian deputy-commander of the garrison, Oberleutnant von Nogay. Kania and his

10.3   The multi-ethnic army, *The Kaiser's Deserters*
(National Film Archive, Warsaw)

companions – in the manner of the good soldier Schweik – give pleasure priority over duty and have no ethnic prejudices. They are open minded; their pacifism and detachment from political questions is portrayed by Majewski as a sign of their modernity. Even their decision to desert demonstrates their rationality – they realise that Austro-Hungary has lost the War and simply adjust to the new situation. Paradoxically, Kania and his comrades are not bad soldiering material. Their teamwork puts the Austrian officers to shame and – in contrast to their superiors who lose one battle after another – they always achieve their objectives.

Von Nogay, in contrast, epitomises the dysfunctions and aberrations of the Austrian military class. He is ambitious, nationalistic, intolerant and sadistic, reminding one of Colonel Redl from Istvan Szabo's film of the same name. His main aim is to change a bunch of layabouts into 'true soldiers of the Kaiser'. Von Nogay is, however, condemned to failure because he lives in a fictional world – the concept of the powerful and monolithic Austro-Hungarian state in which he strongly believes belongs to the past.

Kaiser's Deserters celebrates multiculturalism and promotes the idea of human solidarity transcending national, cultural and religious barriers. Yet, in spite of this, one can discern a hint of nationalism, conveyed in the portrayal of the main characters – Kania, the only Pole among the deserters, is also the cleverest and most charismatic among them. This feature can be explained by the film's literary roots – in the novel by Sejda, first published in the 1930s, when nationalistic ideas were very strong in Poland.

As previously mentioned, Jewish characters are portrayed in both Majewski's films. Although they do not play a large part in the narrative, their relatively sympathetic portrayal indicates the change in social attitude towards them between the 1930s and 1970s or 1980s. *Austeria*, made in 1982 by Jerzy Kawalerowicz and based on a novel by Julian Stryjkowski, the most prominent Polish Jewish writer of the twentieth century, is an even better example of how attitudes towards the Jews have changed in post-1945 Poland. Central to the story is the old fatalistic and sceptical Jewish owner of an inn (*austeria*), named Tag. In 1914, at the outbreak of the War in Galicia, he refuses to abandon his inn. Instead, he provides the refugees with milk and bread and gives shelter to neighbouring Chasids. Being poor and isolated from the wider community of Jews, they had nowhere to go. Moreover, as mystics, concentrating on their dialogue with God and ignoring the material world, Chasids[4] seem to be completely unaware of the danger nearby. They pray, sing and dance ecstatically, becoming more and more entranced.

10.4   *Austeria* (National Film Archive, Warsaw)

The last stage of their bliss is taking off their clothes and running naked to the neighbouring lake. When they reach the water, the sound of exploding bombs is heard.

The last scene of the film, showing the water red with blood, was interpreted as a metaphor of Jewish destiny in the twentieth century – an anticipation of the Holocaust. By comparing the fate of the Jews during World War One with what happened to them in World War Two, the authors of *Austeria* inevitably shift the focus of attention from the peculiarities of 1914 to war as a universal experience of death and destruction. All the political questions and arguments, so fiercely discussed in the films made before 1939, are presented as unimportant or irrelevant in *Austeria*. None of Kawalerowicz's characters, neither Jewish nor Polish, care about Poland or Austro-Hungary. They identify not with a state, a country or a nation, but their town or – as in case of Tag – their house and place of work. The title of the film – *Austeria* – symbolises the importance of the 'small homeland' in the lives of Poles before 1914.

The Jews in *Austeria* contradict cultural stereotypes, being neither a homogenous nor integrated group. On the contrary, they form a society containing people with very different lifestyles and values. Many of them prefer the company of 'outsiders' rather than other Jews. Among them is the aristocratic owner of a large estate who, being a popular figure in Vienna's salons, was admired by the Kaiser himself. Another Jewish woman has an extra-marital affair with a Hungarian officer. Tag has a lover who is his Ukrainian servant and has friends amongst people from many different nationalities. For the rich Jews living in towns, owners of casinos, wholesale businesses and shops, war means only the danger of losing money and property. Chasids, in contrast, do not care for material goods. The only person who seems to have a clear vision of the consequences of the War for Jews and the world as a whole is Tag. As the film progresses, he gains the qualities of a sage and prophet.

Austeria can be regarded as the ideological antithesis to *Florian*. *Florian* promoted the idea of Poland as a country of one language, one nation and one religion, and portrayed the Jews as its enemy; *Austeria* celebrates the multiculturalism of pre-war Galicia, representing Jews as an integral and precious element, and promotes the concept of local patriotism. In *Florian* the condemnation of war was conditional – wars are bad when they serve the interests of Poland's enemies and acceptable when Poland gains from participating in them. *Austeria*, in contrast, denounces all war as a crime against humanity.

Nights and Days (1975), based on an epic masterpiece, written in 1932–4 by the left-wing writer and publicist Maria Dabrowska, although set on the first day of World War One, can hardly be classified as a film about the War as such. It encompasses over fifty years of living in Russian Poland by a couple of disinherited and pauperised aristocrats, Bogumil and Barbara. The film takes the form of a flashback – the first day of the War is the last day of the story, told by Barbara, who in 1914 is an elderly widow, forced to leave her hometown of Kaliniec, which was destroyed by the Germans. Her and her husband's lives, although ordinary, full of hard work and child rearing, are on balance happy, meaningful and worth living. This contrasts with the War, represented as an agent of chaos and destruction of individual lives and a whole culture. *Nights and Days* neither represents the 'good side' of the War nor shows any involvement of Poles in the conflict. Poles, mainly ordinary families who are forced to leave their belongings and flee, are portrayed as victims. One can infer that for these people a secure home meant more than an independent Poland.

As in many films, made before 1939, *Nights and Days* shows people who took part in the nineteenth-century uprisings against Russian authority. The main character, Bogumil himself, took part and was wounded during the 1863 'January Uprising'. However, after this event, which resulted in his family losing their estate and him being forced to work as an estate manager for others, he became very sceptical about the value of military struggle. For Bogumil ordinary life matters more than a glorious death, and everyday work in the fields meant more than fighting for the motherland. Several times in the film he is heard saying: 'It does not matter who possess the fields – Poles or Russians, as long as they are well served' and 'fields last longer and are more important than the people who own them'. I would suggest that the concept of the 'small homestead', represented by both Tag, prepared to stay in his *austeria* even in the event of war, and by Bogumil, devoted to the estate where he worked and spent most of his life and believing in the intrinsic value of the land, oppose the nationalism promoted in films made in the 1920s and 1930s and advocate pacifism.

Pacifism and anti-nationalism are not the only ideological differences between films made before and after World War Two. The representation of women is another indicator of how Poland changed during this period. It is worth remembering that in the films made in the 1920s and 1930s women were portrayed as a valuable part of society, but it was equally assumed that they must conform to the rule of patriarchy.

In the post-1945 films, on the contrary, emphasis is put on World War One as a chance for women to live their own, independent lives. During the War the women in *Austeria, Lesson of Dead Language* and *Kaiser's Deserters* discover their sexuality, enjoy extra-marital liaisons and use their female charm to their own financial advantage. Moreover, they are no longer patriotic – either they hate and despise the War for depriving them of their beloved or enjoy their new situation, marked by greater sexual and social freedom, or are completely indifferent towards the men's affairs of fighting and killing. Many of their lovers are actually 'foreigners' – Hungarian or Austrian officers or local Jewish businessmen who grow rich during the War.

The most suggestive portrayal of the 'new woman', born during World War One, is included in *Bow of Eros (Łuk Erosa;* 1987), directed by Jerzy Domaradzki. This film, based on a novel by Juliusz Kaden-Bandrowski, which in inter-war Poland was regarded as scandalous, places at the centre of the story Maria, the young wife of a university lecturer from Cracow, who leaves home in order to join the Austrian army. Left with very little money and a son to look after, Maria embarks on affairs with men from diverse backgrounds. Some of the men she encounters with genuine interest and sympathy, others become her lovers only because of the money they can offer her.

In *Bow of Eros* the breaking of sexual taboos is accompanied by the breaking of class divisions. During the War Maria's servant, Nastka, a typical, shy 'country-girl' with bad manners, becomes a successful and self-confident businesswoman, keeping a brothel which is visited mainly by the 'high society' of Cracow. It is also Nastka who owns the cabaret where Maria performs. The best indicator of Nastka's new, high status and, simultaneously, the financial and social decline of the upper classes is her marriage to an elderly university professor.

As with the films, discussed previously, *Bow of Eros* advocates pacifism. Those men who left their families in order to fight for their motherland return home disillusioned and bitter. They describe the War as an absurd nightmare and wish they had stayed at home. Some of them even used bribes in order to desert safely from the Austrian army. As in *Lesson of Dead Language*, the end of the War marks the end of the film. Yet, again, nobody celebrates and nobody notices that the end of the War means a new, independent life for their motherland.

In conclusion I would suggest that films made after 1945 try to break away from the nationalism and parochialism, so characteristic of films made in the 1920s and 1930s, and instead portray the War mainly as a universal experience, shared by people irrespective of their ethnicity, class and gender. Moreover, they perceive World War One as a malignant force for destruction of lives and cultures rather than as a beginning of Polish independence. Nostalgia for what was lost in 1914 is much stronger than joy at what was gained in 1918.

One can ask which of the visions, provided by the different films, examined in this study, is closer to historical reality. Although I identify with such films as *Austeria* and *Lesson of Dead Language* and reject *Florian*, I suggest that this question cannot be answered in a categorical way, as historical reality does not exist as such, but is always a product of interpretation or reconstruction, which necessarily contains a degree of subjectivity. My aim has been to show that films about World War One made at various periods have served changing political and cultural purposes – that they were all 'children' of the time of their production. Consequently, all of them provide at least as good an insight into the Polish post-World War One history and the history of Polish cinematography as into the War itself.

NOTES

1   There is considerable controversy surrounding Pilsudski's stance on the question of Polish independence. I present the most common opinion amongst both Polish and foreign historians. However, according to *Encyclopaedia Britannica*, he predicted that 'the Central Powers would be victorious against Russia, but would finally suffer defeat in the west; and that consequently Poles should side with them during the first phase of the war and turn against them later'. See Bernard Newman, *Portrait of Poland* (London: Robert Hale Limited, 1959), pp. 30–1.

2   Compare Wladyslaw Banaszkiewicz and Witold Witczak, *Historia filmu polskiego*, tom I, *1895–1929* (Warszawa: Wydawnictwa Artystyczne i Filmowe, 1966); Barbara Armatys, Leszek Armatys and Wieslaw Stradomski, *Historia filmu polskiego*, tom II, *1930–1939* (Warszawa: Wydawnictwa Artystyczne i Filmowe, 1988).

3   Barbara Armatys, Leszek Armatys and Wieslaw Stradomski, *Historia filmu polskiego*, tom II, *1930–1939* (Warszawa: Wydawnictwa Artystyczne i Filmowe, 1988), p. 259.

4   Hasid, Hassid, Chasid or Chassid: (1) a sect of Jewish mystics founded in Poland about 1750, characterised by religious zeal and a spirit of prayer, joy and charity; (2) a Jewish sect of the second century BC, formed to combat Hellenistic influences. See *Collins English Dictionary* (London and Glasgow: Collins, 1979).

AVAILABILITY OF THE FILMS DISCUSSED

BROADCAST BY TELEWIZJA POLONIA, A SATELLITE CHANNEL OF THE POLISH STATE TELEVISION, AIMED AT POLES LIVING ABROAD, THE MAJORITY OF THEM WITH ENGLISH SUBTITLES

Austeria, (1982), dir. Jerzy Kawalerowicz

Dodek on the Frontier (*Dodek na froncie*; 1935), dir. Michal Waszynski

Florian (1936) dir. Leonard Buczkowski

Heroes of Siberia (*Bohaterowie Sybiru*; 1936), dir. Michal Waszynski

Kaiser's Deserters (*C. K. Dezerterzy*; 1985), dir. Janusz Majewski

Lesson of Dead Language (*Lekcja martwego jezyka*; 1979), dir. Janusz Majewski

Miracle on the Vistula (*Cud nad Wisla*; 1921), dir. Ryszard Boleslawski

Nights and Days (*Noce i dnie*; 1975), dir. Jerzy Antczak

Year 1914 (*Rok 1914; 1932*), dir. Henryk Szaro

AVAILABLE ON VIDEO IN POLAND

Austeria (1982), dir. Jerzy Kawalerowicz
Bow of Eros (*Luk Erosa*; 1987), dir. Jerzy Domaradzki
Kaiser's Deserters (*C. K. Dezerterzy*; 1985), dir. Janusz Majewski
Lesson of Dead Language (*Lekcja martwego jezyka*; 1979), dir. Janusz Majewski
Nights and Days (*Noce i dnie*; 1975), dir. Jerzy Antczak

IN POSSESSION OF POLISH NATIONAL FILM ARCHIVE, WARSAW

Day after Day (*Z dnia na dzien*; 1928), dir. Jozef Lejtes
Grave of the Unknown Soldier (*Mogila nieznanego zolnierza*; 1927), dir. Ryszard Ordynski
Madmen (*Szalency*; 1928), dir. Leopold Buczkowski
Soldier of Victory (*Zolnierz zwyciestwa*; 1953), dir. Wanda Jakubowska
Wild Fields (*Dzikie pola*; 1932), dir. Jozef Lejtes
None of the films are available on video in Britain.

11

The Experience of the First World War and the German Film

Rainer Rother
[translated by Susan Anna Gunther]

INTRODUCTION

In November 1998 when the eightieth anniversary of Armistice Day was remembered the recently elected German Chancellor raised eyebrows by declining to join in the commemorations in France. This non-participation demonstrates a clear difference concerning the importance attached to the official commemorations of the First World War in Britain and France on the one hand and Germany on the other. This difference has existed for decades; the First World War cannot compete in scale with the horrors of the Nazi period which understandably carries more weight in the German mind when trying to reconcile itself with its recent past. This is why virtually all relevant discussions on the 'politics of remembrance' in Germany are almost exclusively concerned with the systematic murder of millions of people during the Second World War.

It is therefore not very likely that a reassessment of First World War events, as happened in Great Britain with changing views on military leadership or in France with a reappraisal of the mutineers of 1917, would cause any great controversy in Germany. Indeed, there are no comparable developments in Germany. It is part of the especially German view of the First World War that it is seen as belonging utterly to the past. As a consequence of this very few post-1945 films ever let that 'distant' war play a part; and if they do it is to show how irrelevant these past events are today.

It is, however, a different matter for the pre-1945 period: here World War One was an important and controversial topic in literature, painting and film, just as in other European states. Germany also shared with her neighbours comparable views on the War, at least up to the Nazi seizure of power. And included in that common ground must be the silence which first shrouded most matters concerning the War, but this is only seemingly a paradox.[1]

Walter Benjamin in his essay 'Der Erzähler' (The Narrator) provides one reason for this. Benjamin treats 'the narrator' as a disappearing character whose form of aesthetic representation is no longer suited to modern circumstances. It is not easy to reconcile Benjamin's main interest with the enthusiasm he affords film as a medium and its ability to 'exercise man in those new conscious perceptions and reactions required by the handling of new technological equipment'.[2] The differ-ence between narration, 'the potential that appeared to us inalienable, the most secure thing amongst secure things',[3] and the new medium of film is obvious. It is hardly exaggeration to assume that in those days 'narration' and 'film' represented in Benjamin's view were not only historically distinct but also aesthetically opposite forms.[4]

The disappearance of narration is based on the loss of narratability; the possibilities offered by narration can no longer catch up with modern society, or so it seemed to Benjamin and other thinkers of his time. The potential that now seems lost to narration is this:

To exchange experiences. The cause of this phenomenon is obvious: experience has been devalued. And it looks as if it is falling into an abyss. Any glance at a newspaper proves that experience has hit a new low, that not only our picture of the external world but also our picture of the moral world has undergone changes over night that nobody would have thought possible. With the World War a new process has surfaced. Had not people noticed at the end of the war that soldiers returned mute from the battlefield? Not richer – but poorer in communicable experience. What ten years later became a flood that poured itself into books on the war was anything but experience that travels from mouth to mouth. And that was by no means strange for never had experiences been more thoroughly proven to be lies, the strategic ones by trench warfare, the economic ones by inflation, the flesh and blood ones by the battles of material, the moral ones by the people in power. A generation that had still been taken to school in the horse-tram found themselves under open sky in a landscape where nothing remained unchanged except the clouds above, and under those clouds in a field of destructive currents and explosions was the tiny, fragile human body.[5]

Benjamin's view, anchored in the philosophy of history, connects the notion of experience with that of narration. The decay of both points indirectly to the alternative: film. If one asks if films produced in Germany about World War One had a similar thinking behind them, then the answer must surely be no. But it must be admitted that the medium of film has the potential to give shape to an 'experience' in a way which is really a denial of the most common characteristics of experience: constancy and communicability. Obviously this potential has rarely been used, and not only in Germany. In the following pages I shall attempt to distinguish those phases in which very different solutions were found for the medium of film either due to technological developments or to differing political circumstances and conditions.

THE GERMAN FILM IN THE FIRST WORLD WAR

The outbreak of war confronted the German film industry with dramatically changed circumstances. Staff were conscripted and the day-to-day working routine became at the least more restricted. Films from enemy countries disappeared, and because of the importance of French films at the time there was a shortage of films for German cinemas.[6] During the first months of the War the public's interest in 'war pictures' provided some compensation for this shortage as did later on the increased production of German companies and the activities of the Danish controlled Nordic Film Co.[7]

Two different phases can be distinguished for feature films as well as topical productions. With documentary films the focus of enthusiasm and interest was initially on military pictures. The fact that footage shown to the public had not been taken at the front became, only later in the War, a problem that was actually discussed in public.[8] During the course of the War the restrictions on cameramen and film companies were touched upon in several film storylines but cinema owners complained that the films either bored the viewers or drove them out of the cinema altogether because these pictures did not contain the spectacular battle scenes the advertisements promised, and which the audience had come to see. The military strictly controlled[9] all access to war locations –

especially the front – that promised interesting footage, but even the military came to realise that their own propaganda was not achieving its aims either at home or in the neutral foreign countries and therefore needed urgent improvement.

A similar development can be observed in feature films. Here, too, productions that treated the war front in the same way as the 1870/1 war were at first quite popular. One could call them 'exploitation movies', but demand for them receded just as quickly as did the hope of a speedy victory. In this genre, endeavours were made from around 1916 to replace those films with scripts that did more justice to reality. The audience had seen enough faked 'original' footage and their preferences reverted to more entertaining pictures. In this respect the German film underwent developments very similar to those encountered in the other combatant countries. An indication of these changes was the fact that from 1916 even film was roped in to launch an appeal for the signing of war loans.[10] During that year the Organisation der Bildpropaganda im Deutschen Reich (Organisation for Picture Propaganda in the German Reich) was reorganised and finally, on 30 January 1917, BUFA, The Bild- und Filmamt (Picture and Film Authority), was founded.[11] This was in no small part a reaction to British and French war propaganda which the German government considered to be far more successful than its own.

The efficacy of this measure was in many ways minimal. For the newsreels and even the 'official' military documentary films that were now produced were little different from what had gone before.

> All the restrictions placed on the newsreel were also placed on the official film. Despite the change in attitude towards film, the restriction on content remained. As a result of this, the overwhelming majority of the preserved footage gives the impression of a war that was traditional in nature and which had simply been given an added dimension in the form of new weaponry.[12]

This revealed itself in the first film, *Bei unseren Helden an der Somme* (*With Our Heroes on the Somme*), which was premiered on 17 January 1917.[13] Here we find under the official seal the promise of 'authentic footage' and the press did indeed treat it as if it was and referred to the film as 'a document of the World War'[14] suggesting that the film would encourage, 'respect for the much-maligned medium of film for here it turns into history'.[15] Obviously the press reaction was intended to support the aims of war propaganda – but in no way can it be assumed that this reflected an honest opinion concerning the achievements of the

11.1   Cover of the booklet based on the propaganda film
Heroes on the Somme (Alf Peacock)

film. The fake scenes, the weak shots taken during manoeuvres used in the film must have been transparent to viewers even at the time. Yet since this BUFA film had been intended to be Germany's answer to Britain's *The Battle of the Somme* anything less than the highest praise let alone any negative criticism would have made patently obvious the failure of German film propaganda. It is difficult to imagine that audiences seeing the film would have felt the same reaction to the image of war that had been achieved by the British film.[16] The somewhat curt and pithy remark by a German diplomat that *Bei unseren Helden* was a well-posed war film is more to the point than the enthusiasm shown by some reviewers.[17]

But this first BUFA film remained a model for subsequent productions. Some of its successors, however, were able to show a marked improvement in one respect: in *Bei unseren Helden* it was unlikely that any 'authentic' footage had been used; mostly it was from manoeuvres which had to stand in for events at the front, a handicap some of the later films were able to avoid. They offered footage that had been recorded *in situ*. But this did not signal an end to other restrictions. Even in later films there were hardly any battle-worn, exhausted or dead German soldiers but only well-cared for wounded men and plenty of Allied prisoners. There were explosions (stock shots), the firing of heavy guns, and marching, advancing and supposedly attacking troops. In a word, it was an ensemble of shots to *suggest* the theatre of war – and even if the real battlefield was shown, the footage had been shot before or after the actual combat. Mühl-Benninghaus quotes the 1917 film *Oesel genommen* (*Oesel Is Taken*) as a good example because it shows the interplay of ships, aircraft and troops, yet no actual battle scenes. This particular restriction of not showing battle seems to have applied to all BUFA productions, despite the urgent requests from Germanophile foreign cinema owners who wanted something to compete with the popularity of *The Battle of the Somme* and which BUFA was simply unable to supply.[18]

Like the Oesel film the 1917 production *Zu den Kämpfen um Tarnopol* (*The Fighting around Tarnopol*) also omits any scenes of the fighting mentioned in the title but simply records Austrian troops advancing, prominent commanders like Prince Eitel Friedrich, General Field Marshal Leopold of Bavaria and even Wilhelm II visiting the troops, Russian POWs, captured weapons and destroyed houses – all the things that offered an interesting perspective on the fighting are here, but nothing more. Even as late as 1918 BUFA produced a film on the German Spring offensive *Vonder Westfront* (*On the Western Front*) which received a devastating assessment by Count Kessler of the German Embassy in Berne,

> My disappointment was indescribable. This film which supposedly was to portray an event of world historical proportions might as well have been pasted together from old Messter newsreels. It does not convey the slightest impression of the battle in the West or the grand scale of events there. There are just a few very dull shots (in most cases quite obviously taken far behind the front) that are strung together with no skill and no uniting thought behind them.[19]

Even films BUFA categorised as 'great military films' – like the 'Seagull film' *Graf Dohna und seine Möwe* (*Count Dohna and His Seagull*) and *DER magische Gürtel* (*The Magic Belt*) did not – according to BUFA's internal assessment – achieve the desired result since they had 'only occasionally been reviewed by the better critics of the newspapers' and 'with a distinct lack of support'.[20] The impact of such films on foreign audiences remained problematic. Thus the sinking of ships was seen in Switzerland more as proof of German barbarism than as a means of making the audience sympathetic towards Germany's cause. This is why the Auswärtige Amt (Foreign Office) sent the following reply to the Netherlands when the 'Seagull film' was requested,

Concerning the Seagull film . . . we do not consider this film as suitable propaganda because of the concern that exists in neutral countries vis-à-vis U-boat warfare. Apart from being shown once in front of an invited audience in Stockholm, the film has only had a release to the general public in Switzerland where it was given a pretty derisive reception so that we had to prevent any further showing. Unless there are special reasons for showing the film in the Netherlands, we have no interest in testing the film on a Dutch audience.[21]

Such self-criticism seems perfectly appropriate because, apart from the above mentioned 'military films', only the handful of films to promote war loans and *Unsuhnbar* (*Unatonable*) by Georg Jacoby, 1917, can be viewed as exemplary. Films that included the promotion of war loans were not produced before the fifth war loan – and even the poster campaign for war loans only used picture designs from the sixth edition onwards.[22] Concerning feature films, those produced by Vaterländischer Filmvertrieb (Patriotic Film Distribution Company)[23] are interesting: aesthetically because they use all kinds of trick shots and aim at an effective and humorous storyline; and politically because they offer an image of the enemy.

As far as propaganda is concerned, the image of the enemy was developed much earlier by the Entente Powers – where the German soldier was depicted as the barbaric Hun with a spiked helmet.[24] Their justification for war was the invasion of neutral Belgium by German troops and the atrocities committed by German soldiers. The propagandist display of war crimes and 'atrocities' went on during the course of the War and the image of the 'Hun' was even further intensified after America's entry into the War. Irrespective of the question of whether these allegations were true or not[25] the German propaganda machine had to respond otherwise neutral countries might see silence as an admission of guilt. Therefore in German films German soldiers were shown in the occupied territories as respectful to the inhabitants and playing with the children to underline their humane conduct.

In German propaganda Britain was pictured as the exploiter of nations and 'John Bull' the aggressive figure that appeared again and again. The film *Das Saugetier* (*Suckling Animal*), 1916, shows Britain as the exploiter of the world – literally draining the life blood from other nations. But such images were only rarely used. Another example is the 1916 production *Der Heimat Schützengraben* (*The Homeland's Protective Trench*) where the appeal for war loans is combined with a depiction of a vicious enemy. A refugee from Eastern Germany comes to a village and tells of his fate – in flashback the viewer sees another village that has been destroyed by Russian troops. The random brutality of the Russians is explained more in the captions than shown in the pictures. But the conclusion is obvious: wife and daughter have been killed and his house destroyed; with the Russians in Eastern Prussia everyone has to do his bit to save the nation from a barbaric enemy. This type of enemy image could, for obvious reasons, only rarely be employed as long as German-troops were on French and Belgian soil. From the middle years of the War the aim of the pictures of destruction and devastation was to document for home audiences the fate Germany would have to suffer if the front did not hold. In other words, the destruction of towns and villages in France was depicted as the potential threat in Germany's future. In most films this message is only implied but is often linked to apportioning the blame for the War to Germany's adversaries. As early as *Bei unseren Helden* a caption blames British and French artillery for the destruction of Péronne just as later films underline the role of enemy artillery as the main cause of devastation in the occupied territories. In purely objective terms it is of course true that after the freezing of the front lines it was indeed Entente artillery that caused the destruction. As the War dragged on, the 'Feldgrauen' were not only portrayed to home audiences as fighting a defensive war but came themselves to believe that that was what they were doing in the face of countless allied offensives.[26]

Films like *Die Räumung einer Stadt im bedrohten Gebiet – Wytschae-tebogen*, BUFA, 1917 (*The Evacuation of a Town in a Threatened Area – Wytschaete*) or *Woevre-Städte als Opfer der Französischen Artillerie*, BUFA, 1917 (*Towns in the French Woëvre Region as Victims of French Artillery*) reinforce this theme more explicitly. The message is particu-larly clearly expressed in a film released by the censors as late as 12 October 1918: *Rentier Kulickes flug zur Front* (*Prosperous Mr Kulicke Is Flown to the Front*). Kulicke, a well-nourished citizen, does not wish to contribute to the latest war loan campaign and is consequently plagued by a nightmare. Two pilots enter his bedroom, pick him up and take him to their plane. Kulicke is then given an aerial tour of the front. He thus gains an insight into the reality of war. This reality consists of devastated countryside and cities, while a caption explains, 'St. Quentin, once a flourishing town with a population of almost 100,000 – famous for its cathedral'. The cathedral, of course, is just as much a ruin as the rest of the town and Kulicke now understands the obvious message: 'Please, aviator, fly me back home, if possible to the White Swan Inn, I must tell the people there how grateful we at home must be to the Army for fighting the war on enemy soil.'

Kulicke explicitly stated a thought that many front-line soldiers had on their minds – they, too, wanted to save the homeland from devastation. But we cannot assume that Kulicke's message, at a time of widespread yearning for peace and in the face of massive German desertions, still possessed any power to convince. In *Rentier Kulicke* we find a striking mixture of reconstructed and original footage, a combination that was to be found in other films like *U-Boote heraus. Mit U-178 gegen Den Feind*, BUFA, 1917 (*U-Boats into Action: With U-Boat 178 against the Enemy*), for example. But feature films also tried to serve the German 'cause' in their way. The first films had counted on uniforms and flags to ensure their success and made little endeavour to achieve credibility or explain the real military situation. However, such films disappeared after the first months of war and were retrospectively criticised as particularly despicable examples of the speculative nature of cinema.[27] Feature films that tried to show at least some of the everyday reality of war remained quite rare during the next years few years as well. The fore-mentioned film *Unsühnbar* tells of sabotage and spying activities on the home front. *Das Tagebuch des Dr. Hart*, Paul Leni, 1916 (*Dr Hart's Diary*) developed its plot from the conflict – as supposed by the Germans – between Polish nationalism and Russian rule – but even here they were unsuccessful, just as German propagandists generally were with their attempts to bring the Polish population onto their side. The film *Der gelbe Schein* (*The Yellow Glow*) 1918, which was only premiered on 22 November 1918, tried to use the sufferings of a young Jewish woman, played by Pola Negri, in Tsarist Russia as an argument in favour of the Central Powers. However, German feature films, even by the end of the War, had never really been able to develop any skill for appropriately communicating the reality of war at the front.

The German film had undergone remarkable changes during World War One. With BUFA the beginnings of a central agency for film propaganda had been created,[28] and with Ufa (Universal Film Company), a year later, a financially strong film combine had been brought into existence. Yet neither the concentration of official propaganda nor the creation of a 'patriotic' combine had, in the final analysis, the desired result. In the field of documentary the restrictions the military imposed on film-makers prevented realistic pictures of the front being shot, and thus robbed the films that were released of all persuasive power. With feature films economic considerations were naturally paramount: at the beginning of the War audiences wanted uniforms and military subjects but very soon tired of this and wanted entertainment. And entertainment was provided by Ufa through comedies, thrillers and adventure films and only exceptionally through films with a propaganda element. Thus we can conclude that while many attempts were made to press the film industry into serving the needs of the War, these attempts were on the whole unsuccessful. No attempt had been made to present on screen the real war of the front line or even conditions at home.

THE WEIMAR REPUBLIC

In 1936 Walter Benjamin observed that for a period of almost ten years after the end of the War hardly any war memoirs had been published, and he could well have included war films as well. It was really Hollywood, through films like *The Four Horsemen of the Apocalypse* (Rex Ingram, 1921)[29] and *The Big Parade* (King Vidor, 1925), that discovered the World War as a subject for cinema and which developed narratives to disseminate the popular view of the War. In marked contrast to the war years with their endorsement and enthusiasm, the Great War in retrospect appeared to be first and foremost senseless. Yet the simplistic friend-foe pattern still emerged in Ingram's film with its German 'barbarians'. Yet even this could no longer hide the general sense of futility. The enemy image which had nowhere been applied in a more stereotypical and one-sided fashion than in some American wartime films was now replaced by stressing the individual suffering that was common to all sides.

In contrast, Germany began to analyse the War in film somewhat later and initially in a different form. Ufa, which itself was born in the spirit of propaganda,[30] released in 1927 *Der Weltkrieg* (*The World War*), a film in two parts[31] (written by George Soldan and Erich Otto Volkmann[32] and directed by Leo Lasko). The film is a compilation that became exemplary for its mixture of original footage and reconstructed scenes and above all its trick shots. Lasko's film was supposed to portray the War without bias, and reference to the original footage used in the film underlined this claim. Part 1, premiered in 1927, fulfilled the expectations of the distributors and proved one of the most successful films of the season.[33] The critics, however, were not universally full of praise, which is not surprising considering the subject.[34] Bernhard von Brentano's judgment exposes the weaknesses of the film in a very precise manner:

> The mistake of this film is its *cowardice*. The authors are constantly beating about the bush . . . they did not want to hurt anyone, but they

offended everyone . . . The authors treat the subject as historical forgetting that the players are sitting in the stalls . . . Of course, one does not want to condemn the attempt to create a film about the war. This kind of film must be produced. There is no other topic of more concern to all of us. But the attempt must be made by courageous men. It is not good enough to view our fate between 1914 and 1918 as neutral . . . The dead are still alive.[35]

So it was not bias but the presumption of impartiality that made critics angry with this film. Indeed nothing at all is found in this film about the experience of the soldiers in the field. Falling back on contemporary 'documentary footage' we have scenes of the soldiers' 'leisure time', marching troops, units attacking, occasionally we see wounded men (mostly Germans) and sometimes soldiers killed in action (mostly French). The weaknesses of this approach are inevitable *and* intended – 'A lot of generals and princes are strutting about the canvas. But the unknown soldier and the unknown mother are missing. Truth is missing. Truth is the task of the Republic'.[36]

Der Weltkrieg is not a very ambitious chronicle. It shows no interest in the causes of the War nor in the consequences for individuals and societies. Nothing is said about German politics, the aims and interests before the War, the configuration of European powers at the time, treaty obligations, mobilisations, or declarations of war. It sees the War as a sort of trial for the German nation and delineates its course mainly with the help of ingenious trick shots which enabled the director to make military operations on the battlefield comprehensible, but the combat footage used was irrelevant due to wartime restrictions.[37]

It is Noldan's trick shots alone that proved innovative: but compilation films enriched with reconstructed scenes found imitators abroad as well as in Germany although sometimes in slightly different form.[38] As far as one can tell from the preserved version of the film, its disadvantage lies not in its political message (which accepts war as natural and is far from critical in its assessment of German politics or the military leaders of the Reich), but in its failure to address the questions that pose themselves to the survivors. Nowhere did Leo Lasko fulfil the demands made by Bernhard von Brentano who stated, with American films in mind,

> It is sad to have to see this great difference: while America approaches the subject with dash and vigour, shooting battle scenes that make you shudder, populating the canvas with soldier types, German and others . . . inspiring uniformed men one can identify with, who a dark and bloody

fate has changed for ever; yet here we shoot such void, daft stuff . . .
nothing that could, even with the best will, help any good cause.[39]

Brentano's complaint, written in connection with Karl Grune's 1927 film
Am Rande der Welt (*At the Edge of the World*) but not restricted to this
film alone, would have been equally appropriate for *Unsere Emden* (*Our
Ship Emden*, 1926, dir. Louis Ralph).[40] None of the German silent movies
would have been able to carry out Brentano's demand and probably
would not have wanted to.

> The whole of Europe has lost the World War but only Germany knows it
> . . . Those in Germany who know that this great war − immeasurably
> heroically conducted and victorious in a thousand battles − was horren-
> dously lost, those will never more help a past to become a future.[41]

This viewpoint strikes one as surprisingly modern because the World
War is not seen in exclusively national terms − but it *is* in Lasko's film.
Here he follows in tone the releases of the Supreme Command and does
not even try to see the War as a European catastrophe. As a portrayal of
the war *experience*[42] it is disappointing and together with its refusal to
inquire into the causes of this putatively unavoidable war it makes *Der
Weltkrieg* a merely corroborating text.[43]

For today's viewer the biggest deficit of the film must be the boredom it
induces − a curse common in many other German films of the Weimar
period. The reason is that they only wanted to approach the subject of the
War with the intention of not causing offence to anyone. They pretended
to analyse the past but were really about the future and reconciliation.
Only a handful of films managed to find a convincing answer to the two
opposing views − to show the War as a heroic event or as an unprecedented massacre. Both types see the war experience as central (and thus
follow the example set by American war films). On the one hand there are
the stories of heroic perseverance and endurance like *Berge in Flammen*
(*Mountains on Fire*, 1931, dirs Karl Hartl, Luis Trenker), or *Morgenrot*
(*Red Sky at Dawn*, 1933, dir. Gustav Ucicky) and on the other stories of
annihilation − *Westfront 1918* (1930, dir. Georg Wilhelm Pabst), *Die
andere Seite* (*The Other Side*, 1931, dir. Heinz Paul) and *Niemandsland*
(*No Man's Land*, 1931, dir. Victor Trivas).

Apart from these films which revealed most clearly how the War was
imagined in the collective memory of society, there were certain genres of
film in which the War formed only a backdrop. Spy films in particular
come to mind like *Die Nacht der Entscheidung* (*The Night of Decision*,

Dimitri Buchowetzki, 1931), *Die unsichtbare Front* (*The Invisible Front*, Richard Eichberg, 1932) and *Unter falscher Flagge* (*Under False Colours*, Johannes Meyer, 1932). At times attempts were made to explain the origins of the War as a mixture of diplomatic failure and intrigue: *1914 – Die Letzten Tage vor dem Weltbrand* (*1914. The Last Days before the War*, Richard Oswald, 1930), for example. The film was at first banned by the censor, mainly because the Foreign Office objected to its release, although it was in no way as controversial as *All Quiet on the Western Front* which provided a welcome excuse for the Nazis for a trial of strength.[44] The commentary at the time in the Social Democratic news-paper *Vorwärts*, in view of the film's obvious endeavour not to burden the German Reich with any blame for starting the War, was to ask

> Why the censor had originally bothered to ban this film only to release it with a pedestrian prologue that would be wholly inexplicable were it not for the Remarque scandal and a certain Mr Goebbels and pink elephants. Our betters, the censors, must have seen the latter quite obviously in the flesh. This piece of censorship is a yardstick for the almost pathological hysteria that has been whipped into film censoring through Goebbels' noisy pantomime. Since 'hysteria' is a foreign word, let's replace it by a good German word: Trembling Cowardice.[45]

Just as the ban was a precautionary reaction to possible protests, in the same way the changes made to the film were an appeasement that finally allowed its showing. The 'Prologue', contributed by the historian Eugen Fischer, did not change anything concerning the basic message of the film but only reinforced it. This is because *1914 – Die letzten Tage vor dem Weltbrand* did indeed look for some culprit who could be blamed for the start of the war and found him to be Tsarist Russia. But neither was this viewpoint nor the varied reception the film received from the press in any way remarkable.[46] The film's reconstruction of the diplomatic activities after the assassination in Sarajevo did not fail because the 'wrong culprit' had been named, rather it suffered from a belief that what prompted the War became the cause of the War – diplomatic intrigue. In the final analysis, according to the film, no one wanted war except the entourage of the Tsar.

Oswald's film could never have achieved any real success because of its obvious aesthetic helplessness. If there was one thing the press agreed on it was the monotony of the scenes, scenes that could offer only constantly changing locations that were somehow always the same and where small secret councils held even more secret conversations. All the dialogue contains similar arguments and it seems to suggest that the start of the War was due to a failure in diplomacy, but it does not take into account the competition between the powers at the time which made a European war possible and in many ways even probable.

This film continued a trend that began with *Der Weltkrieg*: the anxious endeavour to make no false step in the precarious terrain of war memories. This was its weakness and was clearly recognised for what it was in *Vorwärts* but used for its own purposes by the Nazi paper *Völkischer Beobachter*. However, one film did manage to free itself from this self-imposed 'diplomatic' consideration for its political opponents, a film which can be seen as the German equivalent of *All Quiet on the Western Front*, *Westfront 1918*, a film that attempted for the first time to put the front line experience of German soldiers to the fore.[47] But Pabst would not allow himself to be tempted by the lionisation of the trench experience which the reactionary and nationalist guardians of war memory practised. Pabst also deviated from voice-over narration made so popular by Remarque, and which gave Vidor's *The Big Parade* its form. *Westfront 1918* tells of a group of soldiers who die one by one until finally there are no survivors. But the beginning of Pabst's film is different: it does not start in peacetime or show civilians joining the War. His film starts with soldiers who have already been in the trenches for a long time.[48] The participants are slowly and very sketchily identified – they have no 'past' of their own, only distinguishing features.

Consequently the film denies an outlook that transcends the experience of the four infantrymen on the 'Westfront' in 1918.[49] During the whole of the film at no time does a crane shot produce a triumphal synoptic panoramic view. Even scenes in long shot deny an overview of the battlefield. In most shots the sky dominates two thirds of the screen, the attacking masses are seen from the perspective of the trenches. This corresponds with the abandonment of a 'central' episode. There is no real climax. For a fitting portrayal of the War, events such as continuous shelling and attack and counterattack appear aimlessly strung together, the everyday routine of the soldier, so to speak. There are no decisive victories or defeats, only an appalling similarity – the monotonous war in the trenches. In the final scene – in the field hospital – the film prefers to hint that the War is lost rather than stating it explicitly and when the face of the seriously wounded main character is transformed into a skull through a change in the lighting the shot becomes an effective symbol as well as a résumé of the narrative. The main character goes out like a light and the narration stops. It is one of the great achievements of *Westfront 1918* that the dimensions of the War are made more precise by the

11.2   Poster *Westfront, 1918* (Michael Paris Collection)

soundtrack: gun shots and explosions are heard from time to time but it does not even attempt to imitate the inferno of the front. In this understated form the narrative proves itself in other ways too. Thus taboos, like the mass desertions of 1918 in the German Army, the scandalous discrimination in the supplies given to men and their officers, and the loss of life through friendly fire, find expression in almost casual scenes. The gain or loss of territory, which in trench warfare was assumed to be of utmost importance, is of little significance here.

Even the weaknesses of the film make it more consistent: the 'student' character has an affair with a French girl and is killed soon after; the main character, home on leave, finds his wife in bed with the butcher's journeyman. But both these events aim in an almost over-precise way to connect the story back to the framework of the front experience. *Westfront 1918* does not really recognise a 'world' outside the War and the love stories underline this. *Westfront 1918* was the first film in Germany to suggest that the War was 'senseless' and the symbol for this is the lieutenant (played by Claus Clausen). His sense of duty is guaranteed in the rigid expression on his face and in his deeds. But his last attempt to halt the French advance ends in disaster. He is wounded, and perhaps the most memorable sequence is when he is shown on his way to the field hospital taking stock of the losses. Pabst does not show in the battle scenes that the War is lost but in excursions to the overcrowded hospitals where the wounded and the dying receive only cursory treatment.

Amongst the anti-war films *Niemandsland* (Victor Trivas, 1931) must be given a special place. While in *Westfront 1918* the view taken against the War had been awkward in character,[50] Trivas's film portrays the horrors of war by transcending a realistic representation. His film contrasts five individuals who are each shown in the 'normality' of peacetime before the War and who later meet again in a dug-out at the front. The symbolic approach gives the film its structure; its pacifist impetus is obvious and sometimes appears too direct, even clumsy. Contrary to most other anti-war films *Niemandsland* waives any attempt to highlight the horrors in a conventional fashion. There are no characters that are seriously wounded and none that die. The usual scenes that identify a war film are missing. The final scene – which in other anti-war films is usually the point at which the senselessness of war is emphasised – shows the five characters on their way out of No Man's Land. If the lesson of Pabst's film was 'never again war', the lesson here is 'wage war against war'. Trivas's film is a conscious attempt to promote pacifism, which today is no longer very convincing, but it avoids the danger that lies in overemphasising the horror of war.

A third film of the Weimar period that can be seen as an anti-war film was *Die andere Seite* (*The Other Side*, Heinz Paul, 1931), based on the British play *Journey's End*, by R. C. Sheriff. In the spirit of the original the fighting side of war plays little part here and the characters of the original remain British while there is no glorification of the War. For this reason the film found itself on the list of films banned by the Nazis when they came to power two years later. The unheroic view that Heinz Paul expressed here, however, did not stretch to the other war films he made at this time, *Douaumont* in 1931 and *Tannenberg* the following year. Both films concentrate, as the titles indicate, on major battles, episodes that lend themselves to a heroic interpretation of the War. It must be said, however, that both films are markedly weaker from an artistic angle than *Die andere Seite*. In *Douaumont* Paul is ultimately unsuccessful because of the film's small budget. But he is also unsuccessful in tackling the task of producing an 'unbiased' reconstruction of the Battle of Verdun, based on documentary footage and with a disappointingly weak fictional storyline, even though participants of the real assault on Douaumont

11.3   Hauptmann Haupt (left) playing himself attacking the fort of Douaumont, from *Douaumont* (Rainer Rother Collection)

appear in the film – Hauptmann Haupt and Leutnant Radtke, for example. Sadly, their acting is severely limited and neither did the budget allow for expensive battlefield reconstructions. For this reason the film's narrative restricts itself mainly to assertions that are not pictorially backed up. In the tradition of *Der Weltkrieg* this sound film has captions whose task is to offer much-needed explanation. These are combined with trick shots that are also inspired by previous tradition and which explain the course of the military actions with the help of maps and drawings. *Douaumont* is an anachronism, for its technical quality and *mis-en-scène* do not come anywhere near that of other films of its time.[51]

Much the same comments can be made of *Tannenberg*. The battle occurred when the Russian armies invading Eastern Prussia were decisively defeated in 1914. The battle became a symbol of how the War could have been won by the German Reich and created the 'Hindenburg myth', and as such was not without consequence. Paul's film remains strictly within these parameters. Although there is more of a storyline than in *Douaumont* it is nevertheless again dependent on wartime footage, explanatory captions and trick shot maps. Thus this film cannot transcend the outlook of a chronicle. The film also allows more leeway for fiction: a subplot tells of what is happening on a Russian estate, for example. The film's value, however, is to make the battle *comprehensible*, ensuring that the audience can follow and understand its course. But such reconstructive endeavour was in no way able to offer a solution to the traumatic memories of the World War.

Compared to pacifist films *Douaumont* and *Tannenberg* constituted a weak aesthetic response. Paul's films could not satisfy the demand of the right-wing press that the 'front experience' had to be central. However, two other films did fit the bill: *Berge in Flammen* (Karl Hartl and Luis Trenker, 1931) and *Morgenrot* (Gustav Ucicky, 1933). These do indeed show the front experience – but without portraying it as a 'senseless' waste and without letting themselves be thwarted by the 'chronicle' approach. Both films employ well-tried narrative conventions. Thus the Alpine units in the Dolomite mountains just like the U-boat crews form isolated but cohesive groups that are basically cut off from the outside world. Both groups uphold the memory of the homeland and in both films some individuals survive. The storylines employ clearly contoured tasks that are achievable: the sinking of enemy ships, escaping destroyers, fending off an Italian attack, saving their own troops from a mine explosion and so on. By successfully accomplishing these tasks the films offer a satisfying outlook from a narrative point of view: the survivors are heroes.

Both Trenker (who took over directing when Karl Hartl fell ill) and Ucicky are directors of remarkable skill. Their films are fast moving and fluent in style.[52] In their view the War is seen as a test but this does not necessarily make them into chauvinistic films – although in *Morgenrot* the British are shown in particularly bad light when they employ a Q Ship as a U-boat trap. But the main point of the films is the portrayal of the steadfastness of one's own side. Goebbels and Hitler had attended the Berlin premiere of the film and the expression 'perhaps we Germans don't know how to live but we certainly know how to die gloriously' became one of Goebbels's favourites. He thought the portrayal of the home front lacked the necessary severity, however, and he described these scenes as *Gartenlaube* episodes ('roses round the cottage door').[53]

If the lost War with its millions of victims was retrospectively to have had any 'sense' then this sense could not just consist of sacrifice. For this reason these films make an effort to find something positive in the sacrifice, but in the image of men of steel there cannot be a happy ending in any conventional sense. There is no final victory to celebrate, only a successfully tackled in-between stage, a 'getting away with it' is possible. For *Berge in Flammen* this consists at first of repelling an Italian attack – a scene that is told in a remarkable montage. After having secured their own position it seems that there is no immediate danger of an Italian counter-attack. But at night the Austrian troops can hear noises that announce the next threat: the Italians are digging a tunnel under the summit and intend to blow up the Austrian position. Nothing can be done but wait because soldiers cannot abandon their posts. Only when, thanks to the actions of a single hero, the moment of blasting becomes known, can the soldiers retreat from their position for this critical moment and then return to defend it again. This successful achievement acts as a substitute for a general victory.

Berge in Flammen is also remarkable in another respect: the two wartime antagonists are first introduced as mutual friends before the War. Dimai, the Austrian mountain guide, has a friend in the Italian Franchini whom he leads to the summit. In the summit book they write their names and the date – 1 August 1914. As they write they can hear bells ringing in the valley below as the villages are informed of the mobilisation. During the War Dimai and Franchini fight on different sides – indeed, Franchini leads the attack on the Austrian positions. And Dimai, as a defender, fires at his friend. Both survive the War and years later, as shown in the final scene, they climb the mountain again, still friends but perhaps remembering that here they once faced each other as enemies.

Berge in Flammen treats the War as a 'test', a test that even friendship cannot prevent. It is the unquestionable truth of this film that everyone has to do his duty and this is all that matters. There is no doubt whatsoever of that necessity and no despair. The War may not have any ultimate purpose but it has sense. And just as all the male villagers march to war without hesitation and so into battle, there is no waivering, no questioning, only enduring. Similar things can be said about *Morgenrot*, though here the unanimous, near-fatalistic acceptance of the War creates stronger conflicts. In particular, more depth is given to the contradictions of the home front. The initial enthusiasm of the little town of Meereskirchen when it waves goodbye to the U-boat crew seems to evaporate in later years. When the survivors go to sea for the second time the mood is very depressed – too depressed for the captain (Rudolf Forster) who barks at the citizens that Germany needs 'black weather'. 'Even fifty long years of nights will not blind a German'. Such rallying calls to hold out at all costs allude to the *Dolchstosslegende* ('stab in the back') according to which the undefeated military had been let down by the weakness of the homeland. This gives *Morgenrot* a tone that was well-suited for a Germany now under National Socialist control.[54]

THE FIRST WORLD WAR
FROM THE NATIONAL-SOCIALISTS' PERSPECTIVE

The emphasis on the front experience, the shared 'front adventure', was a major part of Nazi ideology[55] and films produced under the new regime show an obvious re-evaluation of the First World War, and the very first propaganda films of the regime demonstrate this. In *Hitlerjunge Quex* (*Hitler Youth Quex*) Heinrich George plays the father who as a communist ends up on the wrong side, but his experiences under the Weimar Republic are seen as responsible for this. The reason is that this veteran of the Great War who had always done his duty had been cheated out of his just reward and thus driven into the arms of the Left. Disappointed veterans frequently appear in Nazi films dealing with the recent past, such as Hans Albers in *Flüchtlinge* (*Fugitives*, Gustav Ucicky, 1934) or Willy Birgel in *Reitet für Deutschland* (*Riders for Germany*, Arthur Maria Rabenalt, 1941). The War itself need not be shown to activate this mechanism, for it is Weimar that is pilloried. In these films Germany's greatness is the lost War, Germany's downfall the Republic.

The homeland and its relationship with the front had often played an important role in earlier films. Thus in *Westfront 1918* and in *Morgenrot* the lack of understanding from those on the home front plays a vital role just as does the inability of the front soldiers to talk about their experiences. The silence and reserve shown by Karl (Gustav Diessl) in Pabst's film corresponds to the restraint of Rudolf Forster in Ucicky's film. This relationship also appears in various forms in the films of other countries but which under the Nazis finds a significant alteration. Films such as *im Trommelfeuer der Westfront* (*Drumfire of the Western Front*, dir. Charles Willy Kayser, 1936), *Stosstrupp 1917* (*Shock Troop*, dir. Hans Zöberlein, 1933/4) and *Unternehmen Michael* (*Codename Michael*, dir. Karl Ritter, 1937) concentrate entirely on the combatants at the front, other films concentrate on showing in detail the tensions between the homeland and the fighting at the front. They are no longer dealing with the incommunicability of 'front experience' but a confrontation between two antagonistic principles. In these films the front is represented by comradeship, honour and duty while the Homeland, in contrast, is subject to political bickering, sharp business-dealing and selfishness that is inimical to the combat soldier.[56]

Films produced in the Nazi period that deal with the subject are different from their Weimar predecessors in that they revert to an unequivocal image of the enemy. However, it is not the military adversary who is the real enemy. Any depiction of combat scenes at the front stress how tough the fighting was and the amazing achievement of German soldiers, thus there is no need to deprecate the other side. The military adversary is not seen with contempt and only rarely is he condemned. This does not mean that the portrayal was 'non-partisan', but one can say that up to 1939 films about World War One showed little anti-British or anti-French propaganda. As is well known all this changed with the outbreak of the Second World War – when the Ufa board were informed by Reich Film Superintendent Fritz Hippler that 'Reich Minister Dr Goebbels desires more anti-British material'.[57]

Films of the First World War were of course not free of enemy images, but these tended to be rare. However, in Herbert Selpin's *Die Reiter von Deutsch-Ostafrika* (*The Riders from German East Africa*, 1934) British troops are accused of transgressions on the German civilian population.[58] Even more open in its depiction of the enemy is Herbert Maisch's *Menschen Ohne Vaterland* (*Men without a Homeland*, 1937) which glorifies the activities of the German Free Corps after World War One in the Baltic region. The anti-Bolshevist bias here gives this film its sharp definition. In the years up to 1939 propaganda films were routinely tinged with anti-communism. But the real focus of most World War films of this period is not to show the German side as more brave or more decent but to show that the War was not 'senseless' but a sequence of noble deeds of the highest meaning. In its final consequence this includes the 'meaningful' sacrifice of the whole nation. In *this* respect these films hark back to the tradition of the heroic film of the Weimar Republic, but they are infinitely harder and more to the point in their conception.

This is not contradicted by showing respect for the enemy soldier. *Im Trommelfeuer der Westfront* takes up anew the tradition of the compilation film using World War One footage combined with newly produced material. Technically this film is more skilful than its predecessors in achieving coherence in spite of the montage of sundry excerpts from footage foreign to the subject. The decisive new element surfaces in the final scene with a pathetic message spoken by an actor in the uniform of the First World War. His gaze firmly directed at the audience, he ends with, 'And men have borne all this/And furthermore they fought bravely/ They suffered, conquered, what no one could/On this side and that side; the heroes of war.'

In the pacifist film *Niemandsland*, too, the soldiers of both sides were the same – human beings and victims. This view allows the film *Stosstrupp 1917*, for instance, to show in great detail the actions of a small unit that continuously act as assault troops on the Western Front. The reason for the assaults is never questioned and the soldiers show no doubt about their orders. The film offers some very authentic-looking footage – the battlefield ploughed up by shells and criss-crossed with trenches – and thus affords, visually at least, something of the war experience. It has no qualms in showing, in one symbolic scene, the proximity of the soldiers in their opposing trenches: the attack of a British unit is repelled, a seriously wounded young British soldier is dragged into the dug-out. There he dies and around him are the sympathetic, silent, helpless German soldiers. The respect that is shown here is primarily due to the unquestioned endorsement of the War: you respect your adversary because he participates in the same war, he is entwined in the same fate.

The re-evaluation of the war experience itself is the main point of these films. Again the horror of battle is no longer seen as evidence of a 'senseless' sacrifice, or the cynical destruction of human beings, but a test through which emerges a new type of human being – hardened by the 'storm of steel'. But when the combatants are made into heroes then defeat in war becomes extraordinarily problematic. According to the narrative logic of the film the blame for defeat cannot lie with the soldiers nor with their leaders. For this the 'stab-in-the-back' myth is engaged; the defeat thereby becomes instrumentalised. This is particularly obvious in a film which abandons combat scenes altogether, *Urlaub auf Ehrenwort* (*Soldiers on Parole*, dir. Karl Ritter, 1937). The film is set out as an excursion through the different layers of the 'home front'. A company (presumably coming from the Eastern Front where an armistice has relieved troops from fighting) is on its way to France and stops over in Berlin for leave. Here the soldiers want to see their wives, lovers, or just get drunk. Their lieutenant grants them leave on their word of honour to return although it is pointed out to him that he is taking a big risk in trusting them.

But they do return, in spite of many obstacles and even in spite of their own scruples. The sergeant almost forgets the time, sleeping in the arms of his wife, but just manages to catch the train. The 'leftie' of the unit, a USPD sympathiser, initially enjoys the dissolute atmosphere of his favourite haunts, but when the 'comrades' try to stop him returning to his unit he starts a fight and breaks free because he understands what this 'unpatriotic rabble' will never understand. This sceptical intellectual, whose friends are planning the downfall of the government, will not shirk his 'damned responsibility' and thus, by returning to the troop, takes his first steps in the right direction. The home front is totally undermined by Bolshevism and only the 'small people', the workers and employees, are free of this. However, the political left and the intellectuals have now become more than just unreliable – they are traitors to their own country. The front soldiers cannot understand this for they no longer recognise political parties, only comrades in arms.

The Weimar mentality began, according to Ritter's film, well before the Armistice; the Berlin of this film is full of signs of decay where sexual promiscurity equals a lack of patriotism.[59] And Ritter continues this theme in a later film, *Pour le merite* (1938). This starts with the Armistice and the refusal of a commander of the air service to hand over his aircraft in accordance with the Armistice conditions. His squadron fly their machines to the homeland where they find a revolution going on. The squadron members are arrested by the revolutionary council but manage to escape before facing the firing squads. Here the enemy image is even more distinct than in *Urlaub auf Ehrenwort*, and again it concentrates on the threat from the enemy within.[60] The main part of the film is devoted to the apparently futile efforts of the squadron commander to preserve the German air service in the face of the conditions imposed by the *Versailles Diktat*. But he fails, just as he fails to secure a decent job for himself. This officer, claims the film, was not made for a position in a world of merchants: what he needs is his military rank and a task appropriate to his rank. For a long time he does not understand the signs that point to a 'new order' emerging, and he ridicules the activities of his former deputy (a member of the Nazi party) who tries to keep aviation alive in Germany by glider flying. Only later does it become clear to him that all this is part of a strategic plan. But before he gains this understanding he is driven to a desperate act of trying to reactivate a hidden warplane. This absurd plan is foiled; he is arrested and is only freed from prison by his comrades. In the final scene he is back in uniform and in command of his old squadron at last but this time under the swastika.

Ritter's films[61] clearly state the connections between 're-heroification' and anti-democratic agitation, and in the years up to 1939 he made it his specialism; he tackles this theme in no less than four films of which one is set entirely in the war years, *Unternehmen Michael*. This deals with the German spring offensive of 1918 which the Supreme Army Command hoped would prove decisive because they knew that never again would they be able to concentrate their efforts and amass men and material on such a scale.

Allusions to historical persons are apparent: the actor Heinrich George with his crew cut reminds us of Hindenburg, and the characterisation of his chief of staff (Mathias Wieman) shows traces of Ludendorff. But the analogies are not binding in every respect; after all we are not dealing with Supreme Command but a combat unit on the front line. The general is therefore given room to air his frustration over lack of support. What is important for the re-evaluation of history is that the film restricts itself to a limited military campaign and symbolically equates the successful outcome of this campaign with the success of the Spring Offensive.[62] At one point the campaign's success is threatened by the unexpected arrival of British reinforcements. Therefore the town has to be taken – the chief of staff himself takes command because his reliable captain has been wounded. Events become more complicated when the German unit stationed in the town become encircled by enemy tanks. The chief of staff can see only one chance of saving his plan: he orders his own artillery to open fire on the town and thus on his own unit. The general, too, knows that there is no alternative if the greater plan is to be preserved and finally gives his approval. The British troops are repelled by German shellfire and the German soldiers in the town perish.

The idea of the 'necessary sacrifice' is a constant motif of Nazi propaganda films and this has rarely been more consistently celebrated than in Ritter's films. *Unternehmen Michael* is without rival in its description of the World War and the re-evaluation of what the experience of war meant for a whole generation, but its re-heroification led another generation to self-destruction.

CONCLUSION

After the invasion of Poland the tasks of Nazi propaganda shifted. Now the First World War no longer played any part in the propaganda war. In this new period there were new enemy images but the home front was, for understandable reasons, no longer shown as problematic or even inimical. Immediately after the end of the Second World War the war film genre became despised in Germany; this changed only in the mid fifties but only rarely did film-makers choose topics from the First World War.

In other countries the First World War is *the* example of a senseless war: *Paths of Glory* (USA, 1957), *Uomini contro* (Italy, 1970) or *Gallipoli* (Australia, 1981), for example, but in Germany it was the *Second* World War that was portrayed as *senseless*. A series of films from *Die Brücke* (*The Bridge*, dir Bernhard Wicki, 1959) to *Stalingrad* (dir. Joseph Vilsmaier, 1993), many of them attracting huge audiences, show the German soldier of World War Two foremost as a victim of the military and political leadership of Nazism. This 'senselessness' is, however, quite different to the senselessness associated with the First World War as perceived in the films of the Weimar Republic. In these post-World War Two German films 'senselessness' has as its inevitable aim a narrative for the exculpation of the individual soldier. These films portray 'heroism' in the face of the 'false cause', while the most important films on the First World War see the War itself as the 'false cause'. In Germany the real challenge of the representation of the past must be concerned with the Second World War and the planned destruction of human beings in the concentration camps. Thus it is understandable that the First World War has disappeared from German cinema.

NOTES

1   It has often been stressed that the first years after the armistice were by no means without some attempts at depicting the events and experiences of war. This is true for the pictorial arts as well as for literature. However, when compared to the flood of war literature at the end of the 1920s the first half of the decade does indeed appear rather silent.

2   Walter Benjamin, *Gesammelte Schriften*, vol. I.2 (Frankfurt am Main: Suhrkamp, 1989), p. 444.

3   Walter Benjamin, *Gesammelte Schriften*, vol. II.2 (Frankfurt am Main: Suhrkamp, 1989), p. 439.

4   For the context in the philosophy of history, see Rainer Rother, *Die Gegenwart der Geschichte: Ein Versuch über zeitgenössische Literatur* (Stuttgart: Metzler 1990).

5   Ibid.

6   See Frank Kessler and Sabine Lenk: 'The French connection: Franco-German film relations before World War I', in Thomas Elsaesser, *A Second Life: German Cinema's First Decades*, (Amsterdam: Amsterdam University Press, 1996), pp. 62–71.

7   The strong market share in Germany of Nordic Film Co. gave rise to protests by the Association of German Film Producers who demanded state intervention. See the documents in Wolfgang Mühl-Benninghaus, *Zur Rolle des staatsmonopolistischen Kapitalismus bei der Herausbildung eines Systems von Massenkommunikation zwischen 1900 und 1933* unpublished thesis (Berlin [DDR]: Humboldt University 1987), pp. 95–107.

8   For further information on this topic and the next see Wolfgang Mühl-Benninghaus, 'Newsreel images of the military and war, 1914–1918', in Elsaesser, pp. 175–84.

9   See in this connection Hans Barkhausen, *Filmpropaganda für Deutschland im Ersten und Zweiten Weltkrieg* (Hildesheim/Zürich/New York: Olms, 1982).

10 See Jeanpaul Goergen and Julius Pinschewer, 'A trade-mark cinema', in Elsaessaer, p. 174.

11 See in this context Hans Barkhausen.

12 Wolfgang Mühl-Benninghaus, p. 183: where it says: 'None of the suffering, death, dehumanisation, nor the destruction of the countryside, of cities or of industry itself, all of which were part of this war, are to be found in the images of war from 1914–18 – images which continue to shape our visual memory even today'.

13 For more details see: Rainer Rother, *'Bei Unseren Helden an der Somme* (1917): The creation of a "social event" ', *Historical Journal of Film, Radio and Television*, 15: 4 (October 1995), pp. 525–42.

14 *Das 8-Uhr-Abendblatt*, 20 January 1917.

15 *Berliner Tageblatt*, 20 January 1917.

16 These effects were due to certain circumstances and could not have been created independently no matter how 'solidly' the propaganda was prepared. See: Nicholas Reeves, 'The power of film propaganda – myth or reality?', *Historical Journal for Film, Radio and Television*, 13: 2 (1993), pp. 181–202.

17 Von Kühlmann, Kaiserliche Deutsche Gesandschaft in Pera, 4 May 1917, Bundesarchiv Potsdam, Bestand R 901, Akte 948, p. 62.

18 In this vein a Herr Bintz who acted on behalf of Germany sent a telegram on 9 January 1917 from Stockholm, saying that the 'Dobruja

film' – presumably we are dealing with *Mackensens siegeszug durch die Dobrudscha* (*Mackensen's Triumphal March through Dobruja*) – had been shown to two distribution companies whose reaction had been 'extraodinarily reserved'. 'The film contains too little action for Swedish tastes. They say that similar pictures have been seen too many times in journals and other war films, they demand battle scenes as cruel and sensational as possible, like the British Somme film' (Bundesarchiv Potsdam, Bestand R 901, Akte 947, p. 161).

19   BA Potsdam, R 901, Akte 954, p. 60.

20   ibid., p. 175.

21   BA Potsdam, Bestand R 901, Akte 949, p. 83.

22   Dieter Vorsteher, 'Bilder für den Sieg: Das Plakat im Ersten Weltkrieg', in Rother, *Die letzten Tage der Menschheit* (Berlin: Ars Nicolai, 1994), pp. 149–62.

23   See the filmography of Pinschewer by Jeanpaul Goergen in the *Lexikon Cinegraph* (Munich: Edition Text und Kritik, 1984).

24   Numerous examples from all pictorial media can be found in Rother, *Die letzten Tage der Menschheit*.

25   Alan Kramer, ' "Greueltaten": Das Problem der deutschen Kriegsver- brechen in Belgien und Frankreich 1914', in Gerhard Hirschfeld, Gerd Krumeich and Irina Renz (eds), *Keiner fühlt sich hier mehr als Mensch . . . Erlebnis und Wirkung des Ersten Weltkrieges* (Frankfurt am Main: Fischer, 1996), pp. 104–39.

26   See in this context Gerd Krumeich, 'Der deutsche Soldat an der Somme: Zwischen Idyll und Entsetzen', in S. Quant and H. Schichtel (eds), *Der Erste Weltkrieg als Kommunikationsereignis* (Giessen: Justus–Liebig– Universität, 1993), pp. 45–62.

27   'But a film works in the 'dramatic' vein, when it projects on the screen the war or a war episode as a dramatic process in five acts embellished with dozens of pictures to the astonishment of its contemporary audience, that is when it is to be rejected on principle as a corruption of art of the most despicable kind' (Johannes Gaulke, 'Kunst und Kino im Kriege', *Die Gegenwart*, annual set 45, no. 44/45, 1916, p. 619). After the end of the War, *Der Kinematograph*, no. 627, 8 January 1919, published a devastating judgement of the 'war weeks': 'They were boring and in most cases did not deserve their name since they too often did not reflect the war but used posed pictures.'

28   For the altercations between BUFA and the German Photographic Society, see Hans Barkhausen, *Filmpropaganda*.

29   This film, more so than later ones, is still close to the propaganda of the war years when especially in American productions the equation German = Hun was applied. The story is based on the simple contrast- ing of French and German attitudes. In particular the scenes of the taking of a village, the killing of civilians and the orgy coupled with the

rape of a servant girl is reminiscent of former atrocity propaganda. It comes as no surprise that the German Foreign Office – though without success – tried to prevent the showing of the film outside the USA. Cf. Thomas J. Saunders, 'German diplomacy and the war film in the 1920's', in Karel Dibbets and Bert Hogenkamp (eds), *Film and the First World War* (Amsterdam: Amsterdam University Press, 1995), pp. 213–22.

30   For the founding history of Ufa see Hans Michael Bock and Michael Töteberg (eds), *Das Ufa-Buch* (Frankfurt am Main: Zweitausendeins, 1992); Klaus Kreimeier, *Die Ufa-Story* (München: Hanser, 1992.

31   Originally as many as three parts were planned but only the first two were produced. The original version of the film is apparently not preserved; the Bundesarchiv/Filmarchiv holds a version that consists of twelve acts. The overwhelming part of the film deals with the events of 1914 to 1916 – in Act 11 the first allied offensive at the Somme is dealt with and only the final act deals with later events of the War.

32   These authors guaranteed a military friendly treatment of the War. Soldan worked in the Reichsarchiv and published as early as 1919 a memorandum on 'German historiography of the World War as a national task'. See Bernd Ulrich and Benjamin Ziemann (eds), *Krieg im Frieden: Die umkämpfte Erinnerung an den Ersten Weltkrieg* (Frankfurt am Main: Fischer 1997), p. 65ff. The Reichsarchiv in its publications did actually translate the aims of this memo into reality and *Der Weltkrieg* is a film in accord with these.

33   'The German cinemas reported full house; at the yearly poll of the cinema owners *Der Weltkrieg* ranked no 5, just one rank behind *Metropolis*' Michael Töteberg, 'Vermintes Gelände', in Bock and Töteberg, *Das Ufa-Buch*, p. 204f.

34   See the review in the *Berliner Morgenpost*, 24 April 1927, partially reprinted in Ulrich and Ziemann (eds), *Krieg im Frieden*, p. 149f.

35   Bernhard von Brentano, *Wo in Europa ist Berlin* (Frankfurt am Main: Insel, 1981), p. 86.

36   Brentano, *Wo in Europa ist Berlin*, p. 87.

37   It is not only the restriction on filming near the front that makes the documentary footage used in this film so imprecise: the origin of the footage played no role whatsoever in its selection. Thus footage from 1917 used in the BUFA film *Bei unseren Helden an der Somme* is used again in *Sieg im Westen* (1940) to illustrate the fighting around Verdun. Documentary footage is not really taken seriously in this compilation film: contrary to protestations of 'authentic' material being used.

38   For examples of compilation films in other countries, see *Met onze Jongens aan den Yser* (Belgium 1929/30, dir. Clemens de Landstheer) and *Gloria* (Italy 1932).

39   Brentano, *Wo in Europa ist Berlin*, p. 143.

40   Ralph recycled the story of the short and successful raiding expedition

of the cruiser *Emden* by using almost the same footage in 1932 for *Kreuzer Emden* and in 1934 for *Heldenkampf und Todesmut unserer Emden* (*The Heroic Death Defying Fight of Our Emden*).

41   Brentano, *Wo in Europa ist Berlin*, p. 171.

42   For the contemporary reception and an evaluation see Garth Montgomery, 'Realistic war films in Weimar Germany: Entertainment as education', *Historical Journal for Film, Radio and Television*, vol. 9, no. 2, 1989, pp. 115–33.

43   It seems likely that only *Heimkehr*, directed by Joe May in 1928 and based on the novel *Karl und Anna* by Leonhard Frank, managed to capture something of the impact the World War had on individuals.

44   For a detailed account see Bärbel Schrader (ed), *Der Fall Remarque: Im Westen nichts Neues. Eine Dokumentation* (Leipzig: Reclam, 1992), and Modris Eksteins, 'War, memory and politics: The fate of the film *All Quiet on the Western Front*', *Central European History*, annual set 13, no. 1, 1980, pp. 60–82.

45   Erich Kuttner, 'Verfilmte Kriegsschuld', in: *Vorwärts*, Abendausgabe, 21 January 1931.

46   The Social-Democrat paper *Vorwärts* suggested that, apart from aesthetic weakness, the film 'does not use any of the means the medium of film has to offer, it lacks all diversion and colour' and that its political stance is 'a finely contrived propaganda piece to blame the war on Tsarist Russia (what a convenient adversary – it is dead and therefore cannot defend itself)', (21 January 1931). The National-Socialist *Völkischer Beobachter* in accordance with Nazi ideology takes a different view: the film's stance cannot be seen as 'objective' because the director is Jewish (31 January 1931).

47   Even when seen on an international scale Pabst's film is a remarkably early example of an attempt to make use of the new technology of sound to portray the War.

48   Hermann Kappelhof, *Der Mobierte Mensch: Georg Wilhelm Pabst und die Utopie der Sachlichkeit* (Berlin: Vorwerk 8, 1984), points out that the beginning of the film works with the somewhat precarious idyll in Yvette's house, where as well as a shift into sexual violence the outbreak of the War itself threatens.

49   Edlef Köppen, who was himself the author of a World War novel, complained that the film was only 'a beginning' and ultimately not decisive enough in its condemnation of the War: 'The Four of the Infantry and a Little Bit of Ready-to-Wear Clothing', *Die Weltbühne*, vol. 26, no. 26, 1930, p. 957.

50   'Even the political happy ending – a wounded Frenchman grips the dead Karl's hand and says: "We are not enemies, we are comrades in arms!" – is foreign to the film, a paper formula, a footnote in the pacifist inventory. When Pabst attempts to establish synthesis, reconciliation and unity, all he has at his command is hollow phrases.' Klaus

Kreimeier, 'G. W. Pabst und seine Filme', in Wolfgang Jacobson (ed), *G. W. Pabst* (Berlin: Argon, 1997), p. 105.

51   For a detailed account concerning reception and context of this film. See my article 'Germany's "Douaumont" (1931): Verdun and the depiction of World War'. *Historical Journal for Film, Radio and Television*, 19, 2, 1999, pp. 217–38.

52   *Morgenrot* was awarded in 1933 the New York film critics' prize for the best foreign film.

53   Elke Fröhlich (ed), *Die Tagebücher von Joseph Goebbels*, vol. 2 (München: Verlag, C. H. Beck), 1987, p. 367.

54   See Rainer Rother, 'Morgenrot', *Ufa-Magazin*, no. 10, Berlin: DHM, 1992, pp. 2–5.

55   See Sabine Behrenbeck, *Der Kult um die toten Helden* (Vierow: SH Verlag 1996).

56   The myth of the hostile reception for the returning soldiers is revised by Richard Bessel, 'Die Heimkehr der Soldaten', in Hirschfeld et al., *Keiner fühlt sich hier mehr als Mensch*, p. 260ff.

57   Bundesarchiv, Akte R 109 I/1033c, p. 133.

58   This is somewhat counterbalanced by the person of a British officer who is friendly with the Germans and receives a positive characterisation throughout the film.

59   See Rainer Rother, '*Urlaub auf Ehrenwort*, *Ufa-Magazin*, no. 15, Berlin: Deutsches Historisches Museum, 1992, pp. 2–6.

60   Ritter directed a film *Patrioten* (1937) which tells how a German pilot (Mathias Wiemann) is brought down behind enemy lines in France and is found by an actress (Lída Baarová). The love story between the two ends in tragedy when they both remember their respective patriotic duties. In this case one cannot really speak of a solid enemy image – but Ritter makes extensive use of anti-Semitic and anti-communist prejudices in *Kadetten* (1939), *Im Kampf gegen den Weltfeind* (1939) and *GPU* (1941/2).

61   For more details on Ritter see Julian Petley, 'Karl Ritter', in *Cinegraph: Lexikon zum deutschsprachigen Film* (München: Edition Text und Kritik, 1984ff.), Rainer Rother, 'Hier erhielt der Gedanke eine feste Form', in Bock and Töteberg, *Das Ufa-Buch*, pp. 422–7; Felix Moeller, *Der Filmminister: Goebbels und der Film im Dritten Reich* (Berlin: Henschel, 1998).

62   In principle *Kolberg* (dir. Veit Harlan, 1945) is a very similar film – only here it portrays the endurance of a town during a siege by superior Napoleonic troops. This endurance transcends into a symbolic portrayal of the situation of the German Reich as a whole. Whether the message was still heard can rightly be doubted. The premiere, simultaneously in La Rochelle and Berlin on the 31 January 1945, was already a *mis-en-scène* with transparent effect.

12

Where is the War?
Some Aspects of the Effects of
World War One on Austrian Cinema

Franz Marksteiner
[Translated by Margit Slosser]

For six months in 1998 Austria presided over the European Union, thus playing a central role in European politics and receiving international media coverage. Heads of State and ministers travelled to this small country, quickening the political pace. Congresses, consultations and meetings of international importance were on the agenda. Hardly a week passed in which the Chancellor or Vice-Chancellor did not appear on national television with news of the imminent solution to the pan-European problem. Receptions, banquets and similar festivities played an important role in the social life of the nation.

From time to time the columnists of the local newspapers and other political commentators praised the ease and finesse with which Austria mastered this organisational feat, fulfilling the international standards required.

Considering Austria's history, there was no reason for concern, especially with reference to the social aspects of the task. In the days of the Viennese Congress, Austrians, above all the Viennese, were so renowned for their celebration of frivolous social events that serious politics and the like were purported to be of lesser importance. This cliché; persistent and by no means unwelcome to the Austrians, was revived by the UFA's well-known production *Der Kongress tanzt* (*The Congress Dances*, dir. Eric Charell) in 1931.[1]

The Austria of today is a modern nation with all the usual problems of a Western democracy. Its entry into the European Union not only marks the end of yet another chapter of Austria's post-war history, it also emphasises the country's will to collaborate in the future maintenance of peace in Europe. Austrian politicians are committed to conveying such an image of Austria to the world. Furthermore the Austrian Vice-Chancellor, Wolfgang Schüssel, often mentions Austria's monarchical past, especially when topics involving the European Union's eastern expansion are on the agenda. The potential rejoining of countries which 'once had belonged together' repeatedly brings the former Austro-Hungarian Empire onto the floor for consideration as a model for a united Europe. If Vice-Chancellor Schüssel did not stress the historical difference in the conditions surrounding the unification of the past and the present, one might feel a tingle of fear.

The support of a middle-European ideology recently dominant in the press often resounds in such statements. Geographically and historically it is understandable that Austria has an interest in such an ideology. This conservative utopia provides a myriad of arguments through which Austria could establish a viable national identity. Austria's present position in the European Union begins to give its citizens an impression of what it means to be a central axis in world politics, but such a position was reality before the ravages of World War One:

> It made our Fatherland small and the outside world once again distant. It robbed us of so much of that which we had loved and showed us the frailty of many things which we had thought to be lasting.[2]

In fact, all of Europe was at first surprised and then shocked by the destructive momentum and ravaging dimensions of this War. Modris Eksteins points out that it was this very element of surprise which deeply destabilised Europe's belief in traditional nineteenth-century values:

> From the perspective of the middle-class world of the nineteenth century, nothing could have been more humiliating than to be taken by surprise. Surprise involved moral failing. The perpetrator of surprise was a scoundrel, the victim of surprise a fool. In the 'Great Surprise' that became the First World War, western civilisation was shattered, as if struck by a shell from Big Bertha, the most fearsome of the German guns.[3]

Today we believe we have a relatively exact picture of this War, through the images passed on by the medium of film. Historically, the advancement of cinema to one of the most influential methods of communication was clearly a result of the First World War. 'No medium has been better able than film to transmit shock, surprise, transcience and, at the same time, the imploring hopes that are so central to our century.[4]

David Bordwell and Kristin Thompson note in their book on film history that 'the war disrupted the free flow of films across the borders' and that 'some national industries benefited from this disruption',[5] and this applies particularly to the Austrian film industry.

Although there were approximately thirty film producers in Austria before the outbreak of the War, the majority of these were French firms working in Austria and producing numerous films. These include rare documentation of the Emperor and his family. Pathé accompanied Franz Joseph on his hunting expeditions to Ischl. The Firm Eclair was responsible for the last living images of the successor to the throne while on that fatal visit to Sarajevo.

At the outbreak of the War the activities of film producers from 'enemy countries' were forbidden; a development which was to the advantage of the local Austrian producers:

> The war effort severely curtailed film-making in the two leading countries, France and Italy. American companies stepped in to fill the vacuum. As of 1926, the United States became the leading supplier of films to the world market, and it has held that position ever since . . . The war isolated several producing countries. For the first time, distinctive national cinemas arose – as opposed to the open flow of films and influences that had previously been the rule.[6]

Based on the last sentence of this quote from Bordwell and Thompson, I would now like to expand on the development of an Austrian national cinema.

For the most part the history of Austrian film has been coupled with, as well as subordinated to, the film history of Germany, often being treated as an appendix.[7] This treatment is understandable within the historical context of economic and private fusions and exchanges between Berlin and Vienna. These had taken place early on in their histories and were further strengthened after 1918, when the borders of Austria were limited to its German-speaking regions.

The Sascha Filmgesellschaft (Sascha Film Society), Vienna, which I will examine later on in this essay, was combined with the production

firm of Oskar Messter, Berlin, in 1916 and renamed the Austro-Hungarian Sascha-Messter Film Society Inc., a fusion which, after the founding
of the UFA in December of 1918, brought the 'concurrence of the largest
German producer with the largest Austrian producer'.[8] The UFA had
purchased Oskar Messter's firm outright.

The history of Sascha-Film seems symptomatic for the beginnings of
Austrian film *per se*. With the support of a large staff it fulfilled the
demands made on Austrian producers, demands still apparent in Austrian film long after 1945. After this time it was relieved of the most
obvious propagandistic and militaristic components and yet still remained basically unchanged. Austrian film was an essential force in
the formation of an Austrian national identity.

In 1914 Count Alexander Kolowrat-Krakowsky entered his firm, the
Sascha Film Factory (Sacha Film-Fabrik), in the commercial register. He
had been active as a producer as early as 1910. The independently
wealthy Count Kolowrat led the life of a dandy who was fascinated by
technology. Countless anecdotes and legends praise his pioneer spirit,
engaging personality and contribution to Austrian film, creating a
situation which obstructs an objective look at his productions.

The following is cited from the 16 August 1914 edition of the *Kine-
matographischen Rundschau* (*Cinematographic Review*):

> Tastefully selected scenes in nature with an air of timelessness, patriotic
> films depicting manoeuvres, drills and the life of our allied troops – taking
> into account the prevailing sentiments and building confidence in our
> troops by conveying their rigidity and poise, all of which will certainly
> meet with approval . . . No more French, English, Belgian and Russian
> films.[9]

It was the *Wiener Kunstifilm* (Viennese Art Film) which first fulfilled the
demands of the public for war news by producing the *Kriegs journal*
(*War Journal*) after 1914. Soon afterwards Sascha-Film produced a
wartime weekly newsreel (*Kriegswochenschauen*) in collaboration with
the distributor Philipp and Pressburger and the Österreichisch-Ungar-
ische Kiniondustriegesellschaft (Austro-Hungarian Film Society).

As an officer in the wartime news headquarters Kolowrat was head of
the film department, co-ordinating the movements of his expanding staff
at the various scenes of war. In at least one instance it is known that a
battle was specially staged for Kolowrat – an artillery offensive at the
Izono Front.

In addition to the wartime weekly newsreel, Sascha-Film also produced an increasing number of short-play feature films. After 1916 long-play feature films were a regular feature of cinema programmes. This development was a reaction to Austria's growing need for movie entertainment. Among the short films produced by Sascha-Film were the state-subsidised patriotic propaganda films, one-reelers which were distributed to the movie theatres free of charge to be shown alongside the featured film. With such titles as *Wir und die Anderen* (*We and the Others*), *Der sichere Weg zum Frieden* (*The Sure Path to Peace*), or *Die goldene Wehr* (*The Golden Defence*) propaganda was continued, even in the years when the final outcome of the War was predictable for its perpetrators.

The feature films of Sascha-Film were chiefly comedies, crime films and the moral and social dramas popular in those days. The films which were used for propaganda were chiefly comedies. The main characters of the production *Wien im Krieg* (*Vienna in War*) are a butcher's son who joins the *Deutschmeisters*, a tram conductress, a mail-woman and other members of the Viennese working class. Characters derived from the working class later play an important role in the newly developed genre *Wiener Film*. From the 1930s to the 1950s this genre was an important and popular product of the Austrian film industry and is still considered to be its most fundamental product.

In 1917, the film comedy *Das Nachtlager von Mischli-Mischloch* (*The Encampment at Mischli-Mischloch*) was produced and then never premiered. Its plot involved the harrowing escape of an Austrian film team arrested by Russian Cossacks. The premiere had been planned for 18 February 1918, by which time Austria had already made peace with Russia.

The plot in the 1916 comedy *Der Nörgler* (*The Malcontent*), produced and 'distributed to theatres free of charge in an effort to convert and inform the critics of the war',[10] uses a dream sequence in which the main character, a Viennese landlord, is presented with the activities of the Austrian military. He 'sees welfare institutions, factories as arsenals, weapons and fighting planes, the troops in formation, fighting in submarines, the fallout etc. – through this dream he is reformed, becomes a patriot and buys war bonds'.[11]

The malcontent, through and through a pessimist, also has his place in the character inventory of *Wiener Film*. The figure of a malcontent also is used in the drama *Die letzten Tage der Menschheit* (*The Last Days of Mankind*) by Karl Kraus, one of the most committed anti-war activists among Austrian writers. Here the malcontent, often assumed to be the author's alter ego, becomes a critic of the increasingly absurd and cruel

War and its agents. Sascha-Film and its collaborators, the producers of propaganda for the warmongers, in Kraus's opinion, receive scathing criticism in this drama. The most emphatic example of this takes place in a scene in which officers are shown a Sascha film which demonstrates the effects of a new weapon, commenting cynically 'bumsti' (nonsense) upon seeing the fallen and dying enemy soldiers.

Retrospectively it seems symbolic that one of Sascha-Film's greatest achievements is its depiction of the final public display of the Habsburg Dynasty in all its magnificence: the funeral of Emperor Franz Joseph in 1916. The death of the Emperor, the end of the monarchy and the War all function as catalysts for the beginning of an Austrian film industry of economic durability and self-initiated aesthetic.

In a show of technical finesse unheard of in those times, Sascha-Films was able to produce and distribute 250 copies of this documentary within three days' of the event. All of Austria was able to view the last days of the 'world's oldest Emperor' on the big screen, the self-same screen which brought about his resurrection and ensured him eternal life.

The fact that Austria's national identity relies disproportionately on its past history rather than being based on the future is well known. One of the corner stones of this country's self-esteem is the Habsburgian Myth – which came into it's own after the monarchy had fallen. The inventor of this term, Claudio Magris, looked for and established this as the dominant theme within Austrian literature and thereby made the many arguments supporting a middle-European ideology possible.

Stefan Zweig coined the phrase *Die Welt von Gestern* (*The World from Yesterday*) in reference to the empire of Franz Joseph I. As in the case of many European writers, he describes the painful caesura caused by the War, the virtual end of the nineteenth century, the destruction of his generation and the consequences Austria suffered in the new order of Europe. The Emperor's all-encompassing, multi-ethnic empire had become a tiny country in which not even its citizens could believe.

In the novels of post-war Austria, it is chiefly the officers who experience the trauma of having learned nothing more than to serve a non-existent country, unable to cope with the reality of a modern world still subservient to out-dated principles. In Joseph Roth's novel *Die Flucht ohne Ende* (*The Escape without End*) the character Franz Tunda crosses post-war Europe and attempts to return home, only to discover his country in ruins. The demise of the empire is thus increasingly transfigured and the desire to return to the myth surrounding the Habsburg Dynasty is born; the aged Emperor became the symbol for durability and security.

Radetzkymarsch (*Radetzky March*), the title of another novel by Joseph Roth, perpetrates the Habsburgian Myth through this tale of three generations in a family of officers and civil servants. The novel ends with the death of the young lieutenant, who falls in the first days of the War.

Although there are many novels which describe the effects of the War on various levels, the above works by Roth, through their superficial treatment of the actual day-to-day experiences of the War, are symptomatic. They bathe the last years of the monarchy in a critical and yet mild light. They mercilessly and yet ever so lovingly see to their hero's destruction. Thus the atmosphere is set for the way in which Austria faces its monarchical past: wistful nostalgia trivialised without end.

Deeply uprooted after World War One, Austria's national identity and its redefinition were concerns of the highest social and political order, especially in the Second Republic after 1945. The historical distance now possible enables an informal re-examination of the legends, image and projections of the former monarchy. In the end Austria had enjoyed great prosperity and enough of this splendour can still be seen today. The First World War, which sealed the fate of this 'World of Yesterday', certainly does not fit into this picture of orderliness, in which all is as it should be with the Emperor seeing to the well-being of his country and his subjects, and seemingly watching over the fate of each individual, the civil servants and military supporting his benevolent rule:

> For those of a nostalgic bent, who look upon the 'World of Yesterday' as a kind of concentrated cultural spectacle, [the war] seems bothersome and out of place. It is as if one would want to excise the violence and destruction out of the history of a previous epoch.[12]

In the years of the monarchy the military was, above all, a representative body. The colourful troops and elegant officers, more apt to arouse romanticised visions of a distant war, were not cut out for the demoralising and devastating material and tactical war which was to follow:

> For all its failings as a military machine, the Austro-Hungarian army served as a pillar of empire. During the 1920s, not a few civilians missed seeing bright uniforms enlivening the streets of Vienna. The army embellished social life, pacified outlying provinces, and furnished soldiers of disparate nationality a focus for patriotism. Thanks to an unwieldly code of honour, refusal to innovate, and pride in the face of disaster, the military reflected the regime that it served. Like Emperor Franz Joseph, the army was more respected than feared, more popular than effective.[13]

This popularity made the portrayal of the Emperor's army seemingly indispensable in Austrian film. Through film the fictional resurrection of the Emperor and his empire was a constant element which not only served to popularise and trivialise the Habsburgian Myth, but also gave the impression of its continuing existence. As the years of monarchical rule slowly lost their political potency, their reconstruction gained strength in the formation of a national identity. Austrian film bears witness to this fact. After 1945, when the policy of reconstructing the monarchical past was no longer politically relevant, the monarchy still formed the central theme in the national characterisation.

Colour film strengthened the popularity described by Johnson even more by returning the empire and its troops to their original gaiety. Since the time of their production in the 1940s and 1950s, these films have been televised time and again to German-speaking audiences in order to ensure high ratings. Painstakingly edited video reproductions, which carry titles such as the *Rex Austria Kollektion*, are increasingly available. The highpoint of this series is the three-part national epic *Sissi* (1955–1957; dir. Ernst Marischka). This film not only serves to reinstate the Habsburgian Myth but also begins the legend surrounding the figure of Romy Schneider.

But where is the War in all of these films? These films have such titles as *Kaiserball* (*The Emperor's Ball*), *Kaiserwalzer* (*The Emperor's Waltz*), *Kaisermanoever* (*The Emperor's Manoeuvre*), *Der Kaiser und das Waeschermaedel* (*The Emperor and the Washergirl*), *Die Deutschmeister* (*The German Masters*), *Hoch klingt der Radetzkymarsch* (*Lofty Sounds: the Radetzky March*). Their heroes are ornate officers and dashing soldiers, all able to win the hearts of ladies. Established comedians and the figure of the Emperor were given much artistic freedom in their appearances. The Emperor makes appearances when it is necessary to disentangle misunderstandings and give the plot a direction, a function that his authority and narrative role allows. But where is the War?

After 1945, the producers of Austrian film favoured the historical setting prior to 1918, a golden era emitting theatrical composure with just enough historical relevance so as to attract a post-war Austria. This applies to the majority of the productions, for the most part comedies. The role the military and its members play are a constant in these films. The comical parts are mostly left to the characters of lower-ranking soldiers and lackeys, the serious roles going to the officers a hierarchy borrowed from the theater and operetta. The War does not exist in these films, in which a drill is only used to allow two lovers to find each other, brought together by the will of the Emperor, and falling into each other's arms.

Even the films which deal explicitly with material of the historical past tend to marginalise the War. One example is Karl Hartl's 1948 production of *Der Engel mit der Posaune* (*The Angel with the Trombone*). With the help of a cast of prominent Austrian actors he describes a Viennese middle-class family, their royal connections and the events of their lives beginning in 1908 and ending after World War Two.

Two thirds of the plot takes place before the outbreak of the First World War. The War itself appears as if it were a law of nature, an inevitable fate which, as the plot develops, is increasingly unable to be influenced by mankind. Interspersed narratives divide the film into episodes, giving it a cyclic nature. The concepts of death and rejuvenation are cited implicitly and used in such a way as to create an almost mythical effect: 'Beginning and end are dark and uncertain'.

The results of the War, the father's handicap, the youngest son's ever more radical tendencies and the collapse and reconstruction of the firm are dealt with more directly than the actualities of the War. Here the idea of victimisation is formulated. One is subservient in matters of love, the code of honour, the will of God. In the end everyone is a victim. Austria

12.1   The pomp and circumstance of the Austrian Army, *The Angel with a Trombone* (Austrian Museum of Film, Vienna)

12.2   *The Angel with a Trombone* (Austrian Museum of Film, Vienna)

writes its history along these lines and thus answers the question of
responsibility which was of such importance especially after 1945.

The assassination at Sarajevo is the subject of another production.
Fritz Kortner produced the film *Sarajevo. Um Thron und Liebe* (*Sarajevo
– of Love and the Throne*, 1955), in which the description of the problems
caused by the morganatic marriage of Franz Ferdinand are treated as
importantly as the depiction of the political confusion and intrigue which
surrounded the heir to the throne.

The two films have a common denominator by allowing the masses to
voice their cry for freedom. Kortner does this by portraying the group
around Gavrilo Princip as young men who are radical and yet insecure.
He then confronts them with the motherly pacifism of the future Em-
press, at whom they scream hateful militant chants.

Both films attest to the failure of the monarchy and yet leave no doubt
as to the sentimental vacuum caused by this failure. Fritz Kortner's
successor to the throne is surrounded by high-handed advisers and
officers who, in the end, are unable to thwart the oncoming catastrophe.
The depiction of these personages is purposely comical, an attribute
which is somewhat irritating in certain scenes of this film, although it is a
device which is usually applied to films dealing with the Hapsburg era.

12.3   Franz Ferdinand in Sarajevo, *Sarajevo – of Love and the Throne* (Austrian Museum of Film, Vienna)

The conception of history, as depicted in Austrian film, was marked by the glorification of the era prior to 1918. It was produced by people who began their careers in the production companies profiting from the patriotic commissions during World War One. These people never ceased to produce propaganda for Austria. Fritz Korner, Karl Hartl, the brothers Ernst and Hubert Marischka and many other directors, authors and producers continued to influence Austria's film industry long after 1945. They all promoted a picture of Austria which based itself on its glorified past. Owing to the political ambivalence towards the old monarchical government, its transfiguration brought about by film and the passage of time, Austria was allowed to cling to its ideal. The War itself remained absent in film. The film result of the War is transfiguration itself.

At the end of the 1960s and the economic decline of the local film industry, Austrian film attempted a new beginning in which television played an important role. As with other subliminated historical periods, the First World War reenters the picture, the ideal of the monarchy loses its glow and Austria's self-portrait becomes torn and cracked.

12.4   The arrest of the assassin, *Sarajevo – of Love and the Throne* (Austrian Museum of Film, Vienna)

The national image of Austria, on which its politicians and citizens prefer to build, has been highly influenced by the film industry. The events of the past years, the developments in Europe, should be the motivation to treat the associations, brought about by this image, with more caution.

> If presently there is a chance to rewrite the history surrounding the First World War, it is due to the changes in middle-eastern Europe . . . The previous affinities and animosities once again play an important role. Thus the majority of European nations are forced to re-examine their historic relations among each other in light of the new developments.[14]

The history of Austrian film-making, as seen superimposed over World War One, is still in its beginning phase. This essay serves merely to provide an impulse articulating this history through focusing on two crucial moments, moments separated by nearly three decades of political chaos and yet linked by a common goal.

NOTES

1   Sigmund Freud, *Studiensausqabe, BD 10. Bildenole Kunst und Literature*, 9. Anflage. (Frankfurt am Main: S. Fischer Verlag, 1969). p. 227.
2   A remake was made by the Austrian director Franz Antel in 1955.
3   Modris Eksteins, 'The cultural impact of the Great War', in Karel Dibbets and Bert Hogenkamp (eds), *Film and the First World War* (Amsterdam: Amsterdam University Press, 1995), pp. 205–6.
4   Ibid., pp. 209–10.
5   David Bordwell and Kristin Thompson, *Film History: An Introduction* (New York: McGraw-Hill, 1994), p. 56.
6   Ibid., p. 54.
7   Not until recent years has Austrian film been the theme of larger studies, wherein the relation to as well as the distinction from German film were treated in depth.
8   Walter Fritz, *Kino in Oesterreich: Der Stummfilm 1896–1939* (Wien: Österreichischer Bundesverlag, 1981), p. 69.
9   Ibid., p. 66.
10 *Paimanns Filmlisten*, No. 48/1916.
11 Ingrid Maria Hübl and Sascha Kolowrat, 'Ein Beitug zur Geschichte der Oesterreichisschen Kinematographie'. Univ. Diss. Wien, 1950, p. 83.

12   Manfried Rauchensteiner, 'Oesterreich im Ersten Weltkrieg', in Rolf Steinminger and Michael Gehler (eds), *Oesterreich im 20, Jahrhundert*, Bd. I (Wien: Boehlau, 1997), p. 74.

13   William M Johnston, *The Austrian Mind: An Intellectual and Social History 1848–1938* (Berkeley: University of California Press, 1972), p. 55.

14   Rauchensteiner, 'Oesterreich in Ersten Weltkrieg', p. 79.

Index